# SUICIDE OR MURDER?

## The Strange Death of Governor Meriwether Lewis

D1051386

Nashville

Murfreesboro

lumbia

.Chattanooga

Huntsville

*Route*
*of the*
**NATCHEZ TRACE**

Gadsden

Josephine Smead

Birmingham

MERIWETHER LEWIS NATIONAL MONUMENT
TENNESSEE

OLD NATCHEZ TRACE

PICNIC AREA

LEWIS GRAVE

SITE OF GRINDERS STAND

VISITOR CENTER

PROPOSED LOCATION NATCHEZ TRACE PARKWAY

PROPOSED BOUNDARY OF NATCHEZ TRACE PARKWAY

N

0   400   800   1200   1600   2000
SCALE IN FEET

Revised 1956    1951  NM-ML 7001

# Suicide or Murder?

## The Strange Death
## of Governor
## Meriwether Lewis

### VARDIS FISHER

**SAGE BOOKS**

THE **SWALLOW PRESS** INC.
CHICAGO

Sage Books are published by
The Swallow Press Incorporated
1139 South Wabash Avenue
Chicago, Illinois 60605


This book is printed on 100% recycled paper


ISBN 0-8040-0616-4
LIBRARY OF CONGRESS CARD CATALOG NUMBER 62-12402

To the memory of
MERIWETHER LEWIS
the greatest American of his breed
and the most neglected

# The Chief Characters

1. Meriwether Lewis, the western hemisphere's greatest explorer, and governor of Upper Louisiana Territory; age: 35.

2. John Pernier (Pernia), his servant; he has been called a Spaniard, a Frenchman, a Creole, a halfbreed, a free mulatto.

3. Capt. Gilbert C. Russell, commanding officer at Fort Pickering, on the present site of Memphis.

4. James Neelly, formerly a major in a State militia, now Indian agent to the Chickasaw Nation. He was probably in his middle years.

5. A Negro servant, probably a slave, who accompanied Lewis, Pernier, and Neelly from the fort to Grinder's Stand.

6. Robert Grinder Sr., owner of Grinder's Stand, a crude inn in the wilderness, 70 miles southwest of Nashville; age, between 34 and 45.

7. Mrs. Robert Grinder, his wife, first name unknown; age, between 34 and 45.

8. Bethenia or Berthenia, the elder Grinder daughter, born in 1800, and so about 10 years old when Lewis died.

9. Malinda, a Grinder slave, said to have been born in 1797, and so about 12 or 13 years old October 11, 1809. It is not certain that she was on the scene.

10. Pete, a Negro, who in old age said he was a Grinder slave, and present when Lewis died. This is doubtful.

11. Polly Spencer, in tradition said to have been the Grinder cook, and about 15 years old. It is doubtful that Polly was present.

12. There was one, perhaps two, Grinder sons present; the elder of the two may have been as young as seven, or as old as 15.

# Table of Contents

# Table of Illustrations

This portrait of Meriwether Lewis
appeared in *Outlook*, Vol. 89, p. 197.

Meriwether Lewis. The Peale painting,
Independence Hall.

William Clark. The Peale painting,
Independence Hall.

Capt. Wm. Lewis of "Locust Hill" Father of Meriwether Lewis. *Courtesy, The Missouri Historical Society, St. Louis.*

The mother of Meriwether Lewis. *Courtesy, The Missouri Historical Society, St. Louis.*

Frederick Bates. *Courtesy, The Missouri Historical Society, St. Louis.*

# What Happened
# at Grinder's Stand?

It seems probable that she was standing in the doorway of one of the two log cabins, facing west, but turning a little to her left to look into the southwest at the man on the horse, coming up from Little Swan Creek on the Natchez Trace. That blazed trail ran from Natchez, on the Mississippi just above New Orleans, 550 miles to Nashville, which was about seventy miles northeast from where the woman stood. Through most of the distance it ran through wilderness and Indian country.

It was late afternoon, possibly just a little before sunset, October 10, 1809.

Stretching endlessly before this woman who was shading her eyes and staring was south-central Tennessee hill-country, covered with dwarfed oak and shrub. The rider on her left, about a hundred and fifty yards from her when she first spotted him, was riding up the path to a small clearing on a ridge, in which stood the two Grinder cabins, called a Stand. This Stand, like a few others along the Trace, offered lodging to travelers. The woman standing there, watching and waiting, was Mrs. Robert Grinder, who was in her middle or late thirties. From North Carolina, she now lived on a physical frontier, with no close neighbors, and within the boundary line of the Chickasaw Indian nation hardly more than a stone's throw from her front door. She had not been at the Stand long, but long enough to have seen, passing her door, going north or south, a great many travelers of many kinds.

The man riding up the slope toward her was Meriwether Lewis, 35 years old, and now governor of the entire Upper Louisiana Territory. This is the Meriwether Lewis of the famous Lewis and Clark team—the Lewis who, with his friend William Clark, led a handful of bold brave men and an Indian girl named Sacajawea for thousands of miles into and across the unknown— up the Missouri to its source and across the Rocky Mountains to the ocean, in one of the greatest feats of exploration in human history. Before that, he had been an officer in various military engagements, and then Thomas Jefferson's secretary. On this October afternoon he was deep in trouble.

As governor of the vast sprawling Louisiana Territory, with headquarters at the frontier river-town of St. Louis, he had had trouble from the beginning. It will be necessary to examine the nature of his difficulties; at the moment it is enough to say that some of his official vouchers had been rejected by the War Department in Washington, rumors about this had spread, his creditors had closed in, and he was making a long and tedious journey in late-summer heat to Washington to try to get matters straightened out.

No doubt the woman had known he was coming. Though it was only a blazed trail through a wilderness there was a heavy traffic over the Trace, going both ways. The Governor had been on it the past six or seven days, and surely someone had left word at Grinder's that this famous man would be passing by, on his way to Nashville and Washington. Mrs. Grinder could hardly have known that he would stop for the night at the rude inn her husband had built only recently, but knowing that he was coming she must have been curious. She knew that he would stop for the night somewhere. On the Trace south of her, toward Natchez, there was no other stand in a day's journey. North of her, toward Nashville, the next one was at a considerable distance.

So it is possible that she thought she might have the famous man as an overnight guest. With her were her small children and one or two youthful slaves. Where her husband was is something that nobody knows: he may have been lurking in the woods and watching this famous man approach, or he may have been, as legend says, off harvesting on his small creek farm. It may be that Mrs. Grinder knew that Governor Lewis was drawing close before he came in sight. It may be that she was astonished to see that he was alone.

He rode up the gentle slope along a winding path, two handsome pistols and a dirk at his waist, a rifle slung along his saddle. About a hundred yards from them he came within sight of the two cabins, but no doubt had seen smoke from the kitchen chimney above the trees long before that. When opposite the cabins he turned off the path, to his right, and rode over to them, across a distance of about fifty yards. What did he see there, what did he say? He must have been weary. On October 7, 8, and 9 he averaged about fifty miles a day over rough hill country. This day, October 10, he had ridden about thirty miles. But he was a polite, even a courtly, gentleman toward women; it is easy to believe that he made a little bow toward her, before dismounting or afterward, and said, "Madam, it is a very pleasant evening."

But what he said and what she said we shall never know. At this point we come face to face with one of the great mysteries in American history. On this spot, at Grinder's Stand, a great American died, when still a young man. He died this evening or night or the next day, and was buried in a split-oak coffin in a hole in the earth, up the ridge about four or five hundred feet north of the cabins. All that is left of him is supposed to be there today, under a shabby monument that was erected more than a century ago.*

Did he kill himself or was he murdered? It should be said at once in plain words that we simply do not know, and can never know, unless evidence turns up of which today we have no knowledge. Many have said it was suicide, many have said it was murder, including on both sides persons who were distinguished.** As late as 1956 a reputable historian published an essay in which he said it was suicide and the matter is settled. But the matter is not settled, as we shall see.

No book and no essay heretofore published has presented more than a part, and usually no more than a small part, of the

---

*See photograph, page 132.          **See Appendix A.

available evidence. This book presents all the evidence that this writer was able to find in two years of research in libraries and historical societies all over the nation. On reading the evidence presented here the reader may think it was murder or he may think it was suicide, or he may feel that an unprejudiced mind can come to no conclusion either way. He will discover that there is little direct and positive evidence to support either view—that any conclusion drawn must rest almost entirely on deduction and inference. Indeed, the case is a fascinating study in the nature of evidence. If the reader is wary, he needs no advice, but even so he may be interested in the fact that a distinguished Boston lawyer, Robert H. Montgomery, has recently published a book on the Sacco-Vanzetti case, in which he presents all the known evidence. He has no doubt that the men were guilty. Another lawyer, Justice Musmanno of the Pennsylvania Supreme Court, has published a book in which he examined all the evidence. He has no doubt that the men were innocent.

When two well-trained, experienced, and distinguished lawyers can reach absolutely opposite opinions on the same evidence we may do well not to be in haste to reach conclusions here. We must assume that factors besides evidence helped to determine the opinion of Mr. Montgomery or Judge Musmanno or both. It is not only bias and preconceived opinions that deceive us; it is that what may seem to be evidence to one person may not seem to be so to another, or may seem to be weaker. This book all the way through will be presenting evidence, or what for various reasons has seemed to be evidence, and the writer hopes that the reader will participate in the effort to evaluate the evidence and determine the probabilities. He may wish to keep in mind, as we have tried to, Prof. Garrett Mattingly's observation in his *Armada*, that when dealing with a character as complex as Queen Elizabeth's it is safer never to be too sure of anything. In this great mystery there are few things more astonishing than the fact that many writers have assumed that they knew exactly how Meriwether Lewis was thinking and acting, during the last weeks of his life. As a man, as a character, he was not that simple.

It is suggested that the reader may wish to study some of the photographs, particularly the Lewis handwriting reproduced here, because the nature of the man and his emotional and mental states during the last weeks of his life are of supreme importance. This is the first time that any of his handwriting, made on days that were crucial to him, has been reproduced, so that the reader can examine it and come to his own conclusions about it.

At the end of the book will be found acknowledgments to the principal persons who assisted in this research; and a body of notes.

Before we return to the scene of his death it seems well to take a look at the kind of man he was, at his problems as governor, at his principal enemy, and at the state of his mind and emotions.

At the Bancroft Library                          VARDIS FISHER
January 4, 1962

# I

## *Governor Meriwether Lewis*

He was born August 18, 1774, about seven miles west of Charlottesville, in Albemarle County, Virginia. According to Thomas
Jefferson's brief account of his life, which appeared as an introduction to the 1814 edition of the Lewis and Clark journals,
Lewis was born "of one of the distinguished families of that state.
John Lewis, one of his father's uncles, was a member of the king's
council, before the revolution. Another of them, Fielding Lewis,
married a sister of General Washington. His father, William
Lewis, was the youngest of five sons of colonel Robert Lewis, of
Albemarle, the fourth of whom, Charles, was one of the early patriots who stepped forward in the commencement of the revolution, and commanded one of the regiments first raised in Virginia
.... Nicholas Lewis, the second of his father's brothers, commanded a regiment of militia in the successful expedition of 1776,
against the Cherokee Indians; ... "

Of Meriwether Lewis's early life we know only a little. His
father died when he was still a small boy. In the same essay
Jefferson says that Lewis was "remarkable even in infancy for
enterprise, boldness and discretion." By "infancy" he probably
had in mind the definition of that word under *Law*: "The status of

an infant, or one under age, or under the age of 21 years." Jefferson told his readers that "When only eight years of age he habitually went out, in the dead of night, alone with his dogs, into the forest.... In this exercise, no season or circumstance could obstruct his purpose."

How much Jefferson knew of Lewis's early life is not known, or what his sources of information were; a few of his statements have drawn scorn from some of Lewis's descendants.* An American historian says, "In the Jefferson papers, filed after Lewis's letter of 7 April 1805, is an undated biographical sketch of Lewis, not in Jefferson's hand, which seems to have been prepared for him by someone who knew Lewis as a boy. It summarizes Lewis's life up to the time he became Jefferson's secretary. One passage reads: '...he was early remarkable for intrepidity...at the age of eight years going alone with his dogs at midnight in the depth of winter, hunting[,] wading creeks where the banks were covered with ice and snow'."

Whether Jefferson's informant knew the facts of Lewis's early life, or whether he freely embellished, is not known. It seems probable that at an early age Lewis learned the use of firearms and prowled alone in the Albemarle forests with his dog —for prowling alone with his dog was a habit with him as a man. His mother seems to have been a "yarb" (herb) doctor and outdoors person, who searched the woods for those herbs which she used in her medicinal concoctions. It may be that mother and son sometimes rambled together, for his attachment to her seems to have been the deepest of his life.

It also seems probable that he was a restless and adventurous child. He had little schooling, though whether he disliked school, or a school was not always at hand, seems not to be known. One of the ablest of those who have written about him says that from the age of 13 to 18 he attended a Latin school. In any case he was still a youngster when he joined the militia, though soon after the Whiskey Rebellion he switched to the regular army. Apparently he liked the military life. "For a short period he had been an ensign in a rifle company commanded by Captain William Clark, and the two had developed an enduring respect for each other." It was because of that respect that, a few years later,

---

*See Notes.

Lewis asked Clark to accept with him equality in leadership and go with him through the vast unknown to the ocean. By the age of 20, Lewis was in the regular army; by the age of 23 he was a full captain; before he was 27 he became Jefferson's private secretary; and at the age of 30 he was leading, with his friend Will Clark, what some have called the greatest exploration in all of history. Not long after he returned from that triumph he became the governor of the Louisiana Territory, succeeding General Wilkinson, whom Chittenden has characterized as "that faithless servant of his country."

To prepare himself to lead the expedition to the ocean Lewis went to Philadelphia, at Jefferson's suggestion, to study those sciences which he would have need of, such as botany and astronomy. He seems to have been an apt student. As a botanist he has never been sneezed at, except by his professional detractors; and as a geographer it was historian DeVoto's opinion that he "clearly ranks with Thompson and Mackenzie." The same historian thought that both Lewis and Clark understood the Indian mind so well that "they must be ranked among the masters of primitive psychology."

Lewis's boldness, his fearlessness in the face of even the most extreme danger, not even those have denied who have written against him. By the age of 16 he begged for a chance to go with an exploring party to the western ocean. He seems never to have thought of himself as a person of extraordinary courage and valor, or even to have been aware of these traits as virtues. A careful reading of his journal to the ocean and back reveals that again and again he missed death by a hair, and wrote about his escapades in a whimsical or droll and always casual way. Typical in his account of his hair-raising adventure with a grizzly bear, June 14, 1805:

"I scelected a fat buffaloe and shot him very well, through the lungs; while I was gazeing attentively on the poor anamal discharging blood in streams from his mouth and nostrils, expecting him to fall every instant, and having entirely forgotten to reload my rifle, a large white, or reather brown bear, had perceived and crept on me within 20 steps before I discovered him; in the first moment I drew up my gun to shoot, but at the same instant recolected that she was not loaded and that he was too

near for me to hope to perform this opperation before he reached
me, as he was then briskly advancing on me; it was an open level
plain, not a bush within miles nor a tree within less than three
hundred yards of me; the river bank was sloping and not more
than three feet above the level of the water; in short there was
no place by means of which I could conceal myself from this
monster untill I could charge my rifle; in this situation I thought
of retreating in a brisk walk as fast as he was advancing untill I
could reach a tree about 300 yards below me, but I had no sooner
turned myself about but he pitched at me, open mouthed and
full speed, I ran about 80 yards and found he gained on me fast,
I then run into the water the idea struk me to get into the water to
such a debth that I could stand and he would be obliged to swim,
and that I could in that situation defend myself with my espontoon; accordingly I ran haistily into the water about waist deep,
and faced about and presented the point of my espontoon, at this
instant he arrived at the edge of the water within about 20 feet
of me; the moment I put myself in this attitude of defence he
sudonly wheeled about as if frightened, declined to combat on
such unequal grounds, and retreated with quite as great precipitation as he had just before pursued me.

"As soon as I saw him run in that manner I returned to the
shore and charged my gun, which I had still retained in my hand
throughout this curious adventure. I saw him run through the
level open plain about three miles, till he disappeared in the woods
on medicine river; during the whole of this distance he ran at full
speed, sometimes appearing to look behind him as if he expected
pursuit. I now began to reflect on this novil occurrence and indea-
voured to account for this sudden retreat of the bear. I at first
thought that perhaps he had not smelt me before he arrived at
the waters edge so near me, but then I reflected that he had
pursued me for 80 or 90 yards before I took the water and on
examination saw the grownd toarn with his tallons immediately
on the imp[r]ession of my steps; and the cause of his allarm still
remains with me misterious and unaccountable. so it was I felt
myself not a little gratifyed that he had declined the combat. my
gun reloaded I felt confidence once more in my strength."

A few minutes later he saw a strange catlike animal which
at first he thought was a wolf. It crouched at a hole, as though

ready to spring, and when he fired it disappeared into the earth. After examining the spot he was convinced that the creature was "of the tiger kind" and that he had hit it—"my gun is true and I had a steady rest by means of my espontoon, which I have found very serviceable to me in this way in the open plains. It now seemed to me that all the beasts of the neighbourhood had made a league to distroy me, or that some fortune was disposed to amuse herself at my expence, for I had not proceeded more than three hundred yards from the burrow of this tyger cat, before three bull buffaloe, which wer feeding with a large herd about half a mile from me on my left, seperated from the herd and ran full speed towards me, I thought at least to give them some amusement and altered my direction to meet them; when they arrived within a hundred yards they mad[e] a halt, took a good view of me and retreated with precipitation. I then continued my rout homewards passed the buffaloe which I had killed, but did not think it prudent to remain all night at this place which really from the succession of curious adventures wore the impression on my mind of inchantment; at sometimes for a moment I thought it might be a dream, but the prickley pears which pierced my feet very severely once in a while, particularly after it grew dark, convinced me that I was really awake, and that it was necessary to make the best of my way to camp."

This charmingly nonchalant account of a day alone among dangerous wild beasts, with a gun that could be fired only once without reloading, is in striking contrast to certain contemporary writing that gives a high order of courage to men who with high-powered automatic weapons, and usually with a guide who is an expert shot, stalk the jungle creatures of Africa. Equally casual and unpretentious is Lewis's account of his deep penetration of Blackfeet country, with three companions; of their encounter with hostile warriors, two of whom they killed; and of a wild ride for their lives for a day and a night. In the annals of this nation it is an exploit which has rarely been equalled in foolhardy courage.

But no one has ever questioned his intrepidity. It would be as foolish to question the woodlore of Daniel Boone, the vision of Jefferson, or the patience of Lincoln. Nor, so far as the records show, has anyone questioned his prudence. This is so much a part of his character and so important in any study of his death that it needs to be made explicit.

When Jefferson asked Livingston to negotiate the purchase of New Orleans from the French, he engaged in ticklish and bold diplomacy; but of all the statesmen of his time he had, according to such historians as the late Bernard DeVoto, the clearest notion of the forces at work in Europe, and of the changes to come. It was a time for a great and daring gamble by the small weak nation known as the United States, and Jefferson was a gambler. He gambled his political life, his administration, and his future place in history (of which he was as conscious as F. D. Roosevelt was to be later) on the bold project of an exploring party across the territory of a foreign and hostile power.

His message to the Congress about it was secret. He took the risk of a deliberate and calculated lie—for he told the Spanish ambassador that he had in mind no more than a small scientific and geographic expedition. His real purpose had to be concealed for a number of reasons, one of which was the immensely rich fur trade in western Canada, on which Jefferson had his eye, and which he hoped in some way to wrest from the British. And he had in mind, of course, that the entire Rocky Mountains area and all the lands beyond it to the ocean should eventually be a part of the United States.

As leader of an exploration who would need the utmost in intrepidity, resourcefulness and prudence we seem not to know whether Jefferson ever had anybody in mind besides George Rogers Clark, an older brother of William Clark, and Meriwether Lewis. He seems to have settled on Lewis when in February, 1801, he summoned him to Washington to serve as his private secretary, for we know that having Lewis act as his secretary was the least of what he had in mind. Jefferson knew that a wish to go to the western ocean had been for Lewis "a darling project of my heart" for years; and so now he wanted to communicate to Lewis his vision, and (it seems likely) to determine from daily observation of Lewis over a period of a year or two whether he was the man for the job. After Lewis's death Jefferson was to say that "While he lived with me in Washington I observed at times sensible depressions of mind . . . ." We don't know whether Jefferson actually saw Lewis in depressed states, or whether on hearing that Lewis had killed himself while deranged he looked back and imagined that he had. In any case, Lewis detested urban life. We know that he had little tolerance of all the protocol and pomp and social emptiness of Washington—not to speak of its streets of mud, his own enforced physical inactivity, and the interminable delay as Jefferson watched the international scene and waited for the right moment. It seems probable that a man like Lewis would now and then have been depressed. So, no doubt, would William Clark have been, or his brother George, or Alexander Mackenzie, the great explorer of western Canada; or any other man whose natural life was leadership on the physical frontiers.

The compelling fact that we should keep in mind is this, that Jefferson entrusted to this man a task that was of supremest importance to him and the nation. He did this after close observation of him for two years. The only possible conclusion is that *at that time* he did not see in Lewis "these distressing affections" that at any moment might plunge him into a "paroxysm," that a few years later Jefferson was to tell his readers he found in him. Otherwise he surely would never have considered him for the leadership of so hazardous a mission: he knew a number of men who by education and experience might have seemed better qualified for the task. As DeVoto says, Jefferson must have "entered office determined to carry out the project as soon as possible and took Lewis into his personal and official household for that purpose." At the end of two years of watching his man Jefferson would not have asked Lewis to lead the expedition if he had had any doubt of his prudence or of his mental and emotional stability.

We must assume that Jefferson opened his mind to Lewis frankly and fully, and revealed to him a great deal more of his vision and his hope than he had dared to put in his confidential message to the legislature. So far as we know, Lewis in no way betrayed his trust. If the nature of his undertaking was not as hidden as Jefferson wished it to be, that was due to no indiscretion in the leadership but to the fact that the Spanish ambassador was not a fool. In our time when trusts have been betrayed by many, and scandals have shaken world capitals, it may seem remarkable that Lewis and Clark kept a secret of such magnitude that it was to change the course of history.

Jefferson called Lewis to Washington in February and took office in March. By the middle of June two years later the as-

tounding news reached Washington that Napoleon had sold Louisiana to the United States. The journey proposed under the
leadership of Lewis and of one other, to be chosen by him, now
became supremely urgent. That Jefferson believed that Lewis
would reach the western ocean, if any man could, and that Lewis
proved to be the man, should be a sufficient answer to anyone
whose tendency is to find in him a weak and ineffectual person,
overrated as an explorer and scientist, a failure as a governor,
and at last a deranged tippler who took his own life. He may have
taken his life—it is our task here to try to determine whether he
did or not—but it is well to set over against the portrait some have
drawn of him the man as he was.

In his essay on him Jefferson said: "Of courage undaunted;
possessing a firmness and perseverance of purpose which nothing
but impossibilities could divert from its direction; careful as a
father of those committed to his charge, yet steady in the main-
tenance of order and discipline; intimate with the Indian character, customs, and principles; habituated to the hunting life;
. . . honest, disinterested, liberal, of sound understanding, and
a fidelity to truth so scrupulous, that whatever he should report
would be as certain as if seen by ourselves; with all these qualifications, as if selected and implanted by nature in one body for
this express purpose, I could have no hesitation in confiding the
enterprise to him."

Those are the words of a friend writing about a friend who
was dead, and like a funeral sermon they embellish; but there
is little to quarrel with down to the word "honest," and possibly
not a great deal after it. It is a fact that on his way to the ocean
and back, every virtue in Jefferson's list that was applicable to
the task of leadership was found in Lewis in remarkable depth
and strength. All this raises a question that is difficult to answer:
How could Jefferson only three years after Lewis's return accept,
apparently without question, the word of a stranger that Lewis
had become deranged and killed himself? This matter will be
examined later.

DeVoto has said that Lewis was mercurial. Mercurial, the
dictionary says, is "likened to the properties of the metal mercury;
as: swift, active, eloquent; clever; crafty; commercial; thievish;
fickle, etc." DeVoto possibly had in mind Lewis's tendency to
strong emotional responses. His journal reveals him to have been

introspective, temperamental, sentimental, lonely and withdrawn, with a habit of self-depreciation. Typical of the latter are his amusing words written on his 31st birthday, August 18, 1805:

"This day I have completed my thirty first year, and conceived that I had in all human probability now existed about half the period which I am to remain in this Sublunary world. I reflected that I had as yet done but little, very little, indeed, to further the hapiness of the human race or to advance the information of the succeeding generation. I viewed with regret the many hours I have spent in indolence, and now soarly feel the want of that information which those hours would have given me had they been judiciously expended. but since they are past and cannot be recalled, I dash from me the gloomy thought, and resolved in future, to redouble my exertions and at least indeavour to promote those two primary objects of human existence, by giving them the aid of that portion of talents which nature and fortune have bestoed on me; or in future, to live for *mankind*, as I have heretofore lived *for myself*." It is hard to tell what he had in mind—possibly all the hours he had spent in wandering in forests, alone, but for his rifle and dog.

Unquestionably he was by nature solitary and lonely. We do not know why. It may have been the shock of losing his father when he was a small lad, or he may have taken the trait from his mother. He seems to have been a bit of what in psychological jargon is called an anxiety neurotic. Too much has been made of his tendency to dose himself with pills and powders when (it seems to be assumed) he had no need of them: after all, the one who detests all pills (and there are such persons) is as much a fanatic as the one unreasonably addicted to them. We don't know that Meriwether Lewis was. Anyone who is so frank in writing about his habits, good and bad, as Lewis was is likely to be taken too seriously. Possibly he took his lively interest in medicines from his mother; or possibly he took it from the famous Dr. Benjamin Rush, whom he consulted, aware that on their long and difficult journey to the ocean he and Clark would have to serve as physicians as well as captains.

Typical of him in an impatient mood, when convinced that persons were unfairly opposing him, is his letter to Clark dated

at St. Louis, May 6, 1804, at a time when he was working to the
limit of his strength to get the expedition under way:

"... I hope all matters will be in readiness for my departure
from this place. Damn Manuel and triply damn Mr. B they give
me more vexation and trouble than their lives are worth. I have
dealt very plainly with these gentlemen, in short I have come to
an open rupture with them; I think them both great scoundrels,
and they have given me abundant proofs of their unfriendly dis-
positions towards our government and its measures. These gentlemen (no I will scratch it out) these puppies, are not unacquainted with my opinions; and I am well informed that they
have engaged some hireling writer to draught a petition and re-
monstrance to Govr. Claibourne against me; strange indeed,
that men to appearance in their senses, will manifest such strong
sumptoms of insanity, as to be *wheting knives to cut their own
throats.*"

He concludes:

"Adieu it is late

Your sincere friend"

A quick, impatient, impulsive, imaginative man, who, like all
such men when they are skilled and able, resented fumbling
bureaucratic controls, or machinations intended to delay or
circumvent him. The Manuel was no doubt Lisa, of whom
Thomas Nuttall wrote in 1810 that he was one of the slipperiest
of the early fur traders: "... he was personally acquainted with
the late *Gov. Lewis* of whose character he has nothing very fa-
vourable to relate; he says, he was fond of exaggerating everything relative to his expedition, & that he was very headstrong,
& in many instances an imprudent man."

What Lisa took to be boasting was possibly no more than
tongue-in-cheek teasing, for Lewis was an inveterate tease. This
he reveals in nothing more than in his attitude toward women,
another matter on which a dreadful lot of nonsense has been
written, by persons who will alter the facts of history to put a man
in love. One writer, Emerson Hough, developed a preposterous
romance between Lewis and Aaron Burr's married daughter, a
calumny on both persons, which has been accepted as historical
fact even by sober people.

William Clark seems to have been a little worried by his friend's apparent indifference to women and to have tried now and then to put an eligible woman in Lewis's way. Clark was married on January 5, 1808, and soon thereafter Lewis wrote him that he was a "musty, fusty, rusty old bachelor . . . . I trust you do not mean merely to tantalize us by the promise you have made of bringing with you some of your Neices, I have already flattered the community of S Louis with this valuable acquisition to our female society." Clark had promised to bring or send a few eligible women to girl-shy St. Louis. He seems to have brought only one, apparently an attractive girl, of whom a St. Louis swain wrote that there was a great agitation among the bachelors in the town, and a "Town meeting has been proposed for the purpose of disposing of her by lot."

Clark's interest in Lewis's unmarried state probably came from a feeling that a wife and children would help to fill the void of his friend's loneliness. In his journal of his western trek Lewis's comments on the female sex are always amusing and usually droll. Typical was his naming of a river:

"The whole of my party to a man except myself were fully pesuaided that this river was the Missouri, but being fully of the opinion that it was neither the main stream, nor that which it would be advisable for us to take, I determined to give it a name and in honour of Miss Maria W——d called it Maria's River. it is true that the hue of the waters of this turbulent and troubled stream but illy comport with the pure celestial virtues and amiable qualifications of that lovely fair one; but on the other hand it is a noble river; . . ."

Reuben Lewis wrote his half-sister Mary that he had had the pleasure of meeting "the accomplished & beautifull" Miss Brackenridge, "one of the most beautifull Women I have ever seen both as to form and features, but unfortunately for his Excellency she left the Neighborhood 2 days after our arrival, so that he was disappointed in his design of addressing her." Reuben surmised that the girl fled because she had heard that Lewis intended to "address" himself to her and thought his intentions too much of a challenge. Possibly she fled, in the immemorial way of women, to measure the strength of his interest. If this was so, she must have been a disappointed young lady, for Lewis never pur-

sued her, or showed half as much interest in her as his brother
Reuben.

At Albemarle, November 3, 1807, he wrote to a friend about
various matters, including the termination of what seems to have
been, on his side, a mild interest in a Miss A—— R——. At this
time he regarded himself as a *"perfect widower with rispect to
love*—thus floating on the *surface of occasion,* I feel all that restlessness, that inquietude, that certain indiscribable something
common to old bachelors, which I cannot avoid thinking my dear
fellow, proceeds from that *void in our hearts,* which might, or
ought to be better filled. Whence it comes I know not, but certain it is, that I never felt less like a hero than at the present
moment. what may be my next adventure god knows, but on this
I am determined, *to get a wife."*

That was as serious as Meriwether Lewis could be about
marriage, and it was not serious enough to move him a single step
toward it. During the remainder of his life he seems to have had
no romantic attachments, however slight, though of course we
do not know what associations he may have had in St. Louis, or
earlier while with Jefferson. It seems likely that when in Washington he was too consumed by a wish to be off to the great adventure to have given any thought at all to women. Wanderlust, he
said, was the strongest force in him—that restlessness, that inquietude; and it may be he never felt that a family was an honorable obligation for a man who was not yet ready to settle down.

For he belonged to the breed, of which this nation has had its
share of distinguished members, who never settle down, as long
as there is a new physical frontier to be reached. It probably was
the one great misfortune of his life, and his most fatal error in
judgment, when he accepted the rather sedentary and confined
position as governor of the territory. He must have known before
he went to St. Louis that it was torn apart by the bickerings and
feuds and plots of ambition and conspiracy, and that his labors
as governor would not be the kind of labors he liked. His problems were to be many, and are so intimately related to his sudden
end that it is necessary to have a look at them, before we leave St.
Louis with him to go down the Mississippi to the present site of
Memphis, and then enter the wilderness with him to journey to
the scene of his death.

His appointment as governor was confirmed by Congress

March 4, 1807. He was governor only about two and a half years. While we examine his life during this period the reader may wish to keep in mind Jefferson's words, that he had observed "distressing affections" in Lewis when Lewis was his secretary in Washington; that after Lewis became governor "these returned upon him with redoubled vigour, and began seriously to alarm his friends"; and that Lewis was "in a paroxysm of one of these, when his affairs rendered it necessary for him to go to Washington."

If Thomas Jefferson was right, there should be in St. Louis some evidence to support him.

## II

# Lewis's Problems
# as Governor

In his history of early St. Louis, Billon says that when Lewis became governor of the Louisana Territory he found it "distracted by feuds and quarrels among the officials, and the people greatly discontented." This opinion, which may be close to the facts, seems to have been Jefferson's view. It was, we should bear in mind, a crude, hell-for-leather frontier outpost, that attracted unprincipled and dangerous men, whose sole purpose was to wrest a fortune from the innocent, from their competitors and rivals, and from the resources of the land. In 1908 Dr. Perley Spaulding wrote: "Lewis found many factions and parties, but his evenhanded justice to all soon established respect for himself, and eventually removed animosities." The second part of Spaulding's statement the Territory's secretary would have hooted at, as we shall see, when we examine the relationship between Frederick Bates and Lewis.

Mr. Dawson A. Phelps, a recent historian, quotes with approval Jefferson's opinion that Lewis found the Territory disturbed by feuds and contentions, and the people divided into factions and parties; and then adds: "The clash of selfish, grasping and ambitious personalities made the position of governor most difficult." Some of those who have been convinced that Lewis killed himself, such as Jefferson and Phelps, may have been inclined to exaggerate the difficulties of Lewis's position, as a part of their explanation that his troubles got him down. We can hardly doubt that his troubles were many and exacerbating, but surely they were not so trying as those which he encountered on his way to the ocean. He was not an inept administrator; on the contrary, he had remarkable skill and tact when handling opposing persons and groups.

DeVoto, while admitting, as any person must, that Clark had greater skill when dealing with Indians, points out that Lewis "was alone at two critical encounters with Indians [on the expedition], the Snakes and the Blackfeet, and he handled them with an experience that no one could have surpassed." This is a typical DeVoto overstatement, but it seems to be a fact that Lewis had extraordinary skill when dealing with Indians, and Indians were one of his major problems as governor. According to Mrs. Grace Lewis Miller, his establishment of a treaty with the Osages was a major accomplishment.

When dealing with the subject of possible suicide, which so intimately touches the nature of a person, one must raise the question of intelligence. Jefferson apparently thought that Lewis's mind was far above average. Frederick Bates, his implacable enemy, never alleged stupidity against him. DeVoto goes so far as to say, of Lewis and Clark, "Both men were of great intelligence, of distinguished intelligence. The entire previous history of North American exploration contains no one who could be called their intellectual equal." Perhaps the question should be, not whether Lewis had the intelligence for his task, but whether he had the temperament for the life of an administrator, with its burden of petty details, and its constant harassment from unscrupulous and scheming men.

There was, for instance, the Burr conspiracy. Arthur Hecht says that a number of military men east of the Allegheny mountains were sent west to testify against Aaron Burr, and their "sworn depositions and testimonies furnished the adminsitration alarming news about the extent of the conspiracy as well as the continued sympathy for Burr." Washington was in fact so alarmed that the Post Master General wrote Lewis, July 28, 1807, as follows:

"The critical state of public affairs, and the extreme distance of the Territory of Louisiana from the General Post Office, which renders the attainment of correct information unusually difficult, have induced me to solicit your particular attention to the conduct of the Agents of this Department in that Territory; and to confide to your discretion and wisdom the power of removing such Officers as are, or may become unfaithful, or not deserving of public confidence; and of appointing suitable Successors in their stead."

It must be admitted that the Post Master General conferred on Lewis extraordinary powers. It may be that such powers were conferred on him by other offices in Washington. We have found no evidence that suggests, much less proves, that he abused such powers, though it is probable that Bates thought he did. The Territory had more than its share of greedy men who were striving in every possible way to win advantages and fill their purses. For Bates, the Territory's secretary, such men were a blight and a curse, and his hostility to Lewis was aroused in large measure because he felt that Lewis was indulgent toward the scoundrels. Bates, then, became one of his major problems. Almost as trying was the arrogant ignorance of certain officials in Washington. One instance will suggest the nature of the whole.

The Federal Government was under a solemn pledge to return a certain Mandan Indian chief and his family to their people; without the promise the chief would not have come down the Missouri with Lewis and Clark, on their return from the ocean in 1806. Before Lewis became governor, Nathaniel Pryor, a sergeant in the Expedition, now an ensign, was placed in command of an armed escort to return the chief and his family. But the Arikaras, who in 1804 had been friendly to Lewis and Clark, were now at war with the Mandans. To Pryor's amazement these Indians attacked his boats, and after fruitless councils attacked a second time. Men were killed or wounded on both sides, including a leading Sioux chief. George Shannon, of the Expedition, had a leg so badly shattered that later it had to be amputated. The whole party was forced to return to St. Louis.

Jefferson was as concerned as any other man to get the chief back home. July 17, 1808, he wrote Lewis, "Since I parted with you in Albemarle in Sep. last I have never had a line from you, nor I believe has the Secretary of War with whom you have much connection through the Indian department. the misfortune which attended the effort to send the Mandane chief home became known to us before you reached St. Louis. we took no steps on the occasion, counting on receiving your advice as soon as you should be in your place, and knowing that your knowledge of the whole subject & presence on the spot would enable you to judge better than we could what ought to be done."

It was unfortunate that an arrogant and bumbling war department did not have the same confidence in Lewis's ability to return a sulking Mandan to his people, at the least expense and without explosive results. There is no exaggeration in the statement that this lack of confidence led directly to Lewis's death. Jefferson was so earnest in his concern, and had so much confidence in Lewis's ability to get the job done, that a month later he wrote the Secretary of War, "I would allow Govr, Lewis the 3 companies of (an illegible word) & military stores as he desires. We are so distant and he is well acquainted with his business, that it is safest for our interests there, & for ourselves after enjoining him to pursue our principles, to permit him to select the means ....I...leave to yourself the detailed answer to Govr. Lewis ...." It seems not to be known if Jefferson ever saw the detailed answer, if indeed there was one.

The very next day he wrote Lewis, "I am uneasy hearing nothing from you about the Mandan chief, nor the measures for restoring him to his country. That is an object which presses on our justice...."

A lot of Indian trouble was brewing in the area. Two weeks later, September 5th, Jefferson wrote the Secretary of War, "I forward you a letter of July 16 from Govr. Lewis from which you will perceive that the cloud between us, the Iowas, Foxes & Sacs is cleared up. he says nothing of the Osages...." One factor in the stupid misunderstanding and the subsequent tragedy was, of course, the slowness of the mail. As Billon says, "Mails from Philadelphia and New York usually about six weeks on their way." He quotes a Territory newspaper of January 25, 1809: "No mail from the east for more than two months."

Another unfortunate aspect of the matter was the fact that Jefferson, who understood the matter and its urgency, and had confidence in Lewis's ability and honesty, would soon leave the

White House. He wanted to get the Mandan chief off his con-
science, for it had been at his urging that the captains had
brought him down the river, and to Washington. Apparently
Lewis was not able to engage a second and larger force and get
it on its way in time to dodge the coming winter. Before that
winter was over, Thomas Jefferson was out as president, and
James Madison, who had barely a portion of his predecessor's
mind and vision, was in. There can be no doubt that if Jefferson
had been president throughout 1809, Meriwether Lewis would
not have died at Grinder's Stand. Madison seems never to have
understood Lewis's problem, that of getting the Mandan chief
back to his people, through hostile Indian nations that were
determined that he would not pass. For his having left his
people and gone to Washington to meet the White Father they
looked on him as a quisling.

Lewis engaged the Missouri Fur Company, experienced and
able, to take the chief and his family to his native village. The
escort left in the early summer of 1809, *after* Jefferson had retired,
under the command of Pierre Chouteau, a topnotch river and Indian man, who had been a member of the former escort. Chouteau's party comprised 125 armed men, many of them expert
riflemen. The chief was delivered to his people September 24,
nineteen days after a frustrated and harassed Lewis had left St.
Louis for Washington, to try to talk sense into the heads of men
who had brought him to the brink of financial ruin.

His difficulties with various departments in Washington
were of a nature with those of many officials who were far removed from the seat of power. Some of them, like William Clark
(though a rejected voucher seems to have been rare in his official life), took a protested bill or an arrogant letter as an inevitable part of government. To Lewis's impatient highstrung spirit
a rejected voucher was not only a reflection on his judgment but
also an impeachment of his honor, to which he seems to have
been extremely sensitive. Apparently without getting specific
consent from the appropriate Washington office he decided to
have the laws of the Territory put in order and copied, and employed one Peter Provenchere for the task. Though the cost of
the project was small it was denied. On receiving the rejection of
his voucher he wrote a letter (see pages 100-101-102) in which
there may or may not be signs of mental derangement. This letter

will be inspected in detail when we come to the subject of his mental condition.

Back in April in the year 1809 the War Department had written him: "No price having been fixed by contract for the ration to be delivered at the military posts up the Mississippi and Missouri your Excellency will oblige the Department by giving your opinion, as to what would be a reasonable compensation for the same, at each of those posts." He must have welcomed this kind of letter, for it clearly implied that by experience and situation he knew more about these Territorial matters than men knew who had never been far from Washington. It may be that he construed such letters to mean that he was allowed a degree of latitude when judging what was needed in the Territory and what should be done.

Seven thousand dollars, a considerable sum in those times, had been approved by Washington for the purpose of equipping and paying a military escort to return the Mandan chief. Because he had heard that the Cheyennes and Arikaras were determined that no boats would pass through their areas, Lewis had, without consulting Washington (he had no time for that), advanced to Chouteau an additional sum, to pay for gifts and bribes. He had also, at about this time, pledged to Chouteau a small sum for an "assaying furnace." Rejecting both, the War Department July 15 wrote Lewis the arrogant and sarcastic letter that precipitated the crisis:

Sir

After the sum of seven thousand dollars had been advanced on the Bills drawn by your Excellency on account of your contract with the St. Louis Missouri Fur Company for conveying the Mandan Chief to his Village; and after this Department had been advised that for this 'purpose the Company was bound to raise, organize, arm & equip at their own expence one hundred and forty Volunteers and to furnish whatever might be deemed necessary for the Expedition, or to insure its success'—it was not expected that any further advances or any further agency would be required on the part of the United States. Seven thousand dollars was considered as competent to effect the object. Your Excellency will not therefore be surprized that your Bill of the 13th of May last drawn in favor of M. P. Chouteau for five hundred dollars for the purchases of Tobacco, Powder, &c. intended as Presents for the Indians, through which this expedition was to pass and to insure its success, has not been honored. It has been usual to advise the Government of the United States when expenditures to a considerable amount are contemplated in the Territorial Governments. In the instance of accepting the volunteer services of 140 men for a military expedition to a point and purpose not designated, which expedition is stated to combine commercial as well as military objects, and when an Agent of the Government appointed for other purposes is selected for the command, it is thought the Government might, without injury to the public interests, have been consulted. As the object and destination of this Force is unknown, and more especially as it combines commercial purposes, so it cannot be considered as having the sanction of the Government of the United States, or that they are responsible for consequences. On another account it was desirable that this Government should have been consulted. Being responsible for the expenditure of Public money made judges in such cases whether the Funds appropriated by the Legislature are applicable and adequate to the object, it is desirable in all practicable cases that they should be advised and consulted when expenditure is required. As the agency of Mr. Chouteau is become vacant by his accepting the command of the Detachment it is in contemplation to appoint a suitable character to supply his place.

Another Bill of your Excellency's in favor of Mr. Chouteau drawn for materials for erecting an assaying Furnace has not been protested, there being no appropriation of this Department applicable to such an object.

The President has been consulted and the observations herein contained have his approval,—and your Excellency may be assured that they are dictated by a Sense of public duty and are perfectly consistent with the great respect and regard with which I have the honor to remain, &c. &c. &c.——

This letter did not reach Lewis until more than a month after it was written. It is easy to imagine with what dismay and mounting anger he read it, and reread it; with what feeling of anxiety he stared at the first part of the concluding sentence—for it told him that all appeal to the President had been cut off; and with what astonishment he must have looked at the second part of that sentence, with its deliberate insolence. We don't know how long he spent thinking of the matter before sitting down to write his reply; his letter is dated August 18th, only two and a half weeks before he set out for Washington. It possibly is the most remarkable letter he ever wrote, and it deserves careful study by those who would understand the state of his mind and emotions at this time.

Saint Louis August 18th 1809

Sir:

Yours of the 15th July is now before me, the feelings it excites are truly painful. With respect to every public expenditure I have always accompanied my Draft by letters of advice, stating explicitly, the object of the expenditure: if the object be not a proper one, of course, I am responsible; but if on investigation it does appear to have been necessary for the promotion of the public Interests, I shall hope for relief.

I have never received a penny of public Money, but have merely given the Draft to the person who had rendered the public service, or furnished articles for public use, which have been invariably [a word was crossed out here] applied to the purposes expressed in my Letters of advice.

I have made advances for the Public from time to time in small sums for recovering of public horses which were lost, for forage for them, expenses attending Sales &C. and have retained from the sales of those horses the sum of eighty five Dollars, for which I have ample vouchers. In these transactions, I have drawn no draft, calculating on going forward long since and settling my Accounts with the Public. The balance of the Sales in Money and Bonds have been lodged with General Clark by the Vendue Master:—to the correctness of this statement, I call my God to witness.

I have been informed Representations have been made against me,—all I wish is a full and fair investigation. I anxiously wish that this may reach you in time to prevent any decision relative to me.

I shall leave the Territory in the most perfect state of Tranquility which I believe, it has ever experienced. I find it impossible at this moment, to explain by letter, and to do away by written explanations, the impressions which I fear, from the tenor of your letter, the Government entertain with respect to me, and shall therefore go on by the way of New Orleans to the City of Washington with all dispatch—Thursday next I have appointed for my departure from Saint Louis. I shall take with me my papers, which I trust when examined, will prove my firm and steady attachment to my Country, as well as the Exertions I have made to support and further its interests in this Quarter.

I do most solemnly aver, that the expedition sent up the Misoury under the Command of Mr. Pierre Chouteau, as a military Command, has no other object than that of conveying the Mandane Chief and his Family to their village—and in a commercial point of view, that they intend only, to hunt and trade on the waters of the Misoury and Columbia Rivers within the Rockey Mountains and the Planes bordering those Mountains on the east side . . . and that they have no intention with which I am acquainted, to enter the Domonions, or do injury to any Foreign Power.

Be assured Sir, that my country can never make "A Burr" of me—She may reduce me to poverty, but she can never sever my Attachment from her.

[We interrupt his letter at this point to say that if the letter from the Secretary of War excited in him painful feelings, as most obviously it did, his reply must arouse in the sympathetic reader emotions no less painful. How much better it would have been if he had replied briefly and with dignity, instead of most solemnly averring, invoking God, and putting his heart on his sleeve for the officials in Washington to look at. It may be that he was drinking and not himself when he wrote this letter. Whatever the reason, he goes on like a man almost beside himself and makes a bad statement worse.]

Those protested Bills from the Departments of War and Treasury have effectually sunk my Credit, brought in all my private debts, amounting to about $4000, which has compelled me, in order to do justice to my Creditors, to deposit with them the landed property which I had purchased in this Country, as Security.

The best proof which I can give of my Integrity, as to the use or expenditure of public Monies, the Government will find at a future day, by the poverty to which they have now reduced me—still, I shall do no more than appeal to the Generosity of the Government by exposing my Claims. I had sooner bear any pecuniary embarrassment than attempt in any manner to wound the Feelings, or injure in the public Opinion, the present Executive, or either of the Heads of Departments, by complaining of Injuries done me, other than in friendly Expostulations.

I am convinced that the Motives expressed in the latter part of your letter, are those which have actuated you; but at the same time, I trust that the Motives that induced me to make the Expenditure, will be found equally pure.

Some weeks after making the Contract with the Misoury Fur Company, for taking the Mandane Chief to his Village, I received information through the Sous and Hahas that the Chyenns had joined the Aricaras and were determined to arrest all Boats which might ascend the River, I conceived it necessary, in order to meet the additional Force and to insure the success of the Expedition conveying the Mandane Chief, to make the further advance with a view, that should it become necessary to engage an auxiliary Force among the friendly Nations through which they would pass, that Mr Chouteau, the Commanding Officer, might be enabled to acquire such aid by means of those Supplies.

You will find from the enclosed Document that if Mr Chouteau does not expend the articles for the purposes mentioned, that he is still held accountable to the Government for such part thereof as may remain unexpended.

With respect to the assaying Furnace I did conceive that such an Establishment was necessary; but, as there is no Appropriation for such objects, arrangements have been made by me, to meet the protested Bill—and no claim will hereafter be made for that object.

I have reason to believe that sundry of my Letters have been lost, as there remain several important Subjects on which I have not received an Answer.

I still hope that Mr. Chouteau will not be removed, he is ordered to return this Fall, or as soon as the military Expedition is at an end, which you will recollect, ceases as soon as he arrives at the Mandane Nation.

Col. Augoust Chouteau of this place, his brother, has agreed with me to act in his place Pro. Tem. The Osage Treaty not having been ratified, would, in my opinion, recommend this Arrangement.

I have the honour to be with much rispect
Your Obt. Servt.
Meriwether Lewis

N.B. The reasons for wishing Mr. Chouteau not to
be displaced is that if the event takes place before one
or the other of the Osages treaties ar ratifyed there
will in my opinion be war with that nation.

How much better it would have been if he had written briefly
and to the point saying that because he had heard that the Cheyennes and Arikaras were determined to stop the boats, and because he had no time to put this matter up to his superiors and
get a reply, he had acted on his best judgment; and concluding:
"I am happy to believe that the motives expressed in the latter
part of your letter are those which actuated you, and that you
will have no doubt of mine." But Meriwether Lewis was at heart
a gentle and kindly man; sarcasm was not his way. We can only
wish that he had called to his side his level-headed friend William
Clark, to advise him in this critical hour.

We don't know whether the letter given here was his first
and only draft, or the last of two or more. It sounds like a first
draft, written out of pain and haste, right from the heart. Possibly
he never knew that he was wasting paper and ink when he confessed to the cold Secretary of War that his credit had been sunk,
for nothing has been found to suggest that the Department relaxed its judgment of him, or abated at all its sarcastic view of him.
Lewis's reply, it must be confessed, is over-emotional, self-pitying,
imprudent, and regrettable; but it reveals a delicacy of feeling for
the sensibilities and honor of the Secretary which the Secretary
obviously did not feel for him. Though in advancing an extra sum
to Chouteau, to be used only if he needed it, Lewis was clearly in
the right, and the Department was clearly in the wrong, Lewis
was sufficiently in possession of himself to be willing to suffer
acute financial embarrassment rather than injure the reputation of
his superiors. The most he would do because of injuries done him
would be to indulge in friendly expostulations! It is possible that
somewhere in the Tennessee wilderness he decided that would
do no good either.

An interesting, but not important, light is cast on the matter by a letter from Chouteau's son to the War Department:

"By the last communications made me by his Excel. 'Gov' Lewis, I have reason to believe that you were not pleased that my Father was employed to reconduct the Mandane Chief and that you consider this mission as being inconsistent with his place of Agent in the Indian Department for the Osage Nation. Perhaps, also, you do not approve the manner in which the affairs of the Department have been managed for some time past; of this, however, I have no certainty,—the Governor not having imparted to me but very superficially the last Instructions which he had received from you. Thus circumstanced, and to prove that my Father's confidence was not misplaced in investing me with his Powers during his absence, I think it my duty to justify him & to acquaint you in detail with the motives and occurrences that have governed his conduct.

"A short time after the arrival of the Governor at St. Louis, complaints were made by some Inhabitants of the Territory against a Party of Osage Indians who had stolen some Horses. From that moment, I may say, the Governor took upon himself the entire direction of Indian affairs, even in the smallest details of the Department, which until then had been confided to the care of my Father. The offence of which the Osages were accused, which previously, among all the other Tribes, had never been expiated in any other way than by the punishment of the guilty individuals, now served as a pretext openly to declare the Osage Tribes *out of the protection of the United States. . . .*"

The brash and aroused son, compelled by an excess of filial devotion, continues in this vein at some length; when, returning to his father, he exclaims, "What would be his grief if he knew that you disapprove his conduct!" Clearly, this long letter from an angry son was not calculated to do Lewis any good in the War Department. The son says his father had invested him with his powers, during his absence; Lewis wrote the Secretary that Chouteau's brother had agreed to act in his stead. This is only one of the many problems which Jefferson possibly had in mind when he said that Lewis was determined to take no sides with any party, but "to conciliate and harmonize them." But Jefferson went so far as to say that Lewis's even-handed justice "soon established a respect for his person and authority" and that "perseverance and time wore down animosities and reunited the citizens again into one family."

As we shall see, Jefferson simply didn't know what he was talking about. The animus of the son toward Lewis is plain in his letter. If Lewis for a while removed from Chouteau's hands most or all of his duties as Indian agent, it seems likely that the father may have felt some bitterness toward him. And there were others whose "animosities" had not been worn down and who had not become part of one happy official family. The outstanding and most outspoken one was young Frederick Bates, the Territory's secretary and Meriwether Lewis's most implacable enemy.

We must now look at this relationship.

# III

# *Meriwether Lewis*
# *and Frederick Bates*

William Clark, after Lewis's death, was governor for about seven years, and so far as we know, Frederick Bates, the Territory's secretary, never spoke about him with malice, or had any serious difficulties with him—indeed, was surprised "to think how well we get along." Why, then, did Bates so quickly become the sworn enemy of Lewis? Was Lewis a hard man to get along with? There is little evidence to support such a view. On the long journey with Clark to the ocean, and back, when hardship, sickness, and dangers tried to the utmost the mettle of both men, the two, DeVoto says, "agreed and worked together with a mutuality unknown elsewhere in the history of exploration and rare in any kind of human association."

We have seen that on becoming governor Lewis inherited problems that a more experienced administrator might have found beyond his powers; and along with these he inherited the secretary, who, says John Bakeless, "privately did everything he could to undermine the Governor's position." How much he did behind Lewis's back we can never know, and Lewis himself probably never knew more than a tithe of it. By the summer of 1809 Bates would no longer speak to him, except when he had to, and would show open contempt for him when he found himself in Lewis's presence.

Bates surely did not plot it that way. April 28, 1807, he wrote Lewis:

"I have not yet experienced so much ill natured opposition as I had expected yet the minds of the many are by no means tranquil. Some of them are shifting their sails to the changing breeze; some plotting schemes of counteraction, others positively predicting that I shall not be six months in the country—and all from the contrary motives of hostility and friendship anxious for your arrival. Now contrary to my first expectations, you must calculate on finding some factions, discontented people by whom your virtues will be dreaded as a scourge, and who will probably anticipate the discountenance into which they must ultimately fall, by commencing the attack.

"For myself, I shall endeavor to remain behind the ramparts of the law, and hope that there I shall be unassaileble. . . ."

It would be interesting to know what Lewis thought of the letter. Was it as plain to him as it is to us? It revealed the man who wrote it—his itching wish to advise and counsel, his tender notion of his own irreproachable honor and integrity, his humorless and pompous manner, and his ambition.

Frederick Bates was born in 1777, the oldest of nine children. His father, a Quaker, had "misfortunes" that made it impossible for him to put his son in college; he was a merchant who was financially ruined by the Revolutionary War. Because his brother Tarleton, and the law partner of another brother, were killed in duels, Frederick abhorred dueling. He had held a number of positions in the government, at one time having been a judge, at another, the land commissioner of Michigan Territory. From April 1, 1807, until Lewis appeared in St. Louis in March, 1808, Bates acted as governor of the Louisiana Territory; and during this time, with William Clark, now Brigadier-General of the militia of the Territory, reorganized the militia. During this time he was also superintendent of Indian affairs, and his biographer says that but for one error he always showed "soundness of judgment." In 1808 he compiled the laws of the Territory. Not long after the death of Lewis he was again acting governor, for two years, or until Clark became governor in July, 1813.

Nobody can read Marshall's two-volume biography of Bates without perceiving that he was, like so many biographers, prejudiced in favor of his subject. He says of him, for instance, "When his mind was once made up, his judgment of men appears to have been almost unerring." This seems to imply that his contempt and scorn of Lewis were justified, an opinion not found elsewhere. Whether Lewis came to detest Bates we do not know. Billon cites a Lewis letter, to one unnamed, just after Bates had been appointed secretary of the Territory:

"The situation of Mr. Bates as a public officer sufficiently shows the estimation in which he is, in my opinion, deservedly held by the Executive of the United States, and consequently renders any further observations in relation to his talents or integrity unnecessary on my part."

In Marshall's opinion, Edward Bates gave a just estimate of his brother when he wrote: "F B was a man naturally of good parts, far above mediocrity, and by life long practice, methodical and exact in business. A constant and observant reader, well versed in the English classics; not ignorant of French literature; and a good historian of all times. He was no public speaker, having never practiced, but his powers of conversation were somewhat remarkable—fluent always, sometimes brilliant, and generally, at once, attractive and instructive. He was a very ready writer, using some diversity of style, but generally clear, terse and pungent. His habits were very retired, perhaps censurable recluse. His friendships few, but strong and abiding."

Wilson P. Hunt wrote Bates that Albert Gallatin had told him, "we had wished to make him Governor, but in the land business we have always considered him a kind of Umpire without whom we should not know how to proceed—we might get as good a man but he is now so well acquainted with the business (and something about the confidence we have in him) we consider him as indispensable."

The Secretary seems to have been able and honest as a public servant, but too selfconsciously, and therefore offensively, virtuous about it all. He was either shrewd or lucky, for his own speculations in land turned out well. He felt that the laws were to be interpreted literally, and enforced to the letter: in 1825, the year after he became governor of the newly-created State, he refused to receive Lafayette officially, on the ground that there were no appropriated funds to entertain him. Meriwether Lewis probably would have said that laws were imperfect things to which common sense must be applied. Though it is plain that this difference in attitude led to the estrangement—that Lewis was far more tolerant of the sharpers and exploiters whom Bates wanted to kick into the river—it is well to let Bates speak for himself, for the reason that his letters so fully reveal him.

He seems to have lived in a state of chronic resentment, because he felt, as he wrote Madison May 6, 1807, that "There are a number of very unworthy men, who hold offices under the territorial Government; But after a few removals, this herd of triflers may be disposed of by a repeal of those very imperfect and indigested laws under which they act. It will then be in the power of a prudent Governor to reestablish the prostrated respectability of Louisiana. . . . It will be in his power to win the affections of the People, who are by no means difficult to govern, and to instruct them in those republican systems with which they are as yet so totally unacquainted."

March 9, the day after Lewis took office, Bates wrote him a short businesslike letter which concluded: "I have not thought that you would require of me a report in writing of the affairs of the Territory. If, however it is your wish, you have only to command me." They exchanged in the next week or two several letters, businesslike but cordial. March 20 Bates wrote an acquaintance: "Governor Lewis arrived on the 8th Inst. and relieved me from the Executive Burthens, at the same time that he gratifies, by his presence the impatient wishes of the people."

Marshall says, "Soon after the arrival of Governor Lewis, the chief executive and the secretary were in disagreement, especially in regard to appointments and Indian policy." By March 24 Bates was writing his young brother Richard: "Affairs look somewhat squally since the arrival of Gov. Lewis. Mighty and extraordinary efforts are making to restore to office some of those worthless men, whom I thought it my duty to remove." One of the "worthless" men seems to have been a John Smith, who was eventually, but vainly, to challenge Bates to a duel. He had been a lieutenant-colonel in the militia, and justice of General Sessions. Marshall thinks that Lewis so relaxed watchfulness over mine speculators that some of them got control of valuable properties without governmental sanction, including Smith, "the most flag-

rant violator of the law." Bates, he says, had "granted leases without fear or favor, and fought relentlessly the unscrupulous and
rapacious speculators who preyed upon the public domain." A
Moses Austin wrote Bates, March 27, that "my confidence in the
correct views of Gov. Lewis are such, that untill I am convinced
by seeing Smith clothed with the Ensigns of his office, I will not
believe him reinstated in the Confidence of the Governor, altho
proclaimed by a thousand tongues."

August 28, Bates wrote the Secretary of War: "Since the
arrival of Gov. Lewis, I have had no interference in the business
of Lead Mines." Their relations seem in fact to have been toler-
able to the end of 1808, though they never saw alike in the matter
of appointments and in the conduct of Indian affairs. During the
winter of 1808-09 Bates must have looked on what the Governor
did with increasing suspicion and hostility, because by April 15
he had to get it off his chest. He wrote to Richard:

"I have spoken my wrongs with an extreme freedom to the
Governor. It *was* my intention to have appealed to *his* superiors
and *mine;* but the altercation was brought about by a circumstance which aroused my indignation, and the overflowings of a
heated resentment, burst the barriers which Prudence and Principle had prescribed. We now understand each other much better.

"We differ in everything; but we will be honest and frank in
our intercourse. I lament the unpopularity of the Governor; but
he has brought it on himself by harsh and mistaken measures. He
is inflexible in error, and the irresistible Fiat of the People, has,
I am fearful already sealed his condemnation." He concludes:
"Burn this, and do not speak of it." Marshall thinks that "Apparently the governor was suspicious of the popular secretary and
fearful that Bates was at the head of a party whose object it was
to bring about his dismissal."

Whether Lewis was suspicious we do not know but he certainly had a right to be, as we shall see in what follows.

July 14 Bates wrote his brother: "Gov. Lewis leaves this in a
few days for Phila. Washington &c. He has fallen from the Public
esteem & almost into the public contempt. He is well aware of
my increasing popularity (for one scale sinks as the other rises,
without an increase of gravity except comparative) and has for
some time feared that I was at the head of a Party whose object

it would be to denounce him to the President and procure his dismission. The Gov: is greatly mistaken in these suspicions; and I have accordingly employed every frank & open explanation which might have a tendency to remove that veil with which a few worthless fellows have endeavoured to exclude him from the sunshine. He called at my Office & personally demanded this explanation. It was made with that independence which I am determined shall mark my conduct on all occasions; and accompanied with an assurance that the path of life, which I had long since prescribed to myself did not admit of prevarication. As a Citizen, I told him I entertained opinions very different from his, on the subject of civil government, and that those opinions had, on various occasions been expressed with emphasis; but that they had been unmixed with personal malice or hostility. I made him sensible that it would be the extreme of folly in me to aspire above my present standing: that in point of *Honor,* my present offices were nearly equal to the government and greatly superior in *emolument*—And that the latter could not, from any motives of prudence be accepted by me, if offered by the President. 'Well' said he 'do not suffer yourself to be separated from me in the public opinion; When we meet in public, let us, at least address each other with cordiality.' My very humanity yielded a prompt assent to this Request, and for this I am resolved to take every opportunity of convincing the People that however I may have disapproved & continue to disapprove the measures of the *Governor,* that as a *man,* I entertain good opinions of him. He used me badly, but as Pope says 'Twas when he knew no better'—In one particular case when he had determined to go to Washington (tho' he did not go) he left certain Executive Business to be performed by *Genl. Clark;* tho' the Laws have expressly provided for his absence. I waited on his Excellency & demanded that the General should be called in. The Gentlemen were then told that I would suffer no interferences &c. &c. &c.—How unfortunate for this man that he resigned his commission in the army: His habits are altogether military & he never can I think succeed in any other profession."

Bates very possibly was right in saying that Lewis's habits were military and that he ought never to have left that profession, but in this long letter to Richard, and in others, he comes out as the kind of self-righteous prig whom Lewis simply could not stand. Clark no doubt could have got along with him. That Lewis asked Clark to take over certain official duties, when he expected to be absent, seems to indicate either suspicion of Bates or a feeling of strong distaste for him. And it reveals another reason why Bates reached the point where he could not think of Lewis without anger and self-pity. If he actually contemplated going to the people to let them know that he approved practically nothing of what the Governor was doing and had done, we can only marvel at Lewis's forbearance; for while Bates was dispatching letters to family, friends and superiors to tell them his opinion of the Governor, Lewis seems to have written nothing about Bates. Perhaps he unburdened himself to his good friend William Clark.

Lewis was not by any means the only person who crossed his path whom Bates could not stand. There was Judge Lucas, of whom he complained constantly to Richard and to the Secretary of War. In the long letter to his brother, of which a portion has just been given, he pours his wrath on Lucas, "who commenced his attacks . . . last year. It was imagined by the whole country that I had done my duty faithfully—& this *good word* was sufficient to excite all the angry malignity of the Judge. He attacked my Report. . . . Foiled in this object he commenced a system of poignant pleasantry at *some times,* and of sarcasm at *others* by which he has frequently raised a storm from which he has been willing enough to retreat. When Lucas & myself quarrel, as we had the indecorum to do last winter, before crowded Audiences of Claimants, Penrose* had the good sense to hold his tongue. He is however a willing Dupe & shares with Lucas the public execrations." After two more pages of pouring out his woes to Richard he says that his "dangerous and delicate" position "will require all the wariness & circumspection of which I am master."

Less than two weeks later, July 25, he was writing to a James Abbott: "Our Gov. Lewis, with the best intentions in the world, is, I am fearful, losing ground. His late preparations for Indian war have not been popular. *He acted for the best.* But it is the fate of great men to be judged by the results of their measures. He has talked for these 12 Mos. of leaving the country—Everybody thinks now that he will positively go, in a few weeks."

Whether Bates was a master of wariness and circumspection

---

*Clement B. Penrose, a member of the Board of Land Commissioners.

is not clear but he certainly was a master of damning with faint praise. Again and again in letters he wrote as he wrote to Abbott, saying on the one hand, with an almost audible sigh of sympathy, that Lewis was a failure, while hastening to add, on the other, that his intentions were of the best. It may well be that Lewis was so sick of Bates's sniping, and no doubt of similar criticism from the Secretary's friends, that for a year he had been talking about leaving the country, which would mean his position and the Territory. It is obvious that he was a goaded man, and that Bates took delight in being the principal goad.

Just three weeks after Lewis left for Washington (by that time he was at Fort Pickering) Bates was writing to the military commander at Fort Madison: "I am much surprised at the suspension by Gov. Lewis, of the trade with the Ioways. The first informations which I had on the subject were from your letters. No record of the transaction has been deposited in the Offices—And as the measure is supported by no principle of Law, Justice, or Policy that I know of I beg that those traders who have regular licenses may suffer no interruptions."

It is unknown why Lewis suspended the trade but we must assume that he had reasons that seemed good to him. The revealing thing in this instance is that he apparently made major decisions without consulting Bates, a matter that must have aroused in Bates the bitterest kind of resentment. Two days later he was complaining to the Secretary of War:

"There is a policy subordinate to, and in execution of the law which the President may doubtless institute for the regulation of Indian Intercourse. But as the Governor has never confided to me the wishes of administration on this, or indeed on any other subjects (except on one special occasion) and as he has left me neither records of his own acts, nor any of his official correspondence, I have nothing but the statute as my guide." In this long letter he confides to the Secretary his opinion that some of Lewis's decisions had been arbitrary, such as granting or revoking hunting and trading licenses—"It has appeared to me that the *right* to *trade* is a right which the Citizen derives from the Laws, and that it is susceptible of very little modification, beyond what the laws themselves have established."

By October 20 (Lewis was dead but Bates did not know it)

he was writing to Penrose to deny that his differences with the
Governor came from a desire on his part to fill the office, rather
than from "an honest difference in opinion, in the transaction of
the territorial business. . . . you have, on very many occasions,
been quite as noisy on the imputed irregularities of the Governor,
as any other person.

"But you still say, that I *have been,* and *am* the enemy of the
Governor,—and that I would be very willing to fill that office myself.—I told you this morning that it was *false*—and I repeat that
it is an impudent stupidity in you to persist in the assertion. How
is it possible that you should know my *wishes,* except from my
declarations or my conduct?—And what declaration of mine, or
what part of my conduct justifies you, in the repetition of *falsehoods* like these?

"In return, for the personal allusions with which you have
honored me, I tender to you, my most hearty contempt."

October 24, still unaware that Lewis was dead, he wrote a
friend: "The term of Gov: Lewis' services, will expire I understand, in Feby or March next. He has been too unfortunate to
expect a second nomination—such, at least is the prevailing opinion." October 31 John B. Treat, Indian agent on the Arkansas,
wrote Bates, "This moment the Secretary of War has mentioned
to me his having by this days Mail received an account of the
extraordinary death of Governor Lewis: for which no one here
undertakes to account for—& certainly the short acquaintance I
had with him S. Louis in June last wholly precludes my having
any reason to offer for his committing an act so very extraordinary
& unexpected."

Those who contend that Lewis killed himself say that he
committed the act while deranged. In all his letters about Lewis
in the summer of 1809, and after Lewis's departure early in September, Bates never once gave any hint, as he surely would have
done, if he had felt that way, that Lewis's behavior was abnormal.

If Bates in the above excerpts from his letters has not revealed himself to the reader for the kind of man he was, then
surely his long letter to Richard, after he heard of Lewis's death,
will bring him forth. It was written on November 9.

"You have heard no doubt, of the premature and tragical

death of Gov: Lewis. Indeed I had no personal regard for him and a great deal of political contempt; Yet I cannot but lament, that after all his toils and dangers he should die in *such a manner*.

"At the *first*, in *Washington* he made to me so many friendly assurances, that I then imagined our mutual friendship would plant itself on rocky foundations. But a very short acquaintance with the man was sufficient to undeceive me. He had been spoiled by the elegant praises of Mitchell & Barlow, and over whelmed by so many flattering caresses of the *high & mighty*, that, like an overgrown baby, he began to think that everybody about the House must regulate their conduct by his caprices.

" '*De mortuis nil nisi bonum*' is a good old maxim; but my character has been assailed, as respects our late Governor, and I owe to those I love some little account of myself.

"I never saw, after his arrival in this country, anything in his conduct towards me, but alienation and unmerited distrust. I had acquired and shall retain a good portion of the public confidence, and he had not generosity of soul to forgive me for it. I was scarcely myself conscious of my good fortune, for the still voice of approbation with which I was favored by the People, was, as yet drowned in the clamours of my enemies. As soon as I was seen in conflict with my associates in business, my friends came forward with a generous and unexpected support.—I bore in silence the supercilious air of the Governor for a long time; until, last summer he took it into his head to disavow certain statements which I had made, *by his order* for, the Secretary's Office. This was too much—I waited on him,—told him my wrongs—that I could not bear to be treated in such a manner—that he *had* given me the orders, & as truth is always eloquent, the Public *would believe* it on my assurances. He told me to take my own course—I shall, Sir, said I, and I shall come, in future to the Executive Office when I have *business* at it.

"Some time after this, there was a ball in St. Louis, I attended early, and was seated in conversation with some Gentlemen when the Governor entered. He drew his chair close to mine—There was a pause in the conversation—I availed myself of it—arose and walked to the opposite side of the room. The dances were now commencing.—*He* also rose——evidently in passion, retired into an adjoining room and sent a servant for General Clark, who refused to ask me out as he foresaw that a Battle must have been the consequence of our meeting. He complained to the general that I had treated him with contempt & insult in the Ball-Room and that he could not suffer it to pass. He knew my resolution not to speak to him except on business and he ought not to have thrust himself in my way. The thing *did pass* nevertheless for some weeks when General Clark waited on me for the purpose of inducing me to make some advances. I replied to him 'NO, the Governor has told me to take my own course and I shall step a *high* and a *proud Path*. He has *injured* me, and he must undo that injury or I shall succeed in fixing the stigma where it *ought to rest*. You come' added I 'as *my* friend, but I cannot separate you from Gov Lewis—You have trodden the *Ups & the Downs* of life with him and it appears to me that these proposals are made solely for his convenience.

"*At last*, I had business at the Executive Office—He pressed me to be seated and made very handsome explanations. I told him that they *sounded* well; but that I could not accept them unless with the approbation of my friend Wm. C. Carr—*He*, with some other Gentlemen were then called in, & *this* particular misunderstanding adjusted to the entire satisfaction of Carr and myself.

Oh Lewis, how from my Love, I pity thee!
'Those who stand high, have many winds to shake them
And if they fall, they dash themselves to pieces'

"I should not speak of these things now, but for the purpose of explaining what followed. Gov. Lewis, on his way to Washington became *insane*. On the arrival of this unhappy news and before we heard of his death, an Honble. Gentleman of this place, a Colleague of mine at the Land-Board, commenced a regular and systematic traduction of my character—He asserted in several respectable companies that the mental derangement of the Governor ought not to be imputed to his political miscarriages; but rather to the *barbarous conduct of the Secretary*. That Mr. Bates had been determined to tear down Gov Lewis, at all events, with the hope of supplanting him in the Executive Office with a great deal of scandal equally false and malicious. The persons who listened most attentively to these accusations, happened to be my very intimate friends Judge Coburn and Doct. Farrar.

"I deliberated with myself 24 hours in what manner I ought to proceed. Clement B. Penrose was worthy of my resentment, as being nearly connected with the 'illustrious House of Wilkinson' as well as on many other accounts. But he has a *Wife* and *family*. A defiance ought not then, if it could be avoided, to come from me. The second day after I had heard these slanders I met him in public, at the Board of Commissioners, after we had adjourned. I charged him with the falsehoods which he had propagated in concise and angry terms. He denied them and explained 'I have said that you were the enemy of Gov Lewis and would willingly be the Governor yourself.' 'You have gone farther than this Sir' said I 'and I will prove it upon you. *I will not submit to your malicious impertinence Mr. Penrose—I will chastise you for it— for two years past, you have been in the habit of gossiping your scandals with respect to me, and I pledge my word of Honor, that if you ever again bark at my heels, I will spurn you like a Puppy from my Path'* These reproaches made no impression upon him—"

After a couple of sentences he says, "Richard, this is a strange world in which we live! I had thought that my habits were pacific; yet I have had acrimonious differences with almost every person with whom I have been associated in public business. I have called myself to a very rigid account on this hand, and before God, I cannot acknowledge that I have been blamable in any one instance. My passions blind me I suppose."

Having in a moment of amazing self-revelation put his finger on the matter, and left nothing for his biographers to say, he then exults, "It is certain, nevertheless, that I float on a flowing tide of popular favor. . . ."

It does seem to be true that he had "acrimonious differences" with practically all the public officials with whom he had official relations. Typical of him are these words to Richard: "You cannot have forgotten, my dear Richard our conversations on the subject of my differences with Judge Griffin. I never did injure the man; but his petulant suspicious ill nature conjured up certain charges which I was very desirous to have personally rebutted."

We have seen that soon after Lewis left for Washington, and before Bates had heard of his death, Bates wrote to various persons to say that Lewis could not expect a second term, in view of the character of his administration. Bates openly solicited support for his friend Judge Coburn; and almost at once, after hearing of Lewis's death, he wrote boldly to President Madison, ". . . the known benevolence of your Character inspires us with Confidence in submitting to you our Wishes"—and his wish was for Coburn as Lewis's successor.

"Whose hell-heart is a sink and a bog of ordure," says Robert Penn Warren of Bates, in his long poem about Lewis and Jefferson. Others have called him Lewis's "bitter enemy." The reader will judge for himself. Whether Bates was right or wrong he certainly was a problem for Lewis in his difficult summer of 1809, but he was not his biggest problem. The matter that filled him with dismay and forced on him the decision to go to Washington was the effectual sinking, as he put it, of his credit, by the rejection of some of his vouchers. We don't know how his creditors heard of the matter, or whether Bates had a hand in bringing it to their attention.

We must now take a brief look at Lewis's debts, his resources, and his desperate but gallant effort to save himself.

## IV

## *Lewis's Financial*

## *Problems, 1809*

Was Governor Lewis caught up in a frenzy of land speculation?
Some writers have said so. The St. Louis *Globe-Democrat* October 8, 1939, said: "It is obvious that Lewis, in 1809, was plunged
into a fever of speculation which raged not less than the smallpox
had raged in the 'little French village under the hill,' exactly a
decade before. It was something from which a man of spirit, and
of adventurous spirit, could scarcely but by miracle escape."

It depends on what is meant by the word *speculate*. The dictionary says that in commerce it is the buying or selling with "the
expectation of profiting by a rise or fall in price; often, to engage
in hazardous business transactions for the chance of unusually
large profits." To buy with an expectation of profit is also what in-
vestors do. A history of Missouri says of Judge J. B. C. Lucas that
when he came to St. Louis in 1805 "he began investing his means
in lands and lots in St. Louis, and laid the foundation of a splendid
family fortune."

Lewis, Clark, Bates, Lucas, and many others in St. Louis had
no doubt that this city would grow, and that the land in and
around it would rise in value. All those who bought land and
were able to hold it realized handsome profits. There can be no

doubt that if Lewis had not had vouchers rejected, and if his creditors had not learned of this and moved on him, he also would have "laid the foundation of a splendid family fortune" and it would not be said of him today that he speculated, but that he wisely invested. It is pretty superficial thinking that finds the origin of his disaster in speculation.

Mrs. Grace Lewis Miller says that within six months after his arrival "he had purchased thirteen handsome parcels of landed property," of which he still owned twelve when he left for Washington. December 1, 1808, about nine months after he arrived, he wrote his mother that he had bought 5,700 acres of land near St. Louis, in four parcels, one of which adjoined the town; a second lay at a distance of six miles, and the third and the fourth were twelve and fourteen miles out. The tract six miles out "contains three thousand acres; the improvements are a field well inclosed of forty acres, a comfortable dwelling house with three rooms with stables and other convenient out houses; a good well and a garden of three quarters of an acre well inclosed."

He paid $3,000 on the lands; $1,500 was due the next May, and $1,200 May 1, 1810. "To meet these engagements it will be necessary to sell the Ivy Creek lands or at least a part of them." To compensate his mother for selling a part of her property, he proposed to give her a portion of those he had bought, possibly one thousand acres, with improvements.

Was he reckless? Was he overreaching his resources? In 1948 Mrs. Miller said she had by that time done research on Lewis in nearly every "important source library" in the United States. In one of her articles she says: "Nothing so pointedly demonstrates the measure of his personal dedication to the public interest . . . as the record of his financial commitments in carrying out the mission which was entrusted to him in 1803. . . . Evidences of experience in handling public treasure and transacting important public business are abundant in the U. S. Accountant's records."

Based on information which she has unearthed she shows that $2,500 was only about five per cent of the total cost of the expedition to the ocean. There was "nearly $21,500 in disbursements by Lewis or his agents for expenses incurred during approximately fourteen months of preparing for the principal part of his journey. . . . In the second year of Jefferson's second Administration his prestige was nothing compared to what it was in the second year of his first term; and conditions for Lewis in 1807, and afterward, were relatively unsatisfactory, in the background, where the financial records were. While the award from Congress for compensation was obtained and disbursed promptly, apparently Lewis's account was not cleared in the same manner; and his subsequent career, and reputation, were affected accordingly. That is, the lustre of his reputation was dimmed."

A part of that comment is rather annoyingly obscure. But whatever his probity and skill in an earlier time in the use of funds, there can be no doubt that in 1808 his tendency was to overreach his own resources, in his eagerness not only to enrich himself but also to see St. Louis grow and to promote its growth. His purchase of lands was not the only demand on his salary of $2,000 a year. The newspaper quoted above is right in saying that "his was the energizing force that brought the first newspaper west of the Mississippi River, by financing Joseph Charless in the establishment of the then Louisiana Gazette, one of the ancestors of your morning's Globe-Democrat." In 1808 Lewis paid over the substantial sum (in those times) of $225 "by myself and others to the said Charless" for the purpose of "establishing a paper in this place." The first issue of the *Missouri Gazette*, Mrs. Miller says, was July 12, 1808. His account book also reveals that he borrowed money to help obtain a charter for the first Masonic Lodge in St. Louis.

For some time (throughout 1807, for instance) he had been paying out various sums toward the forthcoming publication of his journals—$40 to a botanist to make drawings of plants; $20 for paper for the printing of the prospectus; $10 to have it distributed to postmasters. A second sum ($30) went to the botanist for the same purpose; $100 to F. R. Hassler, a West Point instructor in mathematics, for assistance "in the calculation of celestial observations which will be charged to the expense of my works"; $83.50 for "likenesses of the indians &c necessary to my publication to be charged to the expenses of said work"; $150 to Ordway, a member of the Expedition, for his journal; $40 to someone "for drawing the falls of the Missouri"—all these within a few weeks in 1807, besides such sums as $87 for two pistols, and $100 to purchase a horse for his mother. Horses were an expensive luxury in those times: $100 in 1807 was surely equal in purchasing power to $500 today, and very possibly to more than that.

February 15, 1808, he drew $150 as an advance on his salary; March 31 he drew $200, and the next day, $150, the three sums comprising his salary for the first quarter. By April 24 he was drawing $400, "it being in part of my salary becoming due the 1st of July, 1808." Five days later he drew $100 "for this sum in full of my quarter sallery ending the 30th of June 1808." By May 17 he was borrowing $20 from a man named Bates, and on the 25th, $10 from Peter Chouteau. The 28th (of May) he gave his "note on demand" for $200 in one instance, and for $120 in another (for payments on land, no doubt); and on the 28th he borrowed $45 from Chouteau. But by June 7 he had paid Chouteau $400.

June 18 he borrowed $100 from a friend named McFarlane; August 3, $20 from Chouteau, Lewis's contribution toward a Masonic charter. He seems to have kept a careful record of all these matters in his small account book.

In one matter at least he is definitely censurable. As Bakeless has pointed out Lewis received from the War Department $559, which was due in bonus and back pay to John Colter\*. On September 3, 1810, the administrator of the Lewis estate, Edward Hempstead, was served with a summons by an attorney acting for Colter, in which it was claimed that Lewis had withheld from Colter $380 in pay, and $179 as extra pay, allowed by Congress, all of which Lewis had intended "craftily and subtily" to defraud him of. Lewis intended nothing of the kind, of course, but on his willingness to risk Colter's money our censure must be severe. So far as we know, it is the most unworthy act on his record. May 28, 1811, Colter won a judgment, but he should not have had to sue, or to pay a part of what was due him to a lawyer.

It should now be clear what Lewis meant when he wrote the Secretary of War that the rejected vouchers would sink his credit, though it seems rather strange that the rejection of vouchers should so quickly become public knowledge. As his creditors

---

\*His name has been spelled variously, but in his signatures it is Colter. On the return from the ocean, Colter at or near the Mandan villages had turned back up the Missouri with a body of trappers, and had not yet appeared to claim what was due him. Lewis listed his obligation to Colter and called Clark as a witness. He seems then to have spent the money.

came in on him we can imagine with what dismay he faced his immediate future.

A Mrs. Anderson, a relative by marriage, wrote a Mrs. Eva Emery Dye, a novelist who wrote about Lewis more than a half-century ago, that an unfinished letter had been found among Reuben Lewis's papers, written by Lewis to Madison, July 8, 1809. She says the letter inclosed a voucher dated February 6 of that year. This letter, and at least one other, to Madison September 16 from Fort Pickering, have been cited by certain writers as evidence of extreme agitation in Lewis, if not indeed of mental derangement. The reader is invited to examine the letters and determine the matter for himself.* It should be borne in mind that some of his letters, as well as various letters by other men of his time, show that the quality of paper, ink, and pens was often poor. An impatient man, who worked at top speed, as Lewis did, had the habit of striking out words, as better choices presented themselves to his mind. It will be shown later that he did this at times when nobody has thought that he was agitated or deranged. And, finally, the letter below was possibly a rough draft, which he intended to copy.

St. Louis July 8th 1809

Dear Sir

Inclosed I transmit you twenty dollars in bank bills and re-
~~kind~~ your friendly
turn you my sincere thanks for ~~the interest you have taken in my~~
interference  my of eighteen dollars
~~behalf~~ with rispect to ~~my~~ ∧ bill rejected by ~~Mr.~~ the Secretary of
the Treasury. This occurrehce has given me infinite concern as
drawn for similar purposes
~~from it~~ the fate of other bills ∧ to a considerable amount (illegible) cannot be mistaken;—their rejection cannot fail to impress the public mind unfavourably with rispect, nor is this considera-
arise
~~attach~~ in
tion ~~less~~ more painfull than the censure which attached the
for public monies
mind of the executive ~~from my~~ having drawn ~~for~~ without au-
∧

---

*See pages 100-101-102 and 108-109.

thority; a third and not less imbarrassing circumstance attending
   the
~~this~~ ₍ₐ₎ transaction is that my private funds are entirely incompe-
tent to meet these bills if protested.

You will also receive inclosed the voucher on which the bill
of eighteen dollars was predicated on which I shall take the lib-
erty of making a few remarks.—

Previous to ~~my~~ my ~~making any demand~~ drawing any bill of
In the course of the last autumn a Court of Oyer and terminer was held at St. Louis for the trial of a prisoner indicted of
      This duty of presiding in the      to
a felony. This duty Judge   Lucas assigned∧ himself. a few days
          the Judge               to me
previous to the trial ~~fur~~∧ made ~~to me~~ a formal application∧ for
                        of the Territory    ∧
certifyed of the Judiciary and criminal laws   declaring ~~at~~ (ille-
          the court
gible) that unless ~~that I~~∧ was furnished with them he could not
   with
proceed ~~with~~ the trial of the prisoner; under those circumstances
I did not hesitate to cause the copies of those laws to be made
           him.
out and furnished ~~the Judge, and~~ The Secretary of the territory
Mr. Bates previous to my drawing any bill on the (illegible) government for publishing the laws of the territory had informed me
(illegible) ~~had informed~~ me that the expece [expense] of pub-
                  of the territory     in any shape
lishing or promulgating the laws∧ ~~of the territory~~ could not be defrayed by the contingent fund placed under his control consequently ~~there appeared to me to be no other~~ I was compelled to
take the course which I have or suffer a fellon to escape punishment ~~in the transaction I did conceive my self in~~ (illegible) ~~you~~
I shall write more fully to the Secretary of State on this subject
                     which have been
and inclose him my vouchers for the expenses∧ incurred in publishing the laws of the territory as ~~directed by the latter~~ I am im-
peritively directed by

    It is clear that Meriwether Lewis was not up to par when he
drafted that letter, though whether because of anger, impatience,

fatigue, alcohol, or illness it is impossible to say. A fair guess might be that he thought of this as a crucial letter, and found the burden of being both forceful and prudent too much for him at the moment. At the top of the second page he broke off his sentence, leaving it unfinished, as a page later he broke off the letter. If he was drinking immoderately, or even at all, at this time, there is no evidence of it—we can be sure that if he was drinking, Bates would have mentioned the fact in his letters to Richard. Perhaps Lewis had been up most of the night wrestling with his problem and was dog-tired. Though some of his critics have found it easy to condemn him, none of them has told us what Lewis could have done but turn a felon free or furnish a copy of the laws to the judge who demanded it, and hope to have the eighteen-dollars voucher approved.

His administrator filed settlement of the estate February 8, 1815, in which various costs and claims of fourteen persons came to $4,548.31½. Sale of the Lewis properties realized a sum of $4,557.75, leaving to the estate the pathetic sum of $9.43½.

There are at least two ironies in the final settlement, which nobody seems to have mentioned. One is the fact that even Thomas Jefferson, without determining whether Lewis's property would clear his debts, laid a claim against the estate. In a letter dated March 14, 1810, to Captain W. D. Meriwether, Jefferson wrote: "I have some claim on Governor Lewis's estate for monies furnished him some time before he set out on his Western expedition. I do not recollect it's amount, having never looked at it since that time but I have a loose idea of somewhat about 100D." June 23, 1803, Lewis had signed a promissory note to Jefferson for $103.93.

The other irony is more depressing and shocking. On March 4, 1812, two and a half years after Lewis's death, the Washington bureaucracy got around to a confession: "I certify that there is due to the Estate of the late Meriwether Lewis, deceased, the Sum of Six hundred & thirty six Dollars 25/100 being the balance of his Account for disbursements made for the conveyance of the Mandan Chief, and his family to his Village on the Missouri River—including the Damage, Interest, and Cost of protest of three Bills of Exchange drawn by him on this Department in May 1809, for said purposes, which were protested for non-payment— now admitted in conformity to the decision of the Secy of War;

which Sum is to be transmitted by the Treasurer of the United
States to Edward Hempstead, Administrator of the Estate of said
Lewis, deceased, at St. Louis."

So it was honored after all!—the rejected voucher that
brought upon him the sarcasm; that locked the door against him
so that he could not appeal to Madison; that fetched all his creditors against him; that compelled him to give power of attorney to
William Clark and two other friends, so that during his absence
they could take in his behalf any action necessary; that sent him
in the heat of late summer on his way to Washington to see if with
"friendly expostulations" he could obtain justice; that led to his
wretched and mysterious end in a primitive cabin in the Tennessee wilderness; and that aroused malicious gloating in his bitterest enemy, who contrary to his disavowals of interest and ambition would be governor of Missouri before he died.

Mrs. Miller, without citing sources or giving reasons, speaks
of "the weight of opposition he suffered in those times, when he
probably knew his days were numbered." It is doubtful that he
sensed anything of the sort when he set off for Washington. He
was, to be sure, a deeply troubled man. He would soon be a sick
man. Some have believed that soon after leaving St. Louis he was
a mentally deranged man. We must examine this matter and try
to determine his mental and physical condition, during the thirty-
five days between the hour he left St. Louis by boat downriver,
to the late afternoon when he spoke to Mrs. Robert Grinder and
dismounted from his horse.

There is the *myth* of Meriwether Lewis, a myth that has
misled sober historians—the myth of Lewis the drunkard who
with uncombed hair and soiled garments looked like a river rat—
of the haggard face, the yellow skin, the feeble movements. But
our interest is not in myth but in facts and probabilities.* But
first it is necessary to try to reconstruct the Grinder Stand and to
determine who were its occupants on that day, October 10,
1809, when Lewis rode up to the door.

---

*The myth is summarized in Apendix B.

# V

# His Mental

# and Emotional Condition

Those, at least in recent times, who have contended for suicide have said that Meriwether Lewis was mentally deranged off and on during the last weeks of his life, and during the hours he spent at Grinder's Stand. Nobody has ever argued that he killed himself while in possession of his senses. Those who have contended for murder have not been as clear in this matter of his mental and emotional condition, but they seem to feel that he was not out of his mind, at least not at Grinder's during his last hours. It is necessary, therefore, to determine as well as we can the condition he was in.

Those who believe that he killed himself while mentally deranged seem to place almost unlimited faith in the words of Thomas Jefferson, written in August, 1813, for the introduction to the first edition of the Journals. These are his famous words:

"Governor Lewis had, from early life, been subject to hypochondriac affections. It was a constitutional disposition in all the nearer branches of the family of his name, and was more immediately inherited by him from his father. They had not, however, been so strong as to give uneasiness to his family. While he lived with me in Washington I observed at times sensible depressions

of mind: but knowing their constitutional source, I estimated
their course by what I had seen in the family. During his Western expedition, the constant exertion which that required of all
the faculties of body and mind, suspended these distressing affections; but after his establishment at St. Louis in sedentary occupations, they returned to him with redoubled vigor, and began
seriously to alarm his friends. He was in a paroxysm of one of
these, when his affairs rendered it necessary for him to go to
Washington."

Jefferson's words will be examined in some detail later; at
this point, all that we need determine, if we can, is whether he
was deranged before he left St. Louis. One piece of evidence
cited by those who argue for suicide is William Clark's anguished
words, on reading in a newspaper that Lewis had cut his throat,
"I fear O! I fear the weight of his mind has overcome him." That
certainly sounds as if Clark was not surprised to read that Lewis
had killed himself.

On the other hand, Dr. John Bakeless, one of the ablest of
the historians who have written about Lewis, and who leans to
murder rather than suicide, has said: "The story that Lewis was
mentally deranged must also be treated with reserve. He was
certainly ill. He had had difficulties with Bates, a singularly
irritating individual. His personal finances were in a bad way.
He had been drinking heavily [he means not in St. Louis but at
the fort]. His reappointment was in doubt. His accounts were
disputed by Washington auditors. But though the government's
financial methods drive men to distraction, they rarely drive them
to suicide. If they did, the streets of Washington would be lit-
tered with corpses."

The best way to arrive at an opinion of Lewis's condition in
St. Louis is to look at what he did. What would a man in full
possession of his faculties do in such a critical situation? If he
were a man of courage and honor he would put his affairs in order
before undertaking a long and dangerous journey, and that is precisely what Lewis did. Here is his account book, beginning July
17:

July 17         William Christy         Dt
  To this sum paid R. Webster for a         [This is x-ed out in ink of
  horse purchased for the public,         a different color, indicat-
  which sum was allowed you in         ing that it was done later.]
  settlement of your public account $40
Augt. To your duebill on settlement
  20    Genl. Clark                    $81
  except the sum of eighty five dollars Genl. Clark has all the bonds
  notes an money arrising from the
  sales of public horses sold at St.
  Louis.—
August 21st
  On final settlement made me this
  day between Genl. Clark and myself he paid me this sum         $53
  Enquire of Brown at Orleanes for         [These bones seem to have
  the bones of the mamoth sent him         gone astray.]
  by Genl. Clark for the president
  of the U'States—
1809 August 22nd         St. Louis
    A list of private debts due
To John G. Commegyes         $331.45½
To Benjamin Wilkinson         $151.60
To Col. August Chouteau         $10         [James McFarlane and the
To James McFarlane         $657.95         item under the name are
To Do         by Dubill         $ 60.50         x-ed out.]

                             728.45
To Isaac Miller                 10
                             _____
                             718.45


  for which a note is left with Genl.
  Clark                                )    202.87½
Settled with Chouteau by               )
    returning lands                    )    4,355
and if the money is paid by may next is redeemed

Ludwell Bacon payable          )    150
on demand given for            )
disappointment on a sum of     )    [The Bacon item is crossed
money paid 7th June 1808       )    out by lines drawn down
to be first paid               )    through it.]

I owe John Colter this sum        )
having received the same for      )
him at the War office as the      )
gratuity allowed by the go-       )    320
vernment of the U'States          )
for his services on a tour        )
to the Pacific Ocean              )

August 24th. 1809
     John Colt
   paid                           Dr
  To   your order in favor       )
  of Charles Sanganet           )    $125

I have agreed to pay Mr.          )
L Bacon the sum of one            )    [A most revealing confes-
hundred dollars next spring       )    sion!]
or to his order in full           )
for the inconvenience sustained   )
by him in not receiving           )
the amount of                     )
a note given him for 450 dol      )
as agreeable to contract          )

Settle with McFarlane when I meet him.

Gave Judge Stewart a deed
for 708 Acres of land at
partage de Sous—condition
that if I return him $750
with interest thereon before
the 1st day of October 1810.
then the deed be voyd.

――――

  Directed my letters
to be returned to the City
of Washington.—

  deliver a receipt from Mr.
McFarlane to Capt. Russell
at Chickasaw Bluffs.—

――――

Sept. 1st 1809

――――

  Gave James McFarlane my note
payable on demand
for $718.45.—which is in
full of all our private transactions.—

Sept. 3rd
   Gave James McFarlane
my bond for $800.08 Cts
            & account
for his vouchers  for expenses       [This is only two days be-
on a trip to the St. Francis       fore his departure.]
and the Osage Village of
Arkansas when bringing in
the chiefs of that band to sign
the treaty.—

That is the last entry in his account book before he left St. Louis. He also drew four promissory notes to creditors,* and "on the 19th day of August, 1809, appointed his 'three most intimate friends, William Clark, Alexander Stuart, and Wm. C. Carr, his lawful attorneys, with full authority to dispose of all or any part of his property real and personal, and to pay, or receive, all debts due by or to him &c.' executed in the presence of Jeremiah Connor and Sam'l Solomon as witnesses." All this—his handwriting during these last days in St. Louis, his clear and orderly record of his debts, and his investing three friends with the power of attorney, to sell his property during his absence, if creditors should demand it—all this certainly does not look like the behavior of a man in a paroxysm—that is, in "a sudden, violent, and uncontrollable action; a convulsion, a fit." Besides, his letters to his mother during this time were, as Bakeless says, "buoyant with the hope of seeing her soon."

Some writers have seen in him, during this period, and earlier, a neurasthenic concern for his health, and an excessive addiction to medicines. As level-headed a scholar as Bakeless says, "The size of his bill for medicine shows that Lewis was in poor health, or thought he was; and there is no doubt that he was taken genuinely ill on the journey. Jottings in his account book indicate either a variety of maladies or pure hypochondria—or perhaps only that interest in everything medical that characterized Lucy Marks and all her sons. His jottings include: 'billious fever,' 'pills of opium and tartar,' 'Receipt for the best Stomachic,' and 'antibillious pills.' They sound alarming, but you can find the same sort of notes in the Journals of the expedition."

---

*See pages 104-105-106.

From Mr. Bakeless's words the unwary reader is likely to infer a great deal more than is warranted. There is nothing in the whole account book about maladies and medicines except four small pages at the very beginning, all of which seem to have been written at one sitting, and at least a year and a half before he died. They consist only of these few commonplace items: a receipt for the best stomachic; a receipt for making wine; a method of treating bilious fever when unattended by typhus or nervous symptoms; an emetic; pills of opium and tartar; a dose of calomel and jalap; anti-bilious pills; and "alloe pill."

Most of these were in common use on the American frontiers; the writer's parents had all of them, and more, except the receipt for wine. It would be absurd to imply that frontier women, far removed from doctors and forced to act as the family physician, were hypochrondriac because they jotted down this and that about remedies, as these came to their attention.

As for the "size of his bill for medicine" this in no way points to undue concern about his health when we place beside it the fact that we don't know how long a period was covered by $30.75, and from his account book this memo: "Then borrowed of Genl Clark this sum ($49) to pay Doctor Farrow for his attendance on my servant Pernia, an account which I conceive exorbitant but which my situation in life compells me to pay." August 24, 1809, he drew a promissory note to Dr. Saugrain, the most prominent physician in the area, for $30.75, yet one doctor bill for his servant was $49.

The only allusion we have found to medicines that he had with him at the time of his death is in a letter from D. W. Dickson, dated Nashville, February 20, 1810, to Jefferson, saying, in part: "It seems when an inventory was taken at this place of the property of the deceased this article [a miniature of Lewis] being wrapped up with a small parcel of medicine, was over looked, and not discovered until some time after the Inventory had been sent in."

We can, fortunately, let an authority speak on this matter, for a study has been made of Lewis's interest in medicines, and of his talents as a physician, chiefly on the expedition west.* The

*Drake W. Will, "The Medical and Surgical Practice of the Lewis and Clark Expedition," Dept. of Pathology, School of Medicine, UCLA.

conclusions which Dr. Will draws are, to say the least, flattering to Lewis. Even the famous Dr. Rush had said to Jefferson that Lewis "appeared admirably qualified" to lead the expedition. "As would be expected, several of Rush's questions relate to bilious fevers, diseases with which his name and reputation are associated in the history of American medicine." Dr. Will means questions put to Rush by Clark, Lewis, and Jefferson, relative to Indians. Reproduced in this monograph is a set of instructions from Dr. Rush to Lewis, before Lewis headed west: "Unusual costiveness is often a sign of approaching disease. when you feel it take one or more of the purging pills." Again: "1. when you feel the least indisposition, do not attempt to overcome it by labour or marching. rest in a horizontal posture.—also fasting and diluting drinks for a day or two will generally prevent an attack of fever. to these preventatives of disease may be added a gentle sweat obtained by warm drinks, or gently opening the bowels by means of one, two, or more of the purging pills." Dr. Will thinks it probable that Dr. Rush made up a list of medicines for the expedition, "since an item of fifty dozen bilious pills, made to his prescription, was included. . . . Nothing was used more often, to judge by the expedition's journals, than Rush's potent bilious pills." Calomel and jalap were one of Rush's prescriptions and were often mentioned by Lewis in his Journal.

Dr. Will concludes that "the active practice of medicine, somewhat embarrassing to Lewis, but enthusiastically handled by Clark, the more practical field surgeon, undoubtedly eased the party's return journey . . . . Lewis and Clark possessed not only extraordinary common sense but also the medical knowledge common to most educated men of the time, particularly to those who had served as military officers and had seen military physicians at work."

As to the notion, which seems to have prevailed widely, that Lewis was a hypochrondiac, this much at least is certain, that Thomas Jefferson gave birth to it, and a number of writers have accepted his word as gospel. DeVoto said that Lewis was "introverted and mercurial—almost all the bursts of anger and all the depressed moods are his": he means on the journey to the ocean and back. The fact is that DeVoto's words simply are not true, as anyone can determine for himself by reading every word of the Journals. There are a few instances of anger in Lewis, all

of which seem to have been brief and superficial; there are instances of deep anger in Clark. As for depressed moods those who
believe this may take too literally what Lewis wrote about the
state of his emotions. Those who see in an occasional fit of tem-
per, or in confessions of anxiety, the signs of hypochondria should
read the papers of Mackenzie and other explorers. All the men
on the expedition must again and again have felt depressed, for
again and again it looked as if they would perish miserably, in
spite of their heroic efforts.

Thomas Jefferson said that during Lewis's year and a half
in St. Louis "distressing affections" returned to him with "redoubled vigor, and began seriously to alarm his friends." It may be
assumed that Jefferson was not the kind of man who talked out
of his hat, but he had no personal knowledge of what he alleged,
and there is nothing in Lewis's occasional letter to him to suggest
it. We must therefore assume that he based his conclusions on
statements sent to him by persons out there, or on oral reports
from persons who visited him. Diligent search has discovered no
letters bearing such information. Whether persons who visited
him gave him such views of Lewis it is impossible to know.

Opposed to Jefferson's notion of Lewis's condition in St.
Louis are these facts, that right up to the time of his departure
he seems to have been in full possession of himself, and to have
been busy putting his affairs in order; and that a faithful search
of the letters of Frederick Bates, his "bitter enemy," has turned
up no statement, nor even a hint, that Bates thought Lewis was
not himself. It surely seems probable that Bates would have
confided in Richard if he had thought that Lewis was no longer
in possession of himself, or had heard that Lewis was drinking
immoderately. After all, St. Louis was a rather small place, in
which all the important persons knew one another. It seems unlikely that, unknown to Bates and his friends, Lewis could have
been in emotional states violent enough to be called paroxysms.

Unless evidence turns up which until now nobody seems to
have found it must be regarded as probable that before he left
St. Louis there was nothing in Lewis's behavior to justify Jefferson's extreme statements. In his behavior after he left St. Louis
we have a somewhat different view of him, and we shall now try
to determine his condition on his way down the river, at the fort,
and into the wilderness.

# VI

## From St. Louis
## to the Wilderness

As Dr. Bakeless says, after Lewis met August 30 with the Governor's Council, then made further arrangements for the care of his creditors, including power of attorney invested in three close friends, and set off down the river "he had every expectation of going to Washington, visiting Ivy Creek [his mother], and returning to his territory." Every known thing that he did during these last days in St. Louis proves that this is so. He was no more in a paroxysm at that time than Thomas Jefferson was. The question, then, is what happened to him after his departure.

A news item in the *Missouri Gazette* says he set off in good health. If he did set out in good health, he seems not to have remained in good health for many days. The temperature on his journey down the river seems to have been extremely hot and humid. People in this time, and in these primitive conditions, did not of course have the medical care they have in this area today. Joseph Bullen, a missionary to the Chickasaw Indians, observed in 1810 that "There are here a number of sick men from Orleans, mostly Kentucky people; not less than one thousand annually pass this way on their return from market. They go down the Mississippi with their produce, then get horses and return this way [over the Natchez Trace, which Lewis will soon be following]. Those who return after 20th of June, are generally sick."

En route, on September 11, Lewis drew a will, leaving all his real and personal property to his mother:

> after my private debts are paid of which a statement will be found in a small minute book deposited with
> Pernia my Servant                              )
> September 11th 1809                          )     Meriwether Lewis
> in the presence of                             )
> F. S. Trinchard                                 )

Why he did not draw a will before he left St. Louis we do not know. Possibly he was so much under the pressure of his duties and plans for departure that he overlooked it, or possibly he had in mind drawing it after he was on the boat and had more leisure. This servant, whose name he always spelled as in the will, but the correct spelling of which seems to have been Pernier, went with him down the river, and was to be with him almost to, and possibly in, the hour of his death. He is one of the mysterious persons in this story at whom we shall have to take a hard look later.

It seems probable that Lewis became ill at some point on his way down the river. He arrived at Fort Pickering about two o'clock in the afternoon of September 15. Was he a sick man when he arrived? Bakeless says, "Though Lewis was certainly unwell, the wild rumors of his illness that spread need not be taken too seriously." But they have been taken seriously, as we shall see, even by the historians. As a matter of fact the crux of the matter is his physical and mental condition during his first two weeks at the fort. Dr. Bakeless has said that "At Fort Pickering, the army post at Chickasaw Bluffs (Memphis) which he had once commanded, he met old army friends and drank more than he was accustomed to. It is the only mention of intemperance of any kind in his whole career. His entire behavior was odd enough to alarm his friends. Sept. 28, about the time Lewis was starting overland, the news had spread as far as Nashville that the Governor, after arriving at Chickasaw Bluffs 'in a state of mental derangement,' had there 'attempted to put an end to his own existence'."

There was the rumor, which will be stated more fully in a moment. As for drinking with old army friends, Mr. Donald D.

Jackson, Editor of the University of Illinois Press, and one who has done a lot of research on Lewis, feels that "In 1797 when Lewis had served there, it would have been a one-company post with a captain, a couple of lieutenants, and maybe an ensign. It just isn't probable that any of them could have been there still in 1809." The question is less whether Lewis drank with old army friends than whether he drank after arriving. We know that he did. Whether he drank immoderately we don't know. Bakeless thinks that the "best explanation of his odd conduct is malaria, as it is well known that fever of any kind invariably made him light-headed."

It is rather strange that various persons have diagnosed his condition on arriving at the post, and afterward, without letting Lewis himself say anything about it. For he did say something about it, on the very next morning after his arrival. He said it in his famous September 16 letter to President Madison.

Chickasaw Bluffs<br>September 16th. 09

Dear Sir:

         yesterday<br>
I arrived here_∧_ about ~~2 Ock~~ P.M. ~~yesterday~~ very much ex-
<br>                     taken<br>
hausted from the heat of the climate, but having_∧_ medicine feel much better this morning. my apprehsion [apprehension] from the heat of the lower country and my fear of the original papers relative to my voyage to the Pacific ocean falling into the hands of the British induced me to change my rout and proceed by land through the state to Tennessee to the City of washington. I bring with me duplicates of my vouchers for public expenditures &c which when fully explained, or reather the general view of the circumstances under which they were made I flatter myself
<br>        will        sanction &<br>
~~that~~ they_∧_ recieve both_∧_ approbation and sanction.—

Provided my health permits no time shall be lost in reaching Washington. My anxiety to pursue and to fullfill the duties inci-
<br>       the<br>
dent to_∧_ internal arrangements incident to the government of

Louisiana has prevented my writing you [one or two letters here,
                                     more
illegible, were crossed out]∧frequently. ~~Mr. Bates is left in charge~~
Inclosed I herewith transmit you a copy of the laws of the territory of Louisiana.— I have the honour to be with the most sincere
esteem your Obt. ~~and very humble~~
Obt. and very humble Servt.

                                        Meriwether Lewis
James Madison Esq.
President U States

 Olin D. Wheeler says, "It has been my privilege to peruse
the original codices, or note-books of Lewis and Clark, and I
have been much impressed with the manner in which they seem
to serve as exponents of the characters of the two men. Those
written by Lewis are in a fine, regular, symmetric handwriting,
almost as clear and legible as engraving, and evince the conscien-
tiousness of the man in his work . . . . he must have been excru-
ciatingly particular and precise." It is true that his handwriting at
its best resembles engraving, as the reader can see in the instance
referred to; and it is true that in this letter to Madison there may
be, as Mr. Jackson says, "something very strange . . . . it could be
fatigue or malaria, as well as mental distress . . . . " Bakeless
thinks that "its sprawling and uncertain hand and the constant
striking out of words and interlineation of others, to no particular purpose, show clearly that . . . he was far from being his usual
bold and decisive self by the time he reached Chickasaw Bluffs."

 That much it surely does reveal, but his striking out of words
does not necessarily have any significance. It was a habit with
him, as it was with some other men of that time, and no doubt
of any time. Here, for instance, are a few sentences in a letter to
the Secretary of War, July 1, 1808:

 " . . . that the United States at present through mere curticy
permit them ~~at present~~ to exend their trade . . . . "
 "The Osage river at present has not sufficient debth of water
~~at present~~ to admit a peroque or small boat to ascend . . . . "
 " . . . early in April last I ordered ~~ordered~~ all the traders . . . . "
 " . . . however I believe ~~I believe~~ that they are now pretty
well satisfyed . . . . "

"... that the avidity of the traders ~~is such~~ to possess their peltries is such, that they will supply them...."

'... would raise their monthly pay to the sum perhaps of ten dollars ~~pr month~~...."

These are of the same nature as some of his repetitions in the letter to Madison. Possibly he struck out the words about Bates because it occurred to him that Madison already knew that. As a matter of fact, his July letter shows almost as many struck words as his September letter, yet it was written when he was not, so far as we know, ill or exhausted by fatigue or fever. May 30, 1808, he wrote a letter to one Whitlock, which he concluded with "Your friend and Obt Servt." and struck out Obt!

Lewis himself said that he arrived very much exhausted from the heat, took a medicine and felt better the next morning. His words, "provided my health permits," indicate that he felt himself to be ill. There seems to be no sign of insanity or mental derangement in the letter to Madison, but only signs of exhaustion and debility.

The commander at the fort, Capt. Gilbert C. Russell, has left on record his impressions of Lewis's condition on his arrival and during his stay there. We don't know much about him but he seems to have been sober and serious, with little nonsense in him. His letters to the War Department suggest that he was faithful and competent, though like Lewis, and practically all the Government's officials in outlying territories, he had his troubles with Washington. In the Government's summary of a letter's contents, under November 23, 1810, we read that they are "relative to sundry malicious charges brot against him—his repeated applications for leave to visit Washington etc." He had asked for leave to visit Washington so that, as in the case of Lewis, he could go there and explain matters and clear his name.

Among a few items which suggest the nature of the man is this note, April 4th, 1811: "Stating that Some time ago he joined in recommending Sarg. Major Mullen for a commission and now withdraws his name from Said recommendation, because said Mullen married a common prostitute & has prevaricated on oath."

January 4, 1810, almost three months after Lewis's death, Russell wrote Jefferson: "He came here on the 15th September last from whence he set off intending to go to Washington by way of New Orleans. His [this word is illegible—it may be condition] that rendered it necessary that he should be stoped until he would recover which I done and in a short time by proper attention a change was perceptible and in about six days he was perfectly restored in every respect and able to travel."

Almost two years later (November 26, 1811) Russell said in a document which seems to have been a deposition: "On the morning of the 15tht of September, the Boat in which he was a passenger landed him at Fort pickering in a state of mental derangement, which appeared to have been produced as much by
                    The Subscriber
indisposition as by other causes.
being then
The Commanding officer of the Fort on discovering his situation, and learning from the Crew that he had made two attempts to Kill himself, in one of which he had nearly succeeded, resolved at once to take possession of him and his papers, and detain them there untill he recovered, or some friend might arrive in whose hands he could depart in safety."*

In his statement to Jefferson, Russell seems to say that almost at once after arriving at the fort, Lewis again set off down the river, intending to go by New Orleans—for he says, "He came here on the 15 September last from whence he set off . . . . " Did Russell almost immediately overtake him and put him under duress? In his statement nearly two years later he says that Lewis arrived in a state of derangement, and that at once he took possession of him and his papers. Lewis says only that he arrived exhausted, took medicine, felt better the next morning, and health permitting would lose no time in pushing on to Washington. Russell says Lewis arrived on the morning of the 15th, Lewis says he arrived about two in the afternoon. It may be that on the 16th Lewis "set off" to resume his journey down the river, and that, convinced that Lewis was too ill to travel, Russell then put him under restraint.

---

*This document seems to be in the hand of Jonathan Williams, a nephew of Franklin, and the first superintendent of the U. S. Military Academy. The interlineation above is in the same hand that copied the document. Presumably Williams made a copy of the Russell statement.

In his letter to Jefferson, Russell says that "in about six days he was perfectly restored in every respect and able to travel." He certainly was able to write a letter that was par for him in all respects. It was addressed to his friend, Major Amos Stoddard:

> Fort Pickering, Chickasaw Bluffs
> September 22nd, 1809

Dear Majr.

I must acknowledge myself remiss in not writing you in answer to several friendly epistles which I have received from you since my return from the Pacific Ocean. continued occupation in the immediate discharge of the duties of a public station will I trust in some measure plead my apology.—

I am now on my way to the City of Washington and had contemplated taking Fort Adams and Orlianes in my rout, but my indisposition has induced me to change my rout and shall now pass through Tennessee and Virginia. The protest of some bills which I have lately drawn on public account form the principal inducement for my going forward at this moment. an explanation is all that is necessary I am sensible to put all matters right. in the mean time the protest of a draught however just, has drawn down upon me at one moment all my private debts which have excessively embarrased me. I hope you will therefore pardon me for asking you to remit as soon as is convenient the sum of $200. which you have informed me you hold for me.—I calculated on having the pleasure to see you at Fort Adams as I passed, but am informed by Capt. Russell the commanding Officer of this place that you are stationed on the West side of the Mississippi. You will direct to me at the City of Washington untill the last of December after which I expect I shall be on my return to St. Louis.

> Your sincere friend &
> Obt. Servt.
> Meriwether Lewis

In that letter he struck out only one syllable, which he possibly blotted or misspelled, and interlined not at all. He wrote few letters in his lifetime as clear, firm, and straight to the point as that one. Those who favor the theory of suicide seem to feel that during most or all of his two weeks at the fort he was deranged, and so bent on taking his life that Russell had to place him under restraint. This seems improbable. That he was ill during a part of the time there is no reason to doubt, for he speaks of his indisposition, and this word, perhaps taken from Dr. Rush, was his word for illness. But it is hard to believe that a man deranged and bent on self-destruction could have written this letter to Stoddard. He obviously has no thought but to push on to Washington and return to St. Louis.

At some point during his first week at the fort he decided to go overland instead of by water. A number of writers have said that he delayed his departure until James Neelly, Indian agent of the Chickasaw Nation, could go with him to watch over him. There seems to be no evidence to support this claim. He delayed because he expected to go all the way with Russell, and Russell makes this clear in the first of his two letters to Jefferson:

"Being placed then myself in a similar situation with him by having Bills protested to a considerable amount and had made application to the General and expected leave of absence every day to go to Washington on the same business with Governor Lewis. In consequence of which he waited six or eight days expecting that I would go with him but in this we were disappointed & he set off with a Major Neely who was going to Nashville."

There is no conceivable reason why Russell should have misrepresented this part of the situation. He tells us that in about six days after his arrival Lewis was perfectly restored and able to travel, and that Lewis then waited six or eight days, expecting that Russell would get his leave of absence and go with him. When the delay dragged out to a week and Russell's leave did not come through, the impatient Lewis decided to push on, and as far as Nashville to ride with Neelly.

During this period of delay Lewis was not altogether idle. He wrote the letter to Stoddard (the last he is known to have written), primarily, it appears, to call in the $200 and apply it on his debts. Russell says to Jefferson, "At the request of Governor Lewis I enclosed the land warrant granted to him in consideration of his services to the Pacific Ocean to Bowling Robinson, Esq., Secy of the Tr'y of Orleans with instructions to dispose of it at any price about two dollars per acre & to lodge the money in the

Bank of the United States, or any of the branch banks subject
to his order."

While at the fort he made two entries in his account book.

1809
Sept. 17th

Then inclosed my
for 1600 acres to
land warrant    to Bonby [?]          [Capt. Russell gives his
Robertson of New Orleans              name as Bowling Robertson]
to be disposed off for
two dollars pr acre or
more if it can be obtain-
ed and the money sent [?]
deposited in the branch
bank of New Orleans
or the City of Washing-
ton subject to my order
or that of William D
Meriwether for the benefit
of my creditors.    M. Lewis

This entry was made the next day after his letter to Madison
and only two days after his arrival. Its handwriting is rather like
that in the letter to Madison*, but the mind here, as when writing
to Madison, seems to be clear: this suggests that on his arrival
at the fort he was delirious, or otherwise "deranged," because of
heat and fever, and not that he had gone out of his mind because
of his financial and other troubles. The difference between the
two conditions is of great importance in trying to determine how
he died.

If because of his troubles and woes a person feels that further
struggle would be fruitless and that he has come to the end of
the trail, he may steadily become more and more irrational, that
is, insane, and more and more obsessed with the notion that he
ought to destroy himself. This condition is more likely to persist
than to abate, and to manifest itself in repeated attempts at self-
destruction. In derangement because of illness and high fever so
severe that they temporarily overthrow the mind, the person may

---

*The reader can study the handwriting on pages 107-108-109.

indeed make attempts on his life, but this behavior pattern is not likely to persist after he returns to his senses.

Everything that we know about Lewis's behavior at the fort suggests that he was ill, perhaps with malaria, as Bakeless has suggested, on his arrival and for a few days afterward; and that during this period he had irrational moments. During one of these moments he may have made a clumsy attempt on his life, or, more probably, he may only have expressed his delirium in wild actions and talk which someone at the fort, possibly Russell, interpreted as an attempt on his life. After all, no psychiatrist was present at the fort or on the boat, no doctor, nor anyone but rough uneducated frontiersmen whose ideas of what constituted derangement are unknown to us.

That Lewis's behavior abated instead of persisted seems to be established not only by what Russell wrote Jefferson, but also, and far more, by the four documents which Lewis wrote during that period. The last entry in his account book, and the last words he ever wrote, so far as we know, were on September 27, only two days before his departure. It will be observed that this entry is in his customary manner.

September 27th

Then borrowed of Capt.   )
Gilbert C. Russell a check   )   $   $\frac{50}{100}$
on the Branch Bank of New   )   99
Orleans for this sum, for   )
which I gave him my note   )
Dr to the same for     $)   280
two horses——   )

I left the trunk of Capt.
House with Capt. Russell
to be sent to the care of
Wm. Brown of Orleans
Collector to be by him
forwarded to McDonald
and Ridgely of Baltimore
as addressed.

Also left with Capt. Russell
two trunks one containing
papers &c a case for liquor
and a package of blankets

sheets and coverlid to be
sent to William C Carr of
St. Louis for me—unless I
shall otherwise direct.

According to Russell, the one sum was $99.58 instead of
$99.50, no doubt an oversight on Lewis's part. Apparently Lewis
and Russell were friends of some standing: lending a man deep
in financial difficulties the sum of $379.58 was no small matter,
for that surely was equal in purchasing power to more than
$2,000.00 today.

Sometime during Lewis's stay at the fort a rumor had gone
into the wilderness. It is to be found in a famous letter, upon
which those who argue for suicide rest a good part of their case.
It was written from Nashville, September 28, by Captain James
House,* to his friend and Lewis's enemy, Frederick Bates:

"I arrived here two days ago on my way to Maryland—Yester-
day Majr Stoddart of the Army arrived here from Fort Adams, and
informs me that in his passage through the Indian nation, in the
vicinity of Chickasaw Bluffs he saw a person, immediately from
the Bluffs who informed him, that Governor Lewis had arrived
there (sometime previous to his leaving it) in a State of mental
derangement—that he had made several attempts to put an end
to his own existence, which the patroon had prevented, and that
Cap Russell, the commanding officer at the Bluffs had taken him
into his own quarters where he was obliged to keep a strict watch
over him to prevent his committing violence on himself and had
caused his boat to be unloaded at the ferry to be secured in his
stores.

"I am in hopes this account will prove exaggerated—tho' I fear
there is too much truth in it. As the post leaves this tomorrow I
have thought it would not be improper to communicate these circumstances as I have heard them, to you."

So far as is known, that is the only written statement of derangement made *before* Lewis's death. It is only a rumor, of
course. There is no reason to doubt that Major Stoddard saw
someone from the fort, who gave him the story, but we don't
know from whom the informant got it, or with what embellishments. We don't know why Captain House sent the information to

---

*His name is usually given as James Howe.

Bates, or what reason he had, if any, to fear that there was too much truth in it.

The day after Captain House wrote his letter Lewis set off on his disastrous ride into the Tennessee wilderness. As well as we are able we shall now follow him to Grinder's Stand.

# VII

## *Across the Wilderness*
## *to Grinder's*

Lewis waited at the fort about a week for Russell's leave to come through, and when it did not he decided to push on. He had borrowed money from Russell to buy two horses. Russell says that Lewis "set off with two Trunks which contained all his papers relative to his expedition to the Pacific Ocean. Gen'l Clark's Land Warrant, a Port-Folio, pocket book Memo and note Book together with many other papers of both public and private nature and two horses two saddles and bridles a Rifle gun pistols pipe tommy hawk & dirk, all ellegant and perhaps about two hundred and twenty dollars, of which $99 58/100 was a Treasury check on the U.S. Bank of Orleans endorsed by me. The horses one saddle and the check I let him have." Presumably Lewis bought a saddle and two bridles, besides the horses.

He left St. Louis with a considerable body of luggage but this would have been no problem if he had gone all the way by boat. It became a problem when he decided to go by land with packhorses. Russell told Jefferson that "He left with me two Trunks a case and a bundle which will now remain here subject at any time to your order or that of his legal representative." Mr. Boyd, editor of the Jefferson Papers, says that "among other papers pertaining to the expedition, Lewis had in his custody 'Sixteen Note books bound in red Morocco with clasps'—the precise number and sort of journals now in the American Philosophical Society and in the Missouri Historical Society, six of them Lewis journals and eight of them Clark journals. . . ." The inventory, dated at Nashville, November 23, 1809, "has notations in the hand of Isaac A. Coles and William Clark showing the distribution made of the effects after the trunks had been dispatched to Washington. . . . It should be noted, incidentally, that Lewis' personal and official papers were found to be so intermingled that separating them was a difficult task—'Many of the bundles containing at once, Papers of a public nature—Papers intirely private'—"

According to Russell, Neelly was taking with him "a loose horse or two" and offered the use of these to Lewis, as well as some assistance from his Negro servant. How Lewis intended to transport his luggage from Nashville on to Washington we do not know.

On September 29th the little party left the fort and set off on what must have been a pretty rough trail that led to the Chickasaw agency more than a hundred miles in the southeast. It has been widely assumed that only four men rode out of the fort—James Neelly, the Indian agent, who was on his way to the agency and thence over the Natchez Trace to Nashville; Meriwether Lewis, with his servant Pernia; and Neelly's servant, who seems to have been a Negro slave. But in the document which Russell drew up more than two years after Lewis's death it is said that Lewis left the Bluffs "with the Chickasaw agent the interpreter and some of the Chiefs. . . ." It may be that Russell confused this departure with some other; if a group of Indian chiefs rode with Lewis, another element is added to the mystery.

A legend about Lewis that has endured almost down to our time has found expression in a number of places. George R. Gilmer, an ex-governor of Georgia and a friend of some members of the Lewis family, has put it this way in his *Sketches*: "In his expedition to the Pacific he discovered a gold mine. The fact was not made public, nor the place pointed out at the time, lest it might become known to the Indians and Spaniards and thereby be a public injury instead of a public benefit. He informed his friends, upon his return, of the discovery which he had made and his intention of making out such a description of the place that it might be found if he should die before the information could be made useful to the country."

There have been hundreds, even thousands, of legends of lost mines in this country and this may only be one of them. But whether fact or legend hardly matters: if the story had gone abroad that on his journey to the ocean he had found a mine, and had made a map of its situation, this could well have been in the consciousness of his servant, of Neelly, and possibly of the Indian chiefs, not to speak of all the bandits on the Trace and in the wilderness who probably knew that the Governor was coming.

This group of men entering the wilderness would come to the Natchez Trace, at or near the agency, one of the most famous of the country's early primitive roads. Since Meriwether Lewis was to die upon the Trace it may be well to know something about it.

An old Indian trail, at least in most of its length, it ran from Natchez on the Mississippi, north by east to the Tennessee river. In 1801 General Wilkinson effected a treaty with the Chicasaw and Chocktaw, to allow passage through their lands. As Leftwich says, "the inhabitants of the original thirteen colonies were not to be baffled in their determination to secure and settle the richest land on the continent by the closing of the main water routes of travel by a foreign nation and the consequent loss of the means of transportation to the Mississippi Territory and Southwest. So it was that our leaders . . . determined to open up highways through the vast wilderness separating the Mississippi river from the Northeast. The result was the establishment of the Natchez Trace road. . . ."

It was hardly a road, though some writers have called it that; it was really only a trace, a blazed trail, that cut through wilderness to Spanish country. So heavy was to be the travel over it during the ensuing years that in many places it is today clearly visible, for it is worn deep like an old buffalo trail. It became, as Wheeler has said, one link "in a system of 'traces', or primeval roads, from the Atlantic coast settlements to the interior of the West and South. . . ." Elliott Coues examined it in 1891 and found that it was still clearly discernible over most of the distance.

It was over this trace, says a Mississippi historian, that there passed "a steady stream of travellers of every color, occupation and nationality, French, Spanish, English, Canadian *voyageurs*, Arcadians, trappers, in quaint leather hunting suits, military men, painted braves, negro slaves. . . ." The heaviest traffic seems to have occurred some time after Lewis's death, though even by 1809 a number of stands, or inns, had been established along its length, to offer food and lodging to wayfarers.

A Natchez Park historian says there was no banditry on the Trace at the time of Lewis's death. If he is right, a number of others who have written about the Trace are wrong. The Mississippi historian quoted above speaks, perhaps too colorfully, of "those nameless horrors, inflicted by noted bandits, continually harassing, pillaging and murdering those traversing the 'Trace' . . ."; of travelers "heavily loaded with specie, pieces of eight and Spanish doubloons" who were "a most tempting bait to the road pirates." Governor Lewis was tempting bait, if they knew of his coming, and doubly tempting if they thought he had a map of a gold mine. This historian says that most of the stands "were kept by half-breeds, principally under the management of Louis le Fleure"; and Mr. Dawson A. Phelps, the Park historian, says that the Chickasaw Nation "consistently refused to permit any but their own people, that is squawmen or half breeds, to establish or operate stands."

That bandits did rob and kill on the Trace at least in the first decades of the century there can be no doubt. Lewis must have been aware of all this. If he had not heard it as governor, up in St. Louis, he surely heard it while at the fort. As Indian agent, Neelly surely knew about the bandits, and the degree of risk which a famous person like the governor would be taking. It can be imagined that after Lewis got deep into the wilderness he began to cast a practiced eye around him; forested Indian country was the kind of country he was familiar with. It was more than a hundred miles from the fort to the Trace, and at night, when camping, it may be that Neelly talked about some of the more infamous bandits, such as Sam Mason, who from 1799 until his capture in 1804 made a nightmare for travelers of a part of the Trace.

Possibly none of the evil men was more feared than Macajah and Wiley, who announced their presence with the cry, "We are the Harpes!" Their filthy tawny appearance and curly black hair spoke of Negro blood; their hatred of George Washington, of

British sympathies. Late in the preceding century they had pushed westward into central Tennessee, bringing with them a small harem of ferocious women. James Weir saw Knoxville in 1798 and says he stood aghast because of obscene drunken men and women and swarms of almost naked Negro children. He could have heard of the body of one Johnson that had been found in a river, its belly ripped open and filled with stones to sink it; or of the unfortunate pack-peddler named Peyton, his body stripped, his head split open.

After a price was placed on the heads of the brothers, a description of them went forth, for all to read. Macajah was "about six feet high—of a robust make & about 30 or 32 years of age. He was an ill-looking, downcast countenance, & his hair is black and short, but comes very much down his forehead. He is built very straight and is full fleshed in the face. . . ." These two killers, says one of their biographers, made such an "ecstasy of murder" that even the outlaws outlawed them. They could meet a young man, kill him, and then smear his brains on a tree to suggest that he had bashed his own skull in. Another time they murdered William Ballard. A little after that they met the Brassel brothers and for the fun of it cut the throat of one, while the other made a miraculous escape. How many they killed, often for no reason but the wanton hell of it, nobody seems to know—"John Tully, a farmer named Bradbury, the two Triswold brothers, John Graves and his son: they split their head with an axe and threw them out in their own cabin yard, 'where they lay until someone, seeing so many buzzards about, made an investigation and discovered what had taken place'; many others undoubtedly, in the lonely forest, were never discovered—later a directed purpose becomes apparent in the twisting path they have traced through the wilderness. They are looking for Colonel Trabue, seeking him to murder him." They had killed his son, and Trabue had sworn vengeance. Being a justice of the peace, he made moves to protect himself—he drew a will, and broadcast descriptions of his enemies: "The big man is pale, dark, swarthy, bushy hair, had a reddish gunstock. The little man had blackish gunstock, with a silver star with four straight points. . . ." But the Colonel never caught up with them.

A man named Moses Steigal did. Being for some time away from home, he returned late one night to his wilderness cabin, to find his friend, a Major William Love, tomahawked in the attic; his wife dying and his child dead, and his house in flames. Fleeing from this scene the Harpe brothers had met two of Steigal's neighbors and had shot one and brained the other. Insane with rage and grief, Steigal took their trail, and a posse quickly gathered and followed him. The next day Big Harpe was shot down. Before dying (the story goes) he confessed that he was sorry for one murder only, that of his wife's baby, which he had flung by its heels against a tree and left to die in the woods.

The story says that with a butcher knife Steigal cut the monster's head off. He cut it all the way around the neck to the bone, and then wrung it off "in the same manner a butcher would of a hog." On the Trace, in the fork of a tree, Steigal spiked Harpe's head and "for many years the skull hung there, rotted and rain-whitened, grinning down at the traveler." We don't know whether any skulls grinned down at Lewis. The Trace was about 550 miles long, from Natchez to Nashville, and Lewis, during these last days of his life, traversed only about two hundred miles of it, from near the present Houston, to the center of the present county of Lewis, in south-central Tennessee.

There were other highwaymen almost as notorious as the Harpes, on this trail that "plunged straight through the wilderness, swamp-ridden, Indian-infested." A mail route had been established over the entire length of it, and an early post-rider, John L. Swaney, has left us a record of his years over the Trace, and a picture of the wilderness at that time. He left the Nashville settlement Saturday night at eight o'clock, and vanished from the area of lighted cabins into the long dark night. About midnight he reached the Big Branch of Harpeth river, not far from the present Belleview; and when he passed the Tom Davis cabin, with its barking dogs, he left the last dwelling of a white man and entered the wilderness. He carried besides his mail pouch a half-bushel of corn for his horse, food for himself, a greatcoat or a blanket, and a tin trumpet. It took him ten days of hard riding from Nashville to Natchez.

By Sunday morning he reached Gordon's Ferry on Duck River, about fifty miles from Nashville. This was on the border of the Chocktaw Nation. There he fed his horse and ate his breakfast. From this point it was eighty miles to Colbert's Ferry on the Tennessee River; during this long ride, which he made in one day, he rode from north to south down the ridge on which Grinder would build his Stand, and where Meriwether Lewis would pull up for the night and come to his mysterious end.

Across the Tennessee River Swaney came to another stand, where he spent the night. A Mrs. Thomas Martin has left the story that when she stayed overnight at this Tennessee River inn she was assigned to a building where "slept not less than fifty Indians, many of them drunk, while my husband and others sat up all night. It is not their custom to let strangers sleep in the house with their families." We will keep her statement in mind when we examine the stand where Lewis died.

Leaving the Tennessee, Swaney "pushed on deeper into the wilderness." He had been riding into the southwest. He veered more to the south now, and it seems probable that he now approached Harpe country. Not until he reached the Chickasaw agency, more than a hundred miles distant, would he see another cabin, or even an Indian wigwam, and his first night out from the Tennessee he would spend in the woods or a canebrake. Some two hundred miles beyond the Chickasaw agency was the Chocktaw agency; this part of his route lay entirely in Indian country. A hundred miles farther he entered Natchez.

One historian says that it was in the stretch of "canebrake, swamp and desolation ruled by the Chickasaws and Chocktaws, that the dangers to travelers lay. The danger was not in the Indians, or rarely—in whose language the harshest words were 'skena' meaning bad, and 'pulla' meaning mean."

Besides the Harpe brothers there were other trail bandits whose names have been enshrined in American lore—Hare, Mason Murrel, and others. When Hare began to levy on the Trace we seem not to know (a bandit might operate for some time before his name became known), but after he was caught and had served five years in jail, and a year had passed since his release, it was 1818. In that year he robbed a mail coach of $16,900, and a few months later was hanged.

If Hare was preying on the Trace in 1812, it is possible that he was there when Lewis entered it. Some of the bandits, like Sam Mason, spent many years in villainy before they were caught. Swaney, we are told, "rode almost weekly through the Trace, had many a brush with the bandits. Passing, Mason himself would often hail the carrier: 'He was always anxious to know what was

said of him by the public'." Now and then Swaney "stumbled on
the climax of swift tragedy. He heard a man's voice shout, 'Sur-
render!' He heard a shot, and another shot. A great tree had
obscured his view but as he passed it he saw a mounted traveler,
pale, cursing helplessly, his emptied pistols smoking in his hands;
facing him, a bandit, his features unrecognizable in war-paint,
his musket raised. Coolly, the robber fired. The man on horseback jerked about suddenly, then fell face forward, his body
slipping down across the saddle-horn." As Swaney told it, "He fell
across the path with his pistols in his hands."

Most of the books which tell the tales of these bold brigands
may paint the picture in colors too vivid, but there seems to be
no reason to doubt the essential details. In those early years, it is
said, "men had lived hived in their narrow cabins like animals in
a lair, and the early riders of the Trace had robbed, fought pas-
sionately, killed, with the same fierce unpremeditated animal in-
tensity. It had been a dark time. . . ." There came the war of
1812, and though for a little while the Trace seems to have been
quieter, "the bandits still persisted." It was during this "dark
time" that Lewis rode to his death. The banditry seems to have
continued far into the century, for Coates says that "strung out
along the Trace, the wilderness trails and the river, the bandits
kept their strongholds safe."

If it is asked how over such a dangerous trail the mail carrier
could ride in safety, Swaney himself gives the answer. We have
seen his statement that Mason liked to halt him, to ask for news
of the outside world, and to learn what was being said about him.
Mason told him that "no mail-carrier need fear being molested
by him and his men, for mail was of no value to them." The
bandits possibly had a different view of the governor of the Loius-
iana Territory, riding along in what Russell called elegant trappings, with no more bodyguard, during his last day, than two
servants who trailed him.

But if Meriwether Lewis knew about the bandits and of the
risk which he would take going by land, we must suppose that
he gave it little thought. Anyone familiar with his life, or with
no more of it than his journals, must be impressed by the willingness, even the eagerness, it would seem, with which he faced
hostile Indians, grizzly bears, and the unknown. It is also well to
keep in mind the fact that of the small band of men who left their

Old Natchez Trace on Duck River Ridge. *Courtesy, National Park Service.*

This is the Natchez Trace at about the point where Lewis turned off to Grinder's Stand, fifty yards east. Its deep depression, worn by countless feet, is still visible. *Photo by the author.*

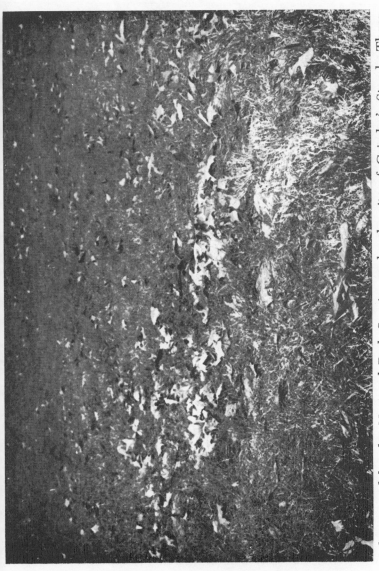

This is said by the National Park Service to be the site of Grinder's Stand. There are a few stones in foreground. Two expert observers long ago said the grave was about 450 feet north of the cabins. The monument (said to be above the grave) is 700 feet north. *Photo by the author.*

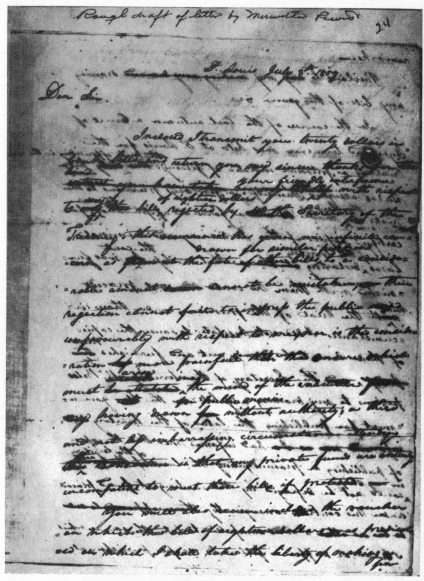

Rough draft of Lewis's July 8 letter, this and following three pages. *Courtesy University of Virginia Library.*

remarks.—

Previous to ~~any my seeking any demand~~ drawing
any bill of the govern' &c

In the course of the last autumn a Court of
Oyer ~~and~~ terminer was held at S' Louis for the
trial of a prisoner indicted of felony. ~~the~~ ~~only presiding in the~~
Lucas assigned himself ~~a few days previous to the~~
~~trial~~ ~~the Judge~~ ~~made to call~~ a formal ~~application for~~ ~~to me~~
certified copies of the Judiciary ~~and~~ criminal
laws, ~~of the territory~~ declaring ~~that this~~ that unless ~~the court~~ was fur-
-nished with them he could ~~the~~ ~~not~~ proceed
~~with~~ ~~with~~ the trial of the prisoner; ~~under these cir~~
-cumstances I did not hesitate to cause the copies
of these laws to be ~~made~~ out and furnished the
~~Judge~~, and The Secretary of the ~~territory~~ M' Bates
previous to my drawing any bill ~~on~~ the ~~the~~ govern-
-ment for publishing the laws of the territory ~~had~~
~~informed me as I~~ had informed me that the expen
of publishing or promulgating the laws ~~of the territory~~
~~in any shape~~ could not be defrayed by the contingent fund placed
under this contract consequently, ~~there appeared to me~~
to be ~~in either~~ ~~I this~~ compelled to take the course which
I have or suffer a fellon to escape punishment.

Rough draft of letter by Meriwether Lewis

24

~~in this transaction I [illegible] concern my self in the~~

you I shall write more fully to the Secretary of State on this subject and inclose him my vouchers for the expences which have been incurred in publishing the laws of the territory as ~~directed by the late [illegible]~~ impe=ratively directed by

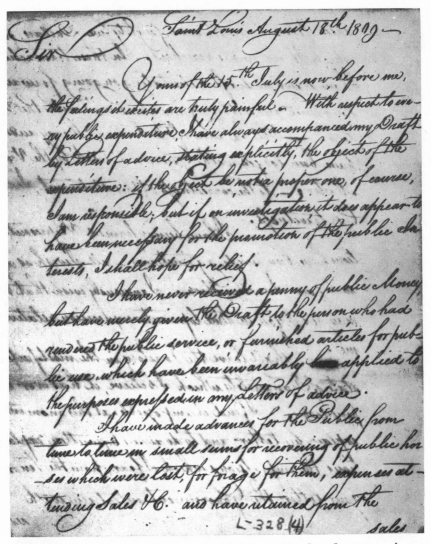

The first page of Lewis's August 18 letter. His handwriting shows he was in top form.

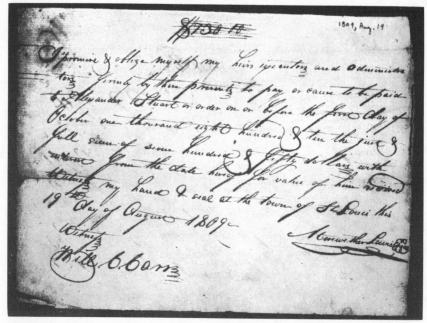

August 19 note. *Courtesy Wisconsin Historical Society.*

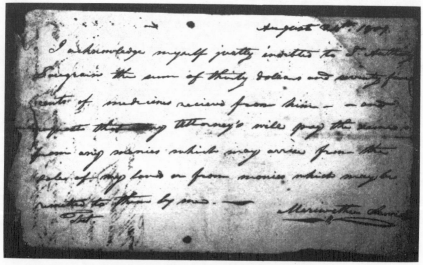

August 24 note. *Courtesy Wisconsin Historical Society.*

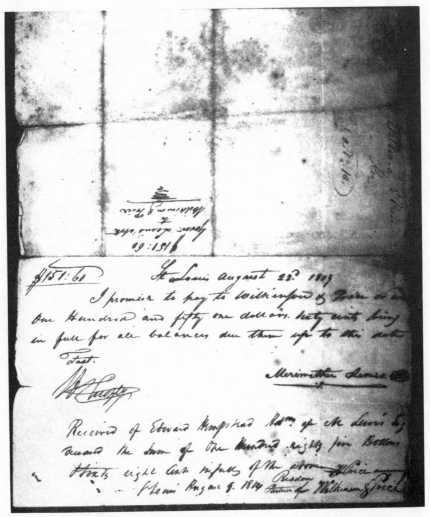

August 22 note. *Courtesy Wisconsin Historical Society.*

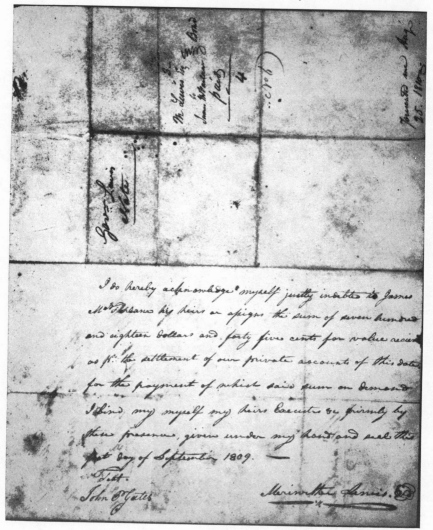

September 1 note. *Courtesy Wisconsin Historical Society.*

39   1809
Sept. 17th

Then inclosed my land warrant for 1600 acres to Bouley Robertson of New Orleans to be disposed off for two dollars pr. acre or more if it can be obtained and the money deposited in the branch bank of New Orleans or the City of Washington subject to my order or that of William D Meriwether for the benefit of my creditors. — M. Lewis

September 17 entry in account book.

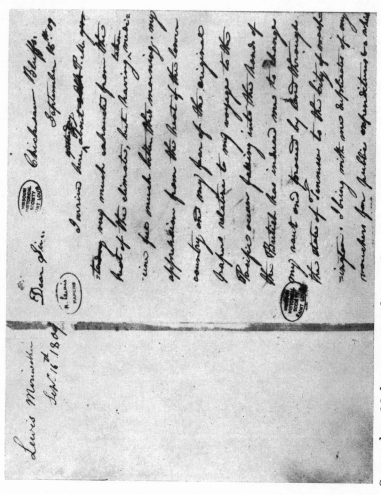

September 16 letter to Madison, this page and next. *Courtesy Missouri Historical Society, St. Louis.*

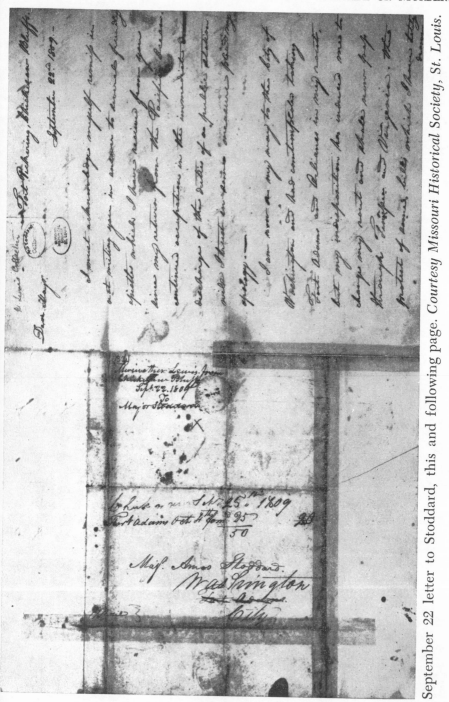

September 22 letter to Stoddard, this and following page. *Courtesy Missouri Historical Society, St. Louis.*

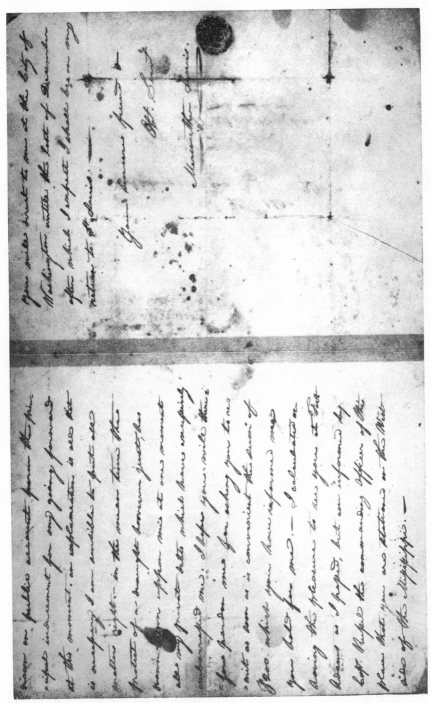

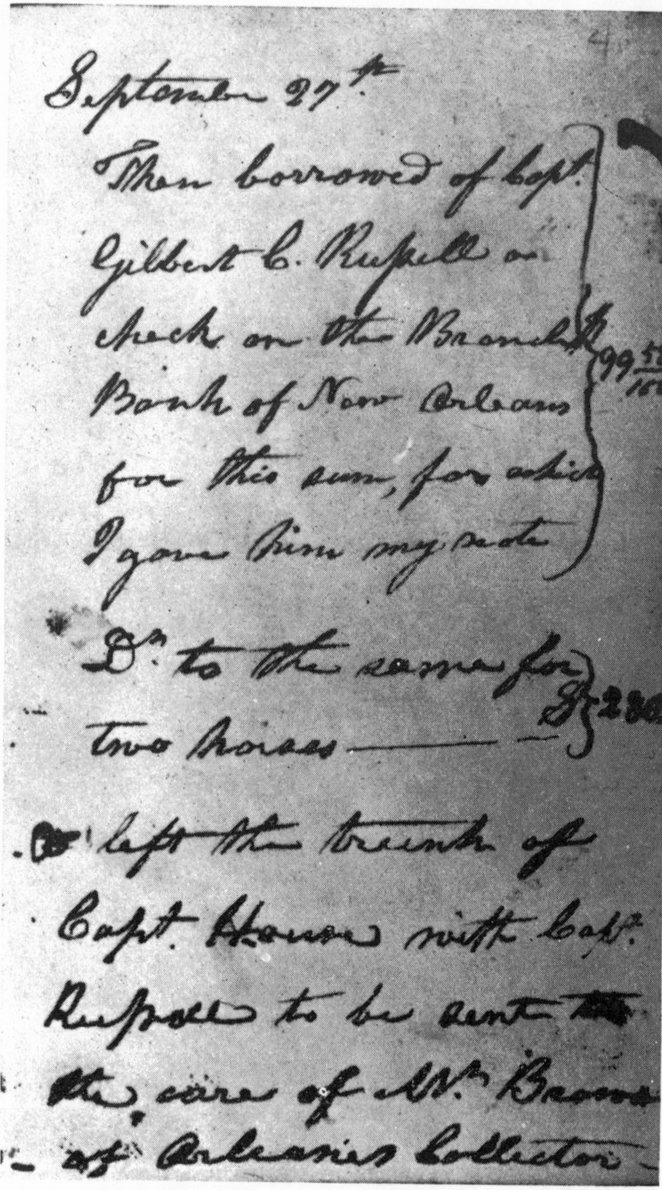

September 27th
Then borrowed of Capt.
Gilbert C. Russell a
check on the Branch
Bank of New Orleans
for this sum, for which
I gave him my note
$99 50/100
Do. to the same for
two horses — $280
left the trunk of
Capt. House with Capt.
Russell to be sent
the care of Mr. Brown
of Orleans Collector

September 27 entry in account book, this and following page.

to be by him forwarded
to M<sup>c</sup>Donald and Ridgly
of Boltimore as addressed,
— Also left with Capt.
Russell two trunks one
containing papers on a
case for liquor and a
package of blankets
sheets and covesl'd to be
sent to William Clark
of S<sup>t</sup>. Louis for me —
unless I shall otherwise
direct. ———

Jefferson Memorial, Washington, D.C. *Photo by author.*

winter camp and went up the Missouri in the spring of 1805, none was cooler with a gun facing an enemy, and probably not more than one or two were better shots, than the tall gangling man who rode out of the fort with James Neelly and two servants.

We don't know on what day the party arrived at the Chickasaw agency, near the present Houston, Mississippi. We don't know what the weather was like. Writing to Jefferson after Lewis's death, Neelly said that "on our arrival at the Chickasaw nation I discovered that he appeared at times deranged in mind, we rested there two days and came on. . . ." If he had malaria when he arrived at the fort it may be that he was again seized by it; or it may be that oppressive heat and fatigue made him behave in a strange manner. Or it may be that Neelly was covering up.

Apparently Russell had been receiving reports from persons who met the travelers. After naming the luggage which Lewis left with him at the fort he told Jefferson: "Enclosed is his memo. respecting them but before the Boat in which he directed they might be sent got to this place I rec'd a verbal message from him after he left here to keep them until I should hear from him again." Why Lewis changed his mind we do not know. One conjecture is that after further thought he was more convinced than he had been that he would return to St. Louis, and saw no reason why luggage left with Russell should go by boat all the way to Washington and from there back to St. Louis.

The other reports that Russell received are more astonishing. In his second, and very angry, letter to Jefferson, in January, 1810, Russell said: "The fact is which you may yet be ignorant of that his untimely death may be attributed solely to the free use he made of liquor which he acknowledged verry candidly to me after he recovered and expressed a firm determination never to drink any more spirits or use snuff again, both of which I deprived him of for several days & confined him to claret and a little white wine."

What an astonishing statement! Was Captain Russell a bluenose? If Lewis drank intemperately at the fort, he did what, as Bakeless says, he is not known to have done at any other time in his life. But Russell's most astonishing statement to Jefferson is in his next paragraph: "But after leaving this place by some means or other his resolution left him and this Agt being extremely fond of liquor, instead of preventing the Govr from drinking or putting him under restraint advised him to it & from every thing I can learn gave the man every chance to seek an opportunity to destroy himself. And from the statement of Grinders wife where he killed himself I can not help believing that Purney was rather aiding & abeting in the murder than otherwise."

This much is clear, that someone reported to Russell that on the trail Neelly urged Lewis to drink. It is also clear that someone told Russell that Mrs. Grinder had said that Pernia "was aiding & abeting in the murder"—that is, in using alcohol to drive Lewis to suicide. As we shall see a little later, this is not what Neelly told Jefferson, and unless she lied or Neelly lied, it is not what Mrs. Grinder told Neelly.

The fact is that of what happened during the twelve days on the trail we know only what Neelly said, what Russell's anonymous informants said, and what an anonymous informant told Henry Bechtle.

For the fiftieth anniversary of the settlement of Cincinnati, various old-timers were asked to contribute to a volume of reminiscences. One of them, Henry Bechtle, wrote in December, 1838, that the wife of a certain man whom he formerly had known "wore the first Petti-coat in the Chickasaw nation. He travelled with Capt. Lewis one whole day but a short time before that meritorious but unfortunate man put an end to his existence." Lewis and his party had been overnight at Perry's Stand, and there Lewis had given this man a prospectus "& had promised to send him one of his large ones when Printed. . . ." Perry, the informant says, thought Lewis the "greatest man in the world." Because Bechtle wrote twenty-nine years after Lewis's death we can't put much faith in what he said. It sounds as if Lewis was full of gab about the projected publication of his journals, and was promoting interest in the project, here and there along the way.

Neelly says that because Lewis appeared at times deranged in mind, they rested at the agency two days. They then rode the Trace north by east, and historian Phelps says they covered a hundred and fifty miles the next three days. That's hard riding over rough hill country; one would not suppose that a deranged man could do it.

They made their last camp together after a day's journey north from the Tennessee River. There "we lost two of our horses,

I remained behind to hunt them & the Governor proceeded on, with a promise to wait for me at the first house he Came to that was inhabited by white people; . . ." Russell, in his deposition nearly two years after Lewis's death, put it this way: "The night preceding this one of his Horses and one of the Chickasaw agents with whom he was traveling strayed off from the camp and in the Morning could not be found. The agent with some Indians stayed to search for the horses, and Governor Lewis with their two servants and the baggage horses proceeded to Mr. Grinders where he was to halt untill the agent caught up."

And so for most of a day Meriwether Lewis rode on alone, but for the two servants who trailed him with the baggage horses. It seems probable that a little before sunset on October 10 he rode up to the Grinder Stand. We shall now examine the premises and the people who lived there.

# VIII

# *The Grinders*
# *and Their Stand*

As early as 1801-02 "travel accommodations, even of the crudest kind, were not available in the Chickasaw country north of the Tennessee River," Mr. Phelps tells us, but by 1805 the Chickasaw agreed "to make three settlements north of the river." They "consistently refused to permit any but their own people, that is squawmen or half breeds, to establish or operate stands." Because, says a National Park Service paper, "of the reluctance of the natives to part with this right it is reasonable to believe that the majority of the inns along the route of the Natchez Trace were kept by Indians or half-breeds who subsisted on the travel over the trace and on the sale of wines and other commodities. Although it is not definitely known that Robert Grinder . . . was an Indian, it is believed that some members [of the Grinder clan] were at least part Indian."

In 1815 a traveler wrote: "The Indian hotels are made of small poles, just high enough for you to stand straight in, with a dirt floor, no bedding of any kind, except a bearskin, and not that in some of their huts. You feel blank and disappointed when you walk in and find a cold dirt floor, naked walls, and no fire. Camping out is far better than such accommodations." Phelps quotes the above and comments: "Such crude types of accommodation, however, were all that were available on the Natchez Trace during the quarter of a century in which it was a nationally important highway."

North of the Tennessee River one of the first of the important stops was John Gordon's ferry across Duck River, about sixteen miles northwest of the present Columbia. "Grinder's Inn . . . came soon after, followed by another stand kept by an Indian called Factor's Son, located about thirty-five miles farther down the Trace, over the Chickasaw line." Phelps says Grinder's was established between January 18, 1803, and October 11, 1809. That is drawing it pretty fine, for it was on October 10 that Lewis rode up to it.

Though Mr. Willam K. Kay, a national park historian, says that "the location and the design of Grinder's Inn are so indefinite as to make it advisable to abandon the original proposal of restoring it on its original site," some conclusions were reached by those who investigated the matter. It is "difficult to obtain any accurate information as to its location, size and construction. . . . The following report on the location, plan and construction of Grinder's Stand is based on facts learned from excavation on the site of the original, information gained from interviews with local residents who saw the building and 'on study of the remains of other old buildings dating back to the early nineteenth century."

His conclusion that there were two cabins the investigator bases on "the account of Malinda Grinder"—that is, of the slave Malinda, who may have used the surname of her master, and of Alexander Wilson, the ornithologist, who inspected the site soon after Lewis's death. It is assumed that two crude log cabins were separated by a "hallway or piazza"—that is, they stood apart from one another twelve or fifteen feet. The Stand "had at least two outside doors facing the Trace and one leading from the south room to the kitchen."\* Each building had a chimney, and the "fireplaces were unusually large. The openings between the logs were often four inches. The cracks were chinked with wood and daubed with clay or some other cement-like material." These investigators concluded that the doors were made of oak, a common wood in the area, but without nails; that they had wooden hinges;

---

\*See sketch, end papers.

that the floor in the kitchen, or north cabin, was of earth, in the other, of puncheons.

We don't know if the stable was north or south of the cabins but presumably it was south, and closest to the puncheon-cabin in which, it is said, Lewis retired. The grave and monument are today about 700 feet north of what is pointed out as the site of one of the cabins. An attorney named Park, whose opinions we shall examine later, visited the site in 1891 and reported that Lewis was buried about 450 feet north of the cabins. Wilson the ornithologist, probably a good judge of distance, said the stable was about 600 feet from the cabins but he did not say in which direction.

A letter from Mr. John H. Saxon, acting superintendent of the Monument, says: "We have your letter in which you inquire about the distance between the site of Grinder's Stand and the Lewis grave. Some years ago the Custodian then assigned to Meriwether Lewis National Monument measured the distance between the two points and recorded it as 700 feet. We assume that the site marked as that of Grinder's Stand is the correct one. Existing rubble, local tradition, and the minor archeological work performed by Messrs. Hagen and Anderson in 1933 all agree in establishing that site as being correct."

In regard to the location of the stable he said, "We have no information, by tradition or otherwise, about the location of the Stand outbuildings. However, we think it highly unlikely that Major Neelly would permit the burial of Lewis's body in an unsuitable place, or that local folklore would not record, to someone's detriment, the choice of a questionable burial place."

Park, as we have just seen, inspected the spot and said that Lewis was buried about 450 feet from the cabins. Elliott Coues, a scientifically trained observer, also examined the site, and said that the grave was "north of the site of the old house, and about 150 yards from it, on the east side of the road." It doesn't seem likely that either man, and especially Coues, would have erred by 250 feet, though when this matter was laid before Mr. Phelps he replied: "I have never regarded either Coues' or Park's statement that the monument was about 450 feet from the cabin site as a matter of importance. Estimates of distance are notoriously unreliable and my guess is that neither of the above-mentioned gentlemen actually paced off the distance. There is no reason to believe that the monument erected by the State of Tennessee has ever been moved. It is believed that the stones used either in a chimney or in the foundation of a cabin mark the cabin site. No other site in the vicinity is marked by such evidence as would identify it as a building site."

The question is not whether the monument has been moved, but whether it was Lewis's bones or those of another person that were exhumed nearly forty years after his death and just before the monument was erected. This matter we shall return to.

Who were the Grinders and where did they come from? In the whole body of literature on Lewis's death possibly nothing is more astonishing than the fact that the writers, including a number of historians, have accepted Mrs. Grinder's version of the death, though they haven't known where she came from, or her first name, or her age or the age of her husband, or her racial background. They haven't even known whether she could read, or write her name. In short, they have known practically nothing about the quality of their witness.

It has not been possible to determine such a simple matter as the correct spelling of their name. The Spences in their history of Hickman county (in which most of the Grinders lived), J.H. Moore, who for a time was the family attorney, the Chattanooga *Times* May 15, 1932, William Bruce Turner, a Columbia judge who has written a history of Maury county, and one or two others have spelled it Griner. In most sources, including all the Tennessee census and court records which we examined, it is spelled Grinder. A search of Lewis, Hickman, and Maury counties discovered no person with either name; it is said there that all the descendants seem to have gone. We did learn at last that the Grinders or Griners came from North Carolina, possibly from Stokes county. In 1807 Josiah Shipp settled at what became known as Shipps Landing or Shipps Bend, in the Duck River area of Hickman county. In Stokes county in 1790 there was a Josiah Ship, a Joshua Grinder, head of a family, and a Mary Grinder, head of a family. Apparently the Grinders and Shipps were close friends, for Robert Grinder's two daughters both married Shipps. Grinder seems to have come to the Duck River area about the time Shipp or the Shipps came.

There served in the Revolutionary War a John Grinder from North Carolina; a Jacob Grinder and a David Griner from Virginia; and a Philip Griner from Georgia. It may be that in an earlier time both Grinders and Griners were of the same family stock, and that the spelling of the name became a matter of choice. In all Tennessee census reports up to 1850 the name is spelled Grinder, and it is to be assumed that at least some member of the family was asked how he spelled his name.

In 1800 Mary Grinder was still in Stokes county but Joshua had left it. It is assumed that the Robert Grinders came from North Carolina because their older daughter, Bethenia or Berthenia, was born there, apparently about 1800, since the 1850 census gives her age as 50.

The Spences say in their history of Hickman county that about 1807 the upper end of Shipps Bend was "settled by Robert Griner, Sr. . . . The next year he moved out on the Natchez Trace, and had an inn near where the Lewis monument now stands. . . . A few years later Griner returned to the north side of Duck River and settled where he had first located. While an inn-keeper on the Natchez Trace, Griner often sold whisky to the Indians. Their love for 'fire water,' as they called it, was so great that they would allow themselves to be bitten by snakes in order to get whisky. . . . The sons of Robert Griner, Sr., were William, John, Albert, Robert, Jr., and the twin brothers, Hulett and Noble. Albert and Noble, in fits of insanity, committed suicide by hanging—Noble, near the old camp ground near the John Thompson place in 1855; and Albert, below the mouth of Indian Creek in 1850."

What we need most to know is what persons were at the stand when Lewis rode up, who they were, and how old they were. We shall find Neelly telling Jefferson that nobody was there but Mrs. Grinder. It is strange that nobody has ever questioned that statement, for the evidence makes it implausible, to say the least. Following are data taken from Tennessee census reports; these seem not to be in all respects trustworthy but we could hardly expect absolute accuracy from census-takers in such primitive conditions when the nation was young.

CENSUS:

| county & year | head of household | husband's age | wife's age | ages of children* |
|---|---|---|---|---|
| Hickman: 1820 | Robert Grinder Sr. | over 45 | over 45 | 3 sons under 10<br>1 son 10 to 18<br>1 son 18 to 26<br>1 daughter 10 to 16 |
| Wayne: 1820 | Robert Grinder Jr. | 18-26 | 26-45 | 3 children under 10 |
| Hickman: 1840 | Robert Grinder | 20-30 | 20-30 | 1 son under 5<br>1 son under 10<br>3 daughters under 5<br>1 daughter 15-20 |
| Wayne: 1820 | John Grinder | 26-45 | 26 45 | 1 son under 10<br>4 daughters under 10 |
| Wayne: 1840 | John Grinder | 20-30 | 20-30 | 1 daughter under 5<br>1 son under 5 |
| Hickman: 1830 | John C. Grinder | 20-30 | 20-30 | 1 daughter under 10 |
| Hickman: 1840 | Albert S. Grinder | 30-40 | 20-30 | 2 sons under 5<br>1 male 15-20<br>1 male 20-30<br>2 daughters under 5<br>2 daughters 5-10 |
| Hickman: 1840 | Hulett W. Grinder (or Hughlett) | 2 males 20-30 | 1 female 50-60 | |

That's a very strange census table, to say the least. The Spences say there were two sons, named William and Noble, but neither appears in the census for these two counties. Looking at the Robert Grinder, Sr., table of children we see that one son in 1809 could have been 15 or close to it; it seems more reasonable that he was still at home than that he had gone. If the figures are correct the two younger Robert Grinders could not have been the same person. Fathers usually give their own name to the oldest of their sons. If the one with the junior title was the senior's son, this son in 1809 was between the ages of 7 and 15, and among the Grinder sons in 1820 could be the son listed between 18-26. If the other Robert was his son, he was not yet born in 1809 or was only an infant. The two John Grinders seem to have been

---

*The children were not necessarily sons and daughters of the heads of the house but presumably were.

father and son. John C. Grinder seems to have been Robert's son, not only because the son would be likely to be in the county where the father lived, but because a John C. appears in a court document related to the sale of Robert Senior's slaves. If John C. had a daughter 5-10 he probably was in his middle twenties in 1830, and in the 1820 census of Robert Senior could have been in either the 10-18 or 18-26 age group.

The census listed besides the head of the household and his wife, not their children, as such, but males and females in certain age brackets. We don't know, then, whether the male 15-20 in the Albert S. home in 1840 was a son. The male 20-30 may have been a son. If Albert had a son 20-30 in 1840 he would have been married by 1820 and would not have appeared in the 1820 census of Robert Senior. He must have been older than 30 in 1840, and so would have been born by 1809 and living with his parents.

Hulett is a riddle. If in 1840 he was no more than 30, and if the female listed as his wife was at least 50, his wife was at least twenty years older. Two males are listed in the 20-30 group, and nobody, male or female, under the age of 20. Possibly the second male was a son of Hulett's wife by a former marriage.

If the 1820 census can be trusted, both Robert Grinder, Sr., and his wife were not less than 34 years old in 1809. In 1820 they apparently had six children at home. In 1809 they had two, possibly three. Bethenia, born in 1800, seems by 1820 to have married William Shipp, born in 1796. There was a son who could have been 15, or as young as 7; if we take the median age he was 11. Robert, Sr., died in 1848. If he was 34 in 1809 he was about 73 when he died. If we take a median age for Robert and his wife they were close to 40 when Lewis rode up to their door.

The ground under us is not much firmer when we come to the Grinder slaves. There is a tradition that at the Grinder Stand in 1809 there were two slaves, Pete, who is said to have been 13, and Malinda, who is said to have been 12. It has not been possible to establish the existence of Pete but there was a Malinda. In any case, a slave named Malinda, belonging to Robert Grinder, Sr., was sold soon after his death. The Grinder slave or slaves seem to have been left to the younger daughter, Mrs. Josiah Shipp, who petitioned for the right to sell them: "John C. Grinder, William G. Grinder and Hughlett M. Grinder and said defendants having failed to appear and plead answer or demur to the petition of petitioners, it is therefore ordered adjudged and decreed by the Court that said petition be taken as confessed as to them and set for hearings expartee."

A boy named Bob was sold for $630; John C. Grinder bought a woman named Patsy for $488; William Shipp bought "Malinda and Malinda's child" and a slave woman named Letty for $325. Robert E. Grinder, Guardian, petitioned at the December term, 1849, to sell the property of "Noble L. Grinder, Lunatick &c.," who according to the Spences killed himself in 1855. Elsewhere the record says that "Noble J. Grinder has been found a_____? & Robert E, his Guardian &_____, and that he is indebted in a sum exceeding five hundred dollars, and that the personal estate of said Noble J. Grinder, exclusive of the slaves is worth about $429. It is therefore ordered, adjudged and decreed by the Court that Robert E the Guardian sell the personal estate of said lunatic, Noble J. Grinder, with the exception of the slaves. . . ." Noble had in 1847 married a woman named Cordelia, who two years later deserted him, whereupon he sought and was granted a divorce.

There is a tradition that a number of the Grinders, besides Noble and Albert, became insane, including the widow of a grandson, and the father of one Dan Grinder. Whether or not the tradition is founded on fact, it is strange that none of those who have been positive that Lewis was deranged, and sympahetic to Mrs. Grinder's problem in the presence of a deranged man, have ever written a word about the insanity in the Grinder family.

It is unfortunate that we don't positively know how many persons were at the stand when Lewis rode up late in the afternoon of October 10. Discussing the "accepted—and very dubious— version of what happened" Bakeless says there is a "local legend that Grinder himself was not nearly so absent as he seemed." We simply don't know whether he was there, or near the premises. It has been said repeatedly that he was away at his farm or ranch, but his settlement on Duck River, if he still had it, was more than twenty miles distant.

Mrs. Grinder was there. With her, we may assume, was Malinda, a slave twelve years old. With her were two, possibly three, of her own children—Bethenia, who was about ten, and a son older or younger. Even if we assume that Mrs. Grinder was only 35, if her daughter was 10 and the son was younger, she did not have her first pregnancy until she was about 24. This certainly is possible but does not seem probable. If she was older than 35, as we have conjectured, and the daughter was her first child, then her first pregnancy was even later than 24. It seems likely that in 1809 she had a son older than Bethenia.

We don't know that Malinda was a Grinder slave in 1809. The Malinda who was sold in 1848 became, in her old age, an "authority" on Lewis's death, for some of the writers who have been convinced of suicide. It is possible that she was acquired after 1809, and having heard from Mrs. Grinder her version (or versions, for she had more than one) of the death, Malinda herself began to tell how it all happened and eventually became convinced that she was present. Or, as seems more likely, she actually was there.

So we may, with some degree of probability, assume that she was present at the stand when Lewis rode up; and Bethenia, about 10, presumably was there; and a son who may have been no more than seven but who may have been older than the daughter. Tradition says that a Polly Spencer was there, the cook, a girl about fifteen. Tradition says that Pete, a Negro slave boy, was there. It is possible in either case, but it doesn't seem probable. The Grinders were hardly prosperous enough to have hired a cook.

The stage is now set for Meriwether Lewis to ride up and die from his own hand or from the hand of another. The next step in this baffling mystery is to see what the primary witnesses had to say about it.

# IX

# James Neelly:

# Chief Witness

Let it be said at once that James Neelly was not the chief witness, for he was not even on the scene when Lewis died and knew nothing about it except what he was told—unless it is to be assumed that he examined the pistols, the wounds, and the premises. It is not known that he did or that he did not; he never mentioned these matters. But Neelly is the chief witness for those who have argued for suicide. According to such evidence as we have, the only persons on the scene who left a record of what happened are Mrs. Grinder and Malinda, and neither of them left a word in writing; of what they saw or pretended to have seen we know only what they are alleged to have told other persons. Pernia was surely on the scene, but his view of the matter, if he ever expressed one, comes to us from the tongue of another person. If Neelly questioned him he left no record of it; if Jefferson questioned him when Pernia went to him the following month, there is no record of that either.

It is an exasperatingly baffling situation. As Olin Wheeler said after doing his best to discover the facts, "The various stories of this sad event are, naturally enough, widely discrepant in detail and conclusive of nothing. In all of them, Neelly, the guardian, is absent hunting horses at the supreme moment and the so-called guardianship proves a farce." But nobody except Neelly, *after* he had gone on to Nashville, and Jefferson, who undoubtedly based his assumption on Neelly, ever said that Neelly was Lewis's guardian. Neelly is a key figure in our mystery and we may as well begin with him.

As Bakeless says, "The entire suicide story, therefore, depends entirely on what the people at Grinder's Stand that night told Neeley the next day, with some possible confirmation from Lewis's two servants, who were sleeping in the stable. . . . If the Grinders really had anything to conceal, their suicide story was the easiest defense to offer. If Lewis really did commit suicide, Mrs. Grinder's own story [not to Neelly but a later version] shows her behaving in a remarkably callous fashion." When he wrote his excellent book Bakeless did not know the correct spelling of Neelly's name or that Lewis had only one servant; but in that paragraph he made a point that should be kept in mind by anyone whose interest is in the facts and probabilities and not in preconceived notions—that if the Grinders had anything to conceal, a story of suicide was the best one they could invent.

Let us try to imagine the scene. James Neelly, according to his story, had remained behind, alone, or as Russell says in his document, with some Indians, to hunt for two horses that had strayed; and some time during the forenoon of October 11 he came up the Trace to Grinder's Stand. Mrs. Grinder had on her hands at the moment a dead and very distinguished man. What had she been doing? Had she sent for her husband?—or the local justice of the peace—or for anyone? Was she beside herself with anxiety, and did she run forward to meet Neelly when she saw him coming? Did Neelly ride up alone, or were Indians with him?

Presumably he was riding a horse and leading one, for he had found only one of the two. Where did he first see the body of Meriwether Lewis—somewhere between the cabins, or in the guest cabin, or by a tree stump? Such questions could be asked endlessly, for the reason that Neelly's account of what he found is one of the most unsatisfactory documents in all of history. This is what he wrote to Thomas Jefferson in Nashville a week later:

"It is with extreme pain I have to inform you of the death of His Excellency Meriwether Lewis, Governor of Upper Louisiana who died on the morning of the 11th instant and I am Sorry to Say by Suicide.

"I arrived at the Chickasaw Bluffs on about the 18th September, where I found the Governor (who had reached there two days before me from St. Louis) in very bad health—It appears that his first intention was to go around by Water to the City of Washington; but his thinking a war with England probable, & that his valuable papers might be in dainger of falling into the hands of the British, he was thereby induced to Change his route, and to come through the Chickasaw nation by land; I furnished him with a horse to pack his trunks, &c on, and a man to attend to them; having recovered his health in some digree at the Chickasaw Bluffs, we set out together. And on our arrival at the Chickasaw nation I discovered that he appeared at times deranged in mind, we rested there two days & came on, one days Journey after Crossing Tennessee River. & where we encamped we lost two of our horses, I remained behind to hunt them & the Governor proceeded on, with a promise to wait for me at the first house he Came to that was inhabited by white people; he reached the house of a Mr Grinder about Sun Set, the man of the house being from home, and no person there but a woman discovering the governor to be deranged. gave him up the house & slept herself in one near it, his servant and mine slept in the stabel loft some distance from the other houses, the woman reports that about three oClock She heard two pistols fire off in the Governors Room; the Servants being awakined by her, came in but too late to save him, he had shot himself in the head with one pistol, & a little below the Breast with the other—when his Servant came in he says; I have done the business my good Servant give me some water. he gave him water,

"he Survived but a short time, I came up Some time after, & had him as decently Buried as I could in that place—if there is any thing wished by his friends to be done to his grave I will attend to their Instructions.

"I have got in possession his two trunks of papers (amongst which is said to be his travels to the pacific Ocean) and probably some Vouchers for expenditures of Public Money for a Bill which he said had been protested by the Secy of War, and of which act to his death, he repeatedly complained. I have also in my care his Rifle, Silver watch, Brace of Pistols, dirk & tomahawk; one of the Governers horses was lost in the wilderness which I will endeavour to regain, the other I have Sent on by his servant who expressed a desire to go to the governors mothers & to Monticello: I have furnished him with fifteen Dollars to Defray his expences to Charlottesville; Some days previous to the Governors death he requested of me in Case any accident happened to him, to send his trunks with the papers therein to the President, but I think it Very probable he meant you—I wish to be informed what arrangements may be considered best in Sending on his trunks &c

"I have the honor to be with Great respect Yr Ob Sert

James Neelly

U.S. Agent to the Chickasaw Nation

"the Governor left two of his trunks at the Chickasaw Bluffs in the Care of Capt Gilbert C Russell, Commanding officer, & was to write to him from Nashville what to do with them."

That, so far as we know, is all that Neelly ever wrote to Jefferson about the matter. There are some astonishing statements in it that no writer on this subject seems to have thought significant enough to mention. He says that there *was no person there but a woman*. Such evidence as we have indicates that Lewis was buried not on the 11th but on the 12th. If, as Neelly wrote Jefferson, he saw him as decently buried as he could, he was at the Grinder Stand or in its area at least one night and probably two. Did he not see any of the children in all that time? If he saw them, did he not think it strange that Mrs. Grinder told him she was alone when Lewis rode up? Or did she tell him that? In two other versions of her tale, which have been recorded, and which we shall examine a little later, she did *not* say that she was alone.

Neelly says that she "gave him up the house & slept herself in one near it." This again is a strange statement, to say the least of it: Neelly must have been at this stand before and he must have known that the cabin with the puncheon floor was for guests, the other for cooking and for the Grinder family. Why did he say that she gave up the house, as though that were not the customary thing to do? Of course she gave him the guest cabin; that's what it was for.

In all the writing on this subject that has dwelt on Neelly,

The Sgt. Floyd Monument near Sioux City, Iowa. According to Olin Wheeler it is 100 feet tall, of "Kettle River, Minnesota, sandstone, a stone of warm, pink color, very durable." *Courtesy Sioux City Chamber of Commerce.*

Meriwether Lewis monument. *Photo by author.*

there has been a curious disposition to find in him a man of irreproachable character, though, as with Mrs. Grinder, the writers have known little or nothing about him.* There is no intention here to impeach him, but only to look at his motives as clearly as we can, and at him for the kind of man he was.

James Neelly was an ex-major but he seems never to have been a major in the regular army, for his name is not to be found in Heitman's *Register and Dictionary of the United States Army.* He probably had been a major in a State militia. Andrew Jackson, a major-general in the State militia, lists a James Neelly, Second Adjutant, in his General Orders of December 13, 1812, as a cavalry officer of the Tennessee Volunteers, who went with Jackson to Natchez at the beginning of the War of 1812.

In the Bureau of Indian Affairs are a few documents related to Neelly. There is his commission as agent of the Chickasaw Nation, dated July 7, 1809; a letter from the Secretary of War the following day, advising him in regard to his duties; an unratified treaty dated July 7, 1811, with the Chickasaw Nation, for the construction of a road through a part of their country; and twenty-eight letters in his own handwriting, between August, 1809, and July, 1812. A letter of June 4, 1812, from the Secretary of War, rather abruptly advised Neelly that he was dismissed as Indian agent and would be replaced by General James Robertson. The reason given for Neelly's dismissal was the hostility of the Indians. This could mean that he had been hitting the bottle and had not discharged his duties with reasonable competence; or it could mean that unlike William Clark he did not understand Indians and was not able to get along with them; or it could mean that with a war coming up it was thought advisable in Washington to put in Neelly's place a man who could handle Indians in a time of crisis.

When he was commissioned agent in July, 1809, he was given a salary of $1,000 a year, with an additional dollar a day in lieu of substance. Within a few weeks he had a voucher rejected, and a number of them before he was removed. May 26, 1810, he was advised that "The compensation claimed by Mr. Allen ... cannot be allowed by this Department." November 24, 1809, the War Department wrote him: "Your letter of the 18th ult. advising

---

*See Notes to this chapter.

a draft of ninety dollars in favor of Jeremiah Love 'for services rendered the United States by guarding and transporting George Lanshart, a prisoner charged with Felony, from the Chickasaw Nation to Nashville,' &c. has been received. The draft has been paid, but will be considered as chargeable to your Private salary account, until more satisfactory evidence than is contained in the letter, shall be exhibited that the United States and the funds appropriated for the Indian Department are properly chargeable with this expenditure."

This was only a month after he wrote Jefferson. If it had been *before*, possibly it would not have occurred to him to say that because of a rejected voucher Lewis had complained repeatedly to the day of his death. May 1, 1811, Neelly was advised that a claim was "totally inadmissable." This rejection of some of his vouchers does not necessarily reflect on his character, but it does suggest, as similar rejections suggest in the case of Lewis, that he had an inadequate notion of the limits of his office.

During his long service as a public official—Indian agent, general, governor—William Clark seems rarely, if ever, to have had a voucher rejected. But he was an extraordinarily prudent man. There is reason to think that Neelly, like Lewis, was impulsive and impetuous. He may have been a hard-drinking devil-may-care sort of fellow, who didn't bother his head with fine distinctions.

We have seen Russell's belief, in his second (and angry) January, 1810, letter to Jefferson, that Lewis would not have died if Neelly had not urged drink on him. Knowing so little of the two men and the circumstances, there is little anyone can say about that that would not be pure speculation. Another matter that aroused Russell's anger puts us on firmer ground.

Russell wrote: "I have lately been informed that James Neelly the Agt to the Chickasaws with whom Govr Lewis set off from this place has detained his pistols & perhaps some other of his effects for some claim he pretends to have upon his estate. He can have no just claim for anything more than the expenses of his interment unless he makes a charge for packing his two trunks from the Nation—and for that he can not have the audacity to make a charge after tendering the use of a loose horse or two which he said he had to take from the Nation & also the aid of his servant."

Those are strong words. They have been completely ignored by those writers who have had no doubt that Lewis killed himself. The words plainly imply that Neelly did not rest very high in the esteem of the fort's commanding officer. Jefferson undoubtedly read this letter, yet we shall find him saying that Neelly made the journey only or largely because he wanted to watch over and take care of Lewis; but Russell says that Neelly had to make the journey as far as Nashville, and that he was taking with him a loose horse or two, on which he told Lewis he could pack his trunks. As for the aid of Neelly's servant, it is not clear that Lewis had need of him, inasmuch as he had a servant of his own.

The angry letter continues: "He seemed happy to have it in his power to serve the Govr — but for his making the offer which was accepted I should have employed the man who packed the trunks to the Nation to have taken them to Nashville accompanied the Govr." That is, if Neelly had not been going to Nashville, and had not offered to assist Lewis with the trunks, Russell would have sent with Lewis the man of whom it has been assumed that he was Neelly's servant. If Russell made a fair statement of the case, he pretty well explodes the myth of Neelly's extraordinary services to Lewis. Russell continues, "Unfortunately for him this arrangement did not take place or I hesitate not to say he would this day be living." That is, if Russell had sent a man with Lewis, not to watch over him because he was deranged, but to assist with the trunks, and presumably to return the pack horses to the fort, Lewis in Russell's opinion would not have died.

Russell continues: "This Neely also says he lent the Govr money which cannot be so for he had none himself & the Govr had more than one hundred $ in notes and specia besides a check I let him have of 99 58/100 none of which it is said could be found. I have wrote to the Cashier of the branch bank of Orleans on whom the checks were drawn in favor of myself an order to stop payt when presented. I have this day authorized a Gentleman to pay the pretended claim of Neelly and take the Pistols which will be held (illegible) to the order of any of the friends of Mr. Lewis free from encumbrance."

What an extraordinary paragraph! He says Neelly had no money of his own, yet Neelly wrote Jefferson that he had given Pernia fifteen dollars to help pay his expenses on the way to Charlottesville. Russell says that Lewis had on him more than a hundred dollars in cash, and the check. The check was found in one of the trunks. The currency was never found, and all but one or two writers on this subject have never mentioned it, apparently thinking it of no significance that Lewis's purse and its contents disappeared during the night of his death. We don't know that Russell was a qualified judge of Neelly, but we should note in passing his contempt for him in such words as "This Neely" and "pretended claim."

In his first letter to Jefferson, Russell said that what had become of Lewis's valuables he did not know, but assumed that they were with Neelly at Nashville. November 26, Jefferson wrote Madison that "Maj Neely" had in his possession two trunks belonging to Lewis. On arriving at Nashville, Neelly presumably had with him all the property Lewis had at Grinder's, except the purse and its contents—and it is a bold person who would say positively that he did not have that.

Russell wrote Jefferson that he had "this day" authorized a man to pay Neelly his claim against the Lewis estate. "This day" was January 31, 1810, or more than three and a half months after Lewis died. At that time Neelly seems to have had in his possession one of Lewis's horses, his rifle, pistols, and dirk—and what else we do not know. Almost two years after Lewis's death, John Hastings Marks, a stepbrother, went to St. Louis to help Edward Hempstead, the administrator, untangle and settle the estate. He then made a long journey to find Neelly. Two years and three months after Lewis's death, January 22, 1812, he wrote his half-brother Reuben Lewis that he had gone by way of Nashville into the Duck River country "in Search of Mr. Nealy to recover the property of Br ML which he had in which I failed in fact . . . ." Mrs. Neelly, he tells Reuben, gave up the horse and the rifle, but Neelly "as I was informed carries the dirk and Pistols constantly with him." It would be interesting to know whether Neelly, if he had been home, would have surrendered the rifle and the horse.

No amount of special pleading can put this man in a decent light in this situation. We don't know whether Russell's man paid Neelly his claim, or offered to pay him and was rejected, or never carried out Russell's instructions. But even if it is assumed that Neelly had a legitimate claim against Lewis, and was not paid, it cannot be assumed that he was justified in taking possession of so many items of valuable property. For the horse alone Lewis paid $140. His weapons, Russell said, were elegant, which probably means that they were the best obtainable. Apparently Neelly's wife told Marks that Neelly carried the dirk and pistols constantly with him. He must have taken a great fancy to them.

It was not a simple task for Neelly to turn the horse over to the administrator or an heir. It would have been a simple task to send the rifle, dirk, tomahawk and pistols along with the trunks —or have turned them over to William Clark and Isaac Coles, who seem to have taken possession of the trunks in Nashville. Was Neelly on the scene when Clark came to take custody of the property? It seems unlikely that he was, for surely Clark knew the kind of weapons Lewis carried, and their worth. Did Neelly ever turn over the dirk and pistols? Apparently he did not; diligent search, including correspondence with a number of persons who have a professional interest in Lewis relics, has found no trace of them.

There is another curious thing about James Neelly. Almost at once, even while he was still in Nashville soon after Lewis's death, stories of how Lewis died were flying from tongue to tongue. Some of them did not agree with, or at least amended, what Neelly reported to Jefferson. Why didn't he clarify the matter? That he did not seems certain, for if he had done so there would be a record somewhere of it. Probably any newspaper in the area, or in the nation, would have been glad to publish anything about it that he cared to write. In view of all the rumors, why didn't he send a fuller report to Jefferson? He continued as Indian agent until June 4, 1812, or for more than two and a half years after Lewis's death. He must have stopped now and then at the Grinder Stand, before the Grinders moved back to Duck River. Did he again hear the story from Mrs. Grinder, and if he did, did she tell the same story twice? Surely the stories appearing in some of the newspapers came to his attention: what did he think of them? We face this astonishing fact: the governor of Upper Louisiana and a famous American died at a wilderness stand in circumstances that some persons in the area must have thought rather mysterious (there seems, for instance, to have been a coroner's jury), yet so far as we know, James Neelly, after a brief letter to Jefferson, maintained complete silence.

From whom did the newspapers get their information? Nobody seems to have asked the question.

Before we dismiss Neelly and proceed to the next witness, we should look at three letters which at least one historian has felt support Neelly's version, and at the strange Russell document, which no writer on this subject seems to have been aware of.

X

# Captain Brahan
# Writes Three Letters

A search of the records has cast little light on the age, background, character, and motives of Captain John Brahan of the 2nd U.S. Infantry. In a War Department Register of Letters, under date of 20 September 1810, is the following:

"Enclosing a printed Paragraph cut from a Public Newspaper, stating the Arrest by Governor Salcedo, of sundry Citizens of the United States known to Capt. Brahan, of very respectable character & connexions,—and that they have been confined as close prisoners, under the charge of being Spies for the French Emperor;—they are said to be in the Castle of St. Eclearia.—Capt. Brahan, in behalf of them & their friends, solicits the immediate interference of the Government of the U.S. to save them from the fatal effects that may proceed from those misrepresentations that have caused their arrest:—etc.etc."

This and a similar item, as well as the three letters, suggest that he was a sober gentleman who took his duties seriously. It is rather remarkable, for instance, that he wrote three letters on the day when James Neelly, so far as we know, wrote only one— or perhaps the remarkable thing is that Neelly wrote only one and not that Brahan wrote three about the suicide or murder of a famous American.

Mr. Phelps says that "Captain Brahan's account, derived from Neely, is identical with that of the Indian agent except for two details." There is no significance in the fact that a report based on another is identical with it; a study of Brahan's phrasing and Neelly's suggests that Brahan had before him Neelly's letter, or had read it with a remarkably retentive memory—for Neelly says, "gave him up the house & slept herself in one near it," and Brahan says, "gave him up the house and slept herself in another house near it." Brahan's letters are not evidence but they do seem to cast a little light on the matter.

It is not known in what order he wrote them. He tells Jefferson that Neelly has informed him that after leaving Chickasaw Bluffs Lewis "appeared some days thereafter while on their journey to be Some what deranged in mind." After two horses strayed from camp, Lewis proposed that Neelly should stay behind and find them. "No person being at home but the wife of Mr. Grinder the woman discovering the Governor to be deranged gave him up the house and slept herself in another house near it the two Servants Slept in a Stabel loft some distance off; about three oclock the woman heard two pistols fire off. being alarmed she went and waked the servants when they came in they found him weltering in his blood. He had shot himself. first it was thought in the head, the ball did not take effect, the other shot was a little below his breast . . . he lived until Sun rise & expired."

Mr. Phelps says Neelly's and Brahan's accounts are identical except for two details: "First, he specified the date—the morning of October 10—that Neelly had remained behind to hunt the horses. Secondly, he failed to mention the highly significant remark that Lewis, after having fired the fatal shots, made as his servant entered the room." A second significant matter, overlooked by Mr. Phelps, is that when talking to Brahan, Neelly said that Lewis *asked* him to stay behind and find the horses. He didn't tell Jefferson that. We do not know whether he overlooked it or did not think it important, or whether, after reflection, he decided to embellish his tale to put a better face on himself. Neelly told Jefferson that Lewis survived the shots "but a short time"; he told Brahan that he lived until sunrise, which would have been around four hours.

Brahan told Jefferson that Neelly had "his Brace of Pistols, his Rifle & Dirk." If he had read Neelly's letter, he was aware that

Neelly had communicated these facts; if he had not read it we must wonder why he felt compelled to tell Jefferson these things. Pernia, he says, will go on to Monticello; he, Brahan, had given him five dollars to put with the fifteen which Neelly had given him, and would have given him more but for the belief that Pernia would drink too much. Again we must wonder what was motivating Brahan: was he familiar with Pernia's drinking habits, or had Neelly told him that Pernia drank too much? It seems unlikely that Brahan knew much about Pernia's habits. If Neelly made a point of Pernia's drinking, possibly he was again trying to put a good face on himself.

Brahan says that Lewis "was a very particular friend of mine" and "I shall remain in this place some time and will with great pleasure attend to any instruction you may think necessary either in sending on the trunks of papers or the other articles . . . . " Since Brahan intended to remain in Nashville, presumably to watch over Lewis's property, why didn't Neelly turn over to him the dirk and pistols?

The same day Brahan wrote to William Eustis, Secretary of War:

"It is with great concern that I announce to you the death of His Excellency Meriwether Lewis Governor of Upper Louisiana, which took place on the morning of the 11th Instant at the house of a Mr. Grinder about Seventy five miles, from this on the Natchez Road—and what renders this unhappy affair more melancholy it is stated from a correct Source that he committed Suicide. Maj. James Neelly Agent for the Chickasaws had travelled with the Governor from the Chickasaw Bluffs until they got within a days Journey of the place when [where] the unfortunate affair took place—they had lost two horses & the Maj. remained behind to hunt them, & the governor proceeded as to get to a house where a white man lived. he reached there before Night, & about three oclock in the morning shot himself with two pistols: the first ball it is said wounded him in the head. the other entered a little below his breast which caused his death in about three hours—Maj Neeley had him intered as decently as he could—and he informs me that he has in his Care two trunks of the Governors containing his Valuable papers, probably his Journal to the pacific ocean, &

perhaps Vouchers for money expended in his Territorial Government; but I have not seen them.

"Major Neeley informs me that he has his Brace of Pistols Rifle, gun & watch which will remain in his hands until he hears what he is to do with them—he has communicated to Mr. Jefferson late President this unfortunate affair, & has informed him what he had got in his hands belonging to the Estate of Governor Lewis. Maj. Neeley informs me that he discovered some days previous to the death of Governor Strong proofs of a derangement in his mind."

If one has complete faith in Neelly's honor, the letter to Eustis passes muster and is filed. If one hasn't, one may look a second time at such expressions as, "it is stated from a correct source"—"the first ball it is said"—"but I have not seen them." These may be only the manner of expression of a literal-minded man who tried with great care to say exactly what he wanted to say; or they may indicate that like Russell he did not take James Neely for granted.

On the same day he also wrote to Major Amos Stoddard, to whom Lewis addressed the last letter of his life. We should note Brahan's statement that "the man of the house was from home" and that the woman of the house "awoke the servants, and they rushed into the Room, and found the unfortunate Governor weltering in his blood; he had shot himself in the head and just below his breast—he died in about three hours; in a few hours Major Neely agent to the Chickasaw came up . . . he had him intered . . . . his servant John Parney will proceed on early in the morning with letters to Mr. Jefferson from Majr Neeley. . . ."

Apparently Neelly said nothing about knife wounds to Captain Brahan. Just a little after Neelly talked to Brahan in Nashville some newspapers were saying that Lewis had knife or razor wounds, and indeed the story that William Clark read in a Frankfort paper only ten days after Neelly wrote Jefferson said that Lewis's throat was cut. It would be pretty far-fetched to assume that the newspapers invented details. If Neelly saw knife wounds and mentioned them to Brahan, then surely Brahan would have put them in his letters, for in all three letters he put the gunshot wounds. We must assume that there were no knife wounds, or that Neelly did not see them, or that for reasons of delicacy (which seems unlikely) or self-interest he did not choose to mention them.

If it was murder, either by Grinder or another party, and if Neelly did not appear on the scene until a few hours after Lewis died, the Grinders, or others, had plenty of time to put the body where they wanted it, to swathe it, and to think of a plausible story. We also must assume that if there was a coroner's inquest, and if Neelly was on the scene at the time, he said nothing to Brahan about it. It seems clear from Brahan's three letters, that he took from Neelly the impression that no persons were there but Mrs. Grinder, Pernia, and the Negro servant. If Neelly had told Brahan that Grinder children and servants were there, it seems unlikely that he would have omitted from all three letters a fact so important. In our opinion, then, it must be assumed that during all the time he was on the premises Neelly never saw the Grinder children and Malinda; and if this is true, they must have been hidden from him. Since Mrs. Grinder did not tell Wilson she was alone, we do not know that she told Neelly that she was alone. This is one of the riddles.

As for Captain Russell, we have seen that three and a half months after Lewis died he had not changed his opinion of Neelly, but on the contrary in an angry letter to Jefferson brought grave charges against him. By November 26, 1811, he was telling a different story. After saying that Lewis arrived at the fort in a state of mental derangement, and that members of the crew told him that twice on the boat Lewis had made attempts on his life, Russell says that "In this condition he continued without any material change for about five days, during which time the most proper and efficatious means that could be devised to restore him was administered, and on the sixth or seventh day all symptoms of derangement disappeared and he was completely in his senses and thus continued for ten or twelve days."

He says next that Lewis left the fort on the 29th, "with his papers well secured and packed on horses. By much severe depletion during his illness he had been considerably reduced and debilitated, from which he had not entirely recovered when he set off, and the weather in that country being yet excessively hot and the exercise of traveling too severe for him; in three or four days he was again affected with the same mental disease. He had no person with him who could manage or control him in his propensities and he daily grew worse untill he arrived at the house of a Mr. Grinder . . . where in the apprehension of being destroyed by enemies which had no existence but in his wild imagination, he destroyed himself, in the most cool desperate and Barbarian-like manner, having been left in the house intirely to himself."

After saying that two horses had strayed and that Neelly with some Indians remained behind to recover them, the Russell deposition continues: "After he arrived there and refreshed himself with a little Meal & drink he went to bed in a cabin by himself and ordered the servants to go to the stables and take care of the Horses, lest they might loose some that night; Some time in the night he got his pistols which he loaded, after every body had retired in a seperate Building and discharged one against his forehead without much effect,—the ball not penetrating the skull but only making a furrow over it. He then discharged the other against his breast where the ball entered and passing downward thro' his body came out low down near his back bone. After some time he got up and went to the house where Mrs. Grinder and her children were lying and asked for water, but her husband being absent and having heard the report of the pistols she was greatly alarmed and made him no answer. He then in returning got his razors from a port folio which happened to contain them and sitting up in his bed was found about day light, by one of the servants, busily engaged in cutting himself from head to foot. He again beged for water, which was given him and so soon as he drank, he lay down and died with the declaration to the Boy that he had killed himself to deprive his enemies of the pleasure and honor of doing it."

A postcript over the name of J. Williams says: "The above was received by me from Major Gilbert Russell of the [blank] Regiment of Infantry U.S. on Tuesday the 26th of November 1811 at Fredericktown in Maryland."

To say the least of it, it certainly is a strange document. One's first thought might be that Russell changed his mind after talking to Neelly—but this is not the Neelly version. This is more like Mrs. Grinder's story to Alexander Wilson, which we will examine in the next chapter. For in this deposition (if that is what it is) Mrs. Grinder is not alone but has her children with her; Mrs. Grinder does not call the servants; and Lewis was not seen in the cabin until one of the servants, presumably Pernia, came over.

Different persons will place different interpretations on some of the details in this version. For us it is little short of ridiculous to assume that Lewis journeyed all day through dangerous wilderness with his pistols unloaded; or that this man for whom the use of firearms was almost second-nature would aim to blow his brains out and do no more than make a furrow across his forehead, and then hold a long-barreled flintlock horse pistol in such a manner that he shoots down through his chest so that the bullet comes out "low down near his back bone." Possibly he bungled both shots. On the other hand, if some person was in that dark cabin shooting at him, a furrow across the skull and a bullet down through the body are not at all improbable.

If this second Russell statement of the case is to be taken at face value, Lewis not only was deranged at Grinder's but was hallucinating. If he was out of his mind, it is conceivable that he felt that a combination of enemies all the way from Bates to the secretary of war was arrayed against him. But for us there is something strangely unlike Russell in his manner of writing this account of Lewis's death. In his two letters to Jefferson his friendship and his feeling for Lewis shone through at every point. Here he says that Lewis killed himself "in the most cool desperate and Barbarian-like manner"—strange words from an army man whose profession was killing with guns.

We have no knowledge whatever of the sources of Russell's information. Did he go to Grinder's himself and talk to the woman? This seems unlikely. More probably he put together his version of the matter on the basis of what he read and heard. If we assume for the moment that the two servants went to the stable, six hundred feet distant, to sleep in the loft, Mrs. Grinder is the key witness in this mystery. We don't actually know what she told Neelly, for the reason that we don't know whether she or Pernia was his chief informant, or how much of what he knew he suppressed. In her second recorded version of what happened we do know what she said, for she talked to a distinguished scientist, who made notes while she talked.

Alexander Wilson's report is, therefore, of compelling significance.

# XI

# A Distinguished

# Scientist Reports

Alexander Wilson, the ornithologist, was born in 1766, and so was in his middle forties when he met Mrs. Grinder. From his earliest years he loved the outdoors and bird-watching. He came to this country in 1794, after a brief jail term for libel, and at once was delighted by all the unfamiliar birds around him. Encouraged by the naturalist, William Bartram, to pursue his interest in birds, Wilson was soon planning a huge project, seven of whose nine volumes were published before his untimely death in 1813—from dysentery, says one source; from complications that set in after he swam a river to capture a rare bird, says another.

The first volume of his monumental work appeared in 1808. He then set out on a long journey to try to find 250 subscribers, at $120 each, so that other volumes could be published. By stagecoach, horse, or afoot he visited settlements from Maine to Georgia. On later journeys he went westward, once setting off down the Ohio alone in a small boat, and persevering by boat, horse, or afoot until he reached New Orleans. He showed great boldness and intrepidity in his forays into the wilderness.

His friend and biographer, George Ord, says that Wilson was "possessed of the nicest sense of honor" but "was of the *Genus*

*irratibile* and was obstinate in opinion . . . . he could not endure
to be told of his mistakes . . . .his features were coarse, and there
was a dash of vulgarity which struck the observer at first view,
but which failed to impress one on acquaintance . . . .almost a
pure type of the bilious temperament, which is best fitted for
constant exertion, and he could bear great fatigue without flinch-
ing." Like Lewis, he had never married, but he was betrothed at
the time of his death.

This remarkably bold and resourceful man was on one of his
journeys to find subscribers, in the late winter or early spring of
1811, when he came to Grinder's Stand and heard from Mrs.
Grinder's lips her story of how Lewis died. We can guess what
his mood was from what he says of the Trace: "the country here
is swarming with wolves and wild-cats, black and brown. According to this hunter's own confession, he had lost sixty pigs
since Christmas . . . .I met a soldier on foot . . . who had been
robbed and plundered by the Chactaws . . . "

He listened to Mrs. Grinder's story, took notes, went on to
Natchez, and wrote a letter to a friend. So now we have a second
version of Mrs. Grinder's story, assuming that Neelly gave us a
faithful report of the first:

"Next morning (Sunday) I rode six miles to a man's house,
of the name of Grinder, where our poor friend Lewis perished.

"In the same room where he expired, I took down from Mrs.
Grinder the particulars of that melancholy event, which affected
me extremely. The house or cabin is seventy-two miles from
Nashville, and is the last white man's as you enter the Indian
country. Governor Lewis, she said, came hither about sunset,
alone, and inquired if he could stay for the night; and alighting,
brought his saddle into the house. He was dressed in a loose
gown, white, striped with blue. On being asked if he came alone,
he replied that there were two servants behind, who would soon
be up. He called for some spirits, and drank a very little. When
the servants arrived, one of whom was a negro, he inquired for
his powder, saying he was sure he had some in a canister. The
servant gave no distinct reply, and Lewis, in the meanwhile,
walked backwards and forwards before the door, talking to himself.

"Sometimes, she said, he would seem as if he were walking

up to her; and would suddenly wheel round, and walk back as fast as he could. Supper being ready he sat down, but had eaten only a few mouthfuls when he started up, speaking to himself in a violent manner. At these times, she says, she observed his face to flush as if it had come on him in a fit. He lighted his pipe, and, drawing a chair to the door, sat down, saying to Mrs. Grinder, in a kind tone of voice, Madam, this is a very pleasant evening. He smoked for some time, but quitted his seat and traversed the yard as before. He again sat down to his pipe, seemed again composed, and casting his eyes wistfully towards the west, observed what a sweet evening it was. Mrs. Grinder was preparing a bed for him, but he said he would sleep on the floor, and desired the servant to bring the bear skins and buffalo robe, which were immediately spread out for him; and, it now being dusk, the woman went off to the kitchen and the two men to the barn which stands about two hundred yards off.

"The kitchen is only a few paces from the room where Lewis was, and the woman being considerably alarmed by the behavior of her guest could not sleep, but listened to him walking backwards and forwards, she thinks, for several hours, and talking aloud, as she said, 'like a lawyer.' She then heard the report of a pistol, and something fall heavily to the floor, and the words 'O Lord!' Immediately afterwards she heard another pistol, and in a few minutes she heard him at her door calling out, 'O madam! give me some water and heal my wounds!'

"The logs being open, and unplastered, she saw him stagger back and fall against a stump that stands between the kitchen and the room. He crawled for some distance, and raised himself by the side of a tree, where he sat about a minute. He once more got to the room; afterwards he came to the kitchen door, but did not speak; she then heard him scraping in the bucket with a gourd for water; but it appears that this cooling element was denied the dying man.

"As soon as day broke, and not before, the terror of the woman having permitted him to remain for two hours in this most deplorable situation, she sent two of her children to the barn, her husband not being home, to bring the servants; and on going in they found him lying on the bed. He uncovered his side, and showed them where the bullet had entered; a piece of his forehead was blown off, and had exposed the brains, without having bled much.

"He begged they would take his rifle and blow out his brains, and he would give them all the money he had in his trunk. He often said, 'I am no coward; but I am so strong, so hard to die.' He begged the servant not to be afraid of him, for that he would not hurt him. He expired in about two hours, or just as the sun rose above the trees.

"He lies buried close by the common path, with a few loose rails thrown over his grave. I gave Grinder money to put a post fence around it, to shelter it from the hogs and from the wolves; and he gave me his written promise that he would do it. I left this place in a very melancholy mood, which was not much allayed by the prospect of the gloomy and savage wilderness which I was just entering alone."

Olin D. Wheeler called this whole thing "an improbable tale" and said of Wilson: "Those who are inclined to accept Wilson's story, aside from Mrs. Grinder's relation to it, should first read Audubon's narration of his experience with Wilson in 1810, as given on pages 30-33 of the *Life of Audubon*, edited by his widow and published by G. P. Putnam's Sons, New York, in order to judge the better as to its entire reliability."

Audubon wrote: "This happened in March, 1810. How well do I remember him as he walked up to me! His long, rather hooked nose, the keenness of his eyes, and his prominent cheekbones, stamped his countenance with a peculiar character. His dress, too, was of a kind not usually seen in that part of the country; a short coat, trousers, and a waistcoat of gray cloth. His stature was not above the middle size. He had two volumes under his arm, and as he approached the table at which I was working I thought I discovered something like astonishment in his countenance . . . . He opened his books, explained the nature of his occupations, and requested my patronage."

Audubon says he was about to subscribe when a friend sitting with him said, in French, not to do it, adding that Audubon was the more important ornithologist. So Audubon did not subscribe. But, he says, he explored the woods with Wilson and offered to correspond with him. Later he read in a Wilson book, "I bade adieu to Louisville, to which place I had four letters of recommendation, and was taught to expect much of everything there; but neither received one act of civility from those to whom I was recommended, one subscriber, nor one new bird; though I delivered my letters, ransacked the woods repeatedly, and visited all the characters likely to subscribe. Science or literature has not one friend in this place."

It is impossible to know why Wheeler thought Audubon's account of the meeting, or Wilson's farewell to Louisville, discredited Wilson as a witness. There seems to be nothing in it but the over-sensitive amour-propre of two distinguished men who were rivals. A testy irascible man Wilson seems to have been; but so was Audubon. The fact that they seem not to have liked one another has nothing whatever to do with Wilson's report of what Mrs. Grinder told him.

Coues, another eminent scientist, says that Wilson was "noted for habitual precision of statement. There is no more reason to doubt Wilson's painstaking correctness than there is reason to doubt his veracity. But the narrative of Mrs. Grinder is very extraordinary!"

Coues thinks there was nothing in Lewis's behavior, as reported, to so alarm a frontier woman that she could not sleep for hours—"she hears two pistol-shots, a heavy fall, and an appeal for help. This, however, only moves her to peep between the cracks in the logs . . . . There she sees her guest staggering, falling, and crawling about in the yard in search of water. Still she does not stir" and only with sunrise "the terror of the woman permits her to give the alarm . . . . Governor Lewis may have committed the deed . . . in a fit of suicidal mania; and the woman's incoherent story may not have been intended to deceive, but may have arisen from confused memories of an exciting night. That is conceivable; but my contention is that the testimony, as we have it, does not suffice to prove suicide, and does raise a strong suspicion that Governor Lewis was foully dealt with by some person or persons unknown—presumably Grinder, or him and some accomplices."

For some persons, it may be, Mrs. Grinder's story as reported by Wilson is explicable on depressingly simple grounds. For others, as for this writer, it may not seem plausible. Wilson's report suggests that he found her attitude rather inexplicable; and it may be significant that he trusted her man so little that he demanded his promise in writing. If only Wilson had described the woman, and given his impressions of her mind and character! We must wonder if Grinder was present while she talked. Did Wilson ask her why in the long hour between daybreak and sunup she made no move to summon help for a dying man? After digging out the facts as well as he was able, Coues decided that there was a "doubt that we have the true date of death within 24 hours." Possibly the simplest explanation of why Mrs. Grinder did not send for help is that at daybreak, and maybe hours before then, Lewis was dead.

It is interesting to compare what she told Wilson with what she may have told Neelly, keeping in mind the fact that only a little more than a year elapsed between the two versions. In Neelly's version "the woman reports that about three o'clock she heard two pistols fire off in the Governors Room"—no one has explained how the woman knew it was a pistol instead of a rifle: are we to assume that after she entered the cabin she looked at the weapons? In the Wilson version there is no three o'clock: two hours passed between the shooting and daylight. Neelly says that no person was present but Mrs. Grinder, and that certainly is what he told Brahan. Unless we assume that Neelly misrepresented the facts we must conclude that the children had been sent away or hidden before Neelly arrived. It would be nonsense to say that for Neelly a twelve-year-old Negress, a ten-year-old daughter, and possibly a son older than either, were not persons. Of all the stories of Lewis's death Wilson's is the one we have to take most seriously, for the reason that he talked to her and made notes and then wrote it all down. In that story Mrs. Grinder says the children were with her. If she told Neelly that she was alone, and if he did not see the children, then murder becomes more probable than suicide. And it takes a lot of credulity to believe that a frontier woman, used to hardship and living in a dangerous wilderness, on a trail infested with bandits, would wait until morning before going herself to the barn, or sending children, to summon the servants, when a mortally wounded man was crawling around and begging for help. It takes even more credulity to believe that a man like Meriwether Lewis when determined to kill himself would have begged for help.

Mrs. Grinder seems to have told Neelly that she went to the stable to bring the servants. She told Wilson that she sent two of the children to bring them. Neelly says the servants were awak-

ened by her but came too late to save him—and he survived but
a short time. That is *not* the story she told Wilson. She told him
she was too terrified to do anything before daylight, and that
Lewis did not die until the sun was above the trees. It may be,
as Coues said, that she was confused. Or it may be that she could
not tell the same story twice, for the reason that the truth was
not in it.

Why within a few months did she change her story? We can
only conjecture. If she was not a stupid woman, she had a reason
for doing it. If she was a stupid woman, it is conceivable that
she had no wish to deceive and was simply unable to tell a plausible story. She told Wilson that she was terrified and peered
between two logs at a man crawling around in her yard. Bakeless says pioneer women were not like that. The one who writes
these words was born of one and as a child knew no other kind.
He never knew one who would have remained behind a barred
door and refused water to a dying man.

So at this point in the mystery we have a choice of two possibilities. One is that Mrs. Grinder told the truth—that she actually
did not dare to venture out and give help to a man begging for
it. The other is that she perceived the advantage to her and her
family in saying that Lewis was violent, and was a grave threat to
her own life. Whether she got the idea of derangement before
she talked to Neelly, or after, we do not know. In the Wilson
version it is significant that she said that Lewis was talking like
a lawyer—not talking to himself but talking like a lawyer. We
suspect that that is what he did, if he paced back and forth and
talked aloud.

It hardly seems likely that if Lewis was determined to kill
himself and shot himself twice he would then rush forth to beg
a woman to heal his wounds, or beg Pernia to take his rifle and
blow his brains out, when he could so easily have taken the rifle
himself. As for money in the trunk, there was none, except the
check on the New Orleans bank. It may be that Lewis was attacked, wounded, robbed, and left to die, and that he did then
crawl or stagger forth and beg for water and help. If this were
so, and her husband was not a party to it, Mrs. Grinder's unwillingness to open the door is understandable, for she may have
thought that murderers were still on the scene. Or it may be
that she invented this part of the story. One familiar wih Lewis's

life is not going to find it easy to believe that in one moment he made a furious attempt on his life, and in the next went begging for help.

As for the statement he is alleged to have made, "I am no coward, but I am so strong, so hard to die," there are several possibilities. It may be that when Wilson visited Lewis in St. Louis, he heard the story about the grizzly bears. Lewis used those words in his journal and .it may be that when telling about the grizzlies he said, "They are so strong, so hard to die." Another possibility is that during the evening after his arrival Lewis talked to Mrs. Grinder and the others present about his journey to the ocean, and when telling about the grizzlies used words that Mrs. Grinder remembered, and used when talking to Wilson. A third possibility is that Lewis was attacked and shot and actually did live for a while. It is even conceivable that he was fired on, and that Mrs. Grinder assumed, without knowing any better, that he had shot himself. Possibly he did not tell her that he had been attacked. Perhaps he assumed that she knew it. In any case, according to her story to Wilson she remained inside the kitchen with the door barred until morning came. If Lewis was still alive then, and knew that he was mortally wounded and must die, and wished to get it over with and be done with it, possibly he said that he was strong and hard to die. A fourth possibility is that Pernia heard him tell about the grizzly bears (as likely as not, more than once), and seeing his master wounded, yet clinging to life for two hours or more, said to Mrs. Grinder that Lewis was so strong, so hard to die.

If Malinda were on the scene, as she claimed to have been, she was in the kitchen with Mrs. Grinder during those hours of terror. We would expect to find her telling the story again and again. In fact, she did. We would expect it to agree in its essentials with Mrs. Grinder's story to Wilson. We shall find that in some esesntials it does not agree, but before we look at it there is a third recorded version from Mrs. Robert Grinder.

# XII

# Mrs. Grinder's
# Third Version

No doubt Mrs. Grinder told her story many times over a period
of years. She was still telling it in 1839, thirty years after Lewis's
death. The *Dispatch* in New York said, February 1, 1845, "We
find in the North Arkansas, a paper published at Batesville, Ark.
[some] singular and not generally known facts" about the death of
Meriwether Lewis. The preliminary statement says that the
writer "is at present a teacher in the Cherokee Nation, and says
that he is personally acquainted with the circumstances which
he relates." In 1839 he visited the Lewis grave and "found it
almost concealed by brambles, without a stone or monument of
any kind, and several miles from any house. An old tavern stand,
known as Grinder's once stood near by, but was long since burned.
The writer gives the following narrative of the incidents attending the death of Capt. Lewis, as he received them from Mrs.
Grinder the landlady of the house where he died in so strange
a manner."

Mrs. Grinder in 1839 was not less than sixty-four years old,
and possibly was no more than seventy. It seems reasonable to
assume that she was still in full possession of her faculties when

she talked to the school teacher. How did she tell the story after thirty years?

"She said that Mr. Lewis was on his way to the city of Washington, accompanied by a Mr. Pyrna and a servant belonging to a Mr. Neely. One evening a little before sundown, Mr. Lewis called at her house and asked for lodgings. Mr. Grinder not being at home, she hesitated to take him in. Mr. Lewis informed her that two other men would be along presently, who also wished to spend the night at her house, and as they were all civil men, he did not think there would be any impropriety in her giving them accommodations for the night. Mr. Lewis dismounted, fastened his horse, took a seat by the side of the house, and appeared quite sociable."

So far that sounds pretty convincing. Lewis rode up, asked for lodgings, found the woman reluctant, and in his rather courtly way toward women tried to reassure her. He sat by the house, waiting for the two servants to come up, and was sociable. But we are not prepared for what comes next.

"In a few minutes Mr. Pyrna and the servant rode up, and seeing Mr. Lewis they also dismounted and put up their horses. About dark two or three other men rode up and called for lodging. Mr. Lewis immediately drew a brace of pistols, stepped towards them and challenged them to fight a duel. They not liking this salutation, rode on to the next house, five miles. This alarmed Mrs. Grinder. Supper, however, was ready in a few minutes. Mr. Lewis ate but little. He would stop eating, and sit as if in a deep study, and several times exclaimed. 'If they do prove anything on me they will have to do it by letter.' Supper being over, and Mrs. Grinder seeing that Lewis was mentally deranged, requested Mr. Pyrna to get his pistols from him. Mr. P. replied, 'He has no ammunition, and if he does any mischief it will be to himself, and not to you or anybody else.' In a short time all retired to bed, the travellers in one room, as Mrs. G. thought, and she and her children in another."

What are we to make of that? In a letter to us a historian says, "I submit that 30 years is a good long time for an uneducated, not-too-bright woman to tell the same story." We simply don't know how bright Mrs. Grinder was. That Lewis rushed out and challenged two or three men to a duel merely because they asked for lodgings is so fantastically improbable that we must assume either that Mrs. Grinder invented it to support her story of derangement, or got Lewis mixed up with another lodger on another occasion. Thirty years is a long time, but Mrs. Grinder in her version to Wilson asked us to believe that she spent a sleepless night of terror. That kind of night writes details deep in memory.

"Two or three hours before day Mrs. G. was alarmed by the report of a pistol, and quickly after two other reports, in the room where the travellers were. At the report of the third, she heard someone fall and exclaim, 'O Lord! Congress, relieve me.' In a few minutes she heard some person at the door of the room where she lay. She inquired, 'Who is there?' Mr. Lewis spoke and said, 'Dear madam, be so good as to give me a little water.' Being afraid to open the door she did not give him any. Presently she heard him fall, and soon after, looking through a crack in the wall, she saw him scrambling across the road on his hands and knees."

If this is true, where was Lewis going? If he crossed the road he was going in the direction of Little Swan creek, which he had crossed on his way in. He could have been going to water, or he could have been fleeing from enemies.

"After daylight Mr. Pyrna and the servant made their appearance, and it appeared they had not slept in the house, but in the stable. Mr. P. had on the clothes Mr. L. wore when they came to Mrs. Grinder's the evening before, and Mr. L's gold watch in his pocket. Mrs. G. asked him what he was doing with Mr. L's clothes on; Mr. P. replied, 'He gave them to me.' Mr. P. and the servant then searched for Mr. L., found him and brought him to the house, and though he had on a full suit of clothes, they were old and tattered, and not the same as he had on the evening before, and though Mr. P. had said that Lewis had no ammunition, Mrs. G. found several balls and a considerable quantity of powder scattered over the floor of the room occupied by Lewis; also a canister with several pounds in it.

"When Mr. L. was brought to the house, [illegible] his shirt bosom and said to Mrs. G.: 'Dear madam, look at my wounds.' She asked him what made him do so? He replied, 'If I had not done it somebody else would.' He frequently asked for water, which was given to him. He was asked if he would have a doctor sent for, he said not. A messenger, however, went for one but did not get him. He attempted to cut his throat, but was prevented.

Some of the neighbors were called in. He frequently cried out, 'Oh how hard it is to die, I am so strong.' He, however, soon expired. Major Neely was sent for, and he and Mr. P. buried him, and took possession of his effects. Mrs. G. heard that Pyrna went to see Mr. Lewis' mother, and that she accused him of murdering her son; and he finally cut his own throat, and thus put an end to his existence.

"I make no comment on the above; it is all wrapt up in mystery. I have heard that Capt. Clarke, the worthy colleague of their tour, was highly honored and handsomely rewarded by the government, while Lewis was neglected, and that this had an effect to produce alienation of mind. If this be true, are there not some living who are acquainted with the fact?"

What a beautiful opportunity this school master had to dig out the truth! He seems to have felt that he did not have the truth, for he said after listening to Mrs. Grinder that it was all wrapped in mystery and he would make no comment. It is obvious that this school teacher knew nothing about Neelly's report, or Wilson's. It is plain that he actually talked to Mrs. Grinder, for some of the things he wrote down he could have got from nobody else. One question, then, is why Mrs. Grinder did not tell Wilson the same story she told Neelly, and why after thirty years she told a third story that in significant details is different from both. Thirty years is a long time, but she remembered not only Neelly's name but also the fact that he was addressed as Major Neelly.

We can never know whether she changed her story because she was stupid and confused, or because the years had taught her to try to tell a better story, in defense of herself and her family. If, as tradition says, her husband was arrested and tried for murder, it is only natural that Mrs. Grinder, telling the story time after time, would allow self-interest to choose the details. After so many years, what we may have is a mixture of facts and fabrications.

One startling change in her tale is having all three men go to the cabin to sleep. We suspect that this is exactly what they did. In any case, this version throws out her awakening of the servants, as in the Neelly report, or sending two children to fetch them, as in the Wilson report. And now we have three shots, not two, which implies either that he reloaded one of the pistols, or also fired the rifle. Having Lewis cry out, "Congress, relieve me"

takes us into the realm of farce; we would conjecture that during
the evening, before supper, or afterward, he talked about his
difficulties, and said that possibly it would take an act of the
Congress to give him relief. In this third version he does not return to the cabin and remain there, after searching for water, but
falls to hands and knees and goes off across the Trace. As Bakeless says, gunshot wounds usually produce an intolerable thirst,
so it may be that, denied water, he headed for Little Swan creek.

What we must wonder, when reading this version after thirty
years, is how Mrs. Grinder's mind was working and what her
motives were. Had the passing of the years convinced her that
her first stories were not all that they should have been? For now,
at daylight, she has Pernia and the Negro come to the cabins, and
she concludes that they had not slept with Lewis after all, but in
the stable. If Pernia did have on Lewis's clothes, and have his
watch (he would also in this case have his money), he becomes
suspect number one. He could not have had a gold watch, unless
Lewis had two watches with him, for the one at the Missouri
Historical Society is described as "Watch, with double, or hunting
case of silver, made in London, England, in 1796-97, carried by
Meriwether Lewis on the Expedition to the West Coast." It is
possible, of course, that Lewis had two watches. Some members
of the Lewis family, notably his mother, seem never to have
wavered in their belief that Pernia killed his master. But if Mrs.
Grinder suspected that he was a murderer, why didn't she tell
Neelly that? It is not easy to believe that Mrs. Grinder invented
all these new details about Pernia; on the other hand, it is not
easy to believe that she would have told neither Neelly nor Wilson,
and Wilson especially, how Pernia appeared after daybreak in
Lewis's garments and carrying his watch. We do know that Lewis
owed Pernia back wages, and that after he left Nashville he went
straight to Jefferson, and we have reason to believe to Lewis's
mother, to try to collect them. If Pernia told the truth, Lewis
owed him about $240, or more than Lewis had with him, includ-
ing the check.

In this third recorded version Mrs. Grinder says she wanted
to send for a doctor but Lewis said no. It has not been possible
to find any record of a doctor in that area at that time. The
simplest conjecture is that some person or persons listening to her
story of that night, and the way Lewis crawled around and begged

for water and lived for hours, asked her why she didn't send for a doctor, and that at last she perceived the wisdom of putting the doctor in. And this could easily be so, whether it was suicide or murder. We are asked to believe that neighbors were called in and that Neelly was sent for, for the reason that she had come to realize that these things ought to have been done. Somewhere down the years she may have been made conscious of the fact that her treatment of Lewis, as she reported it to Wilson, was unspeakably cruel. We may even suppose that the astonished school teacher said, "But didn't you send for a doctor?" and that she replied quickly, "Why, yes, I wanted to but he wouldn't let me." And knowing what ought to be said, she added, "I sent for one anyway but did not get him." If there was anything to hide, she could hardly have dared get one, for a doctor would have examined the corpse and very possibly would have made a report.

But in Mrs. Grinder's third recorded version nothing is more incredible than the implication that after being shot two or three times Lewis crawled away across the Trace and vanished; that the two servants "after daylight" made their appearance and Pernia had on the clothes Lewis had been wearing when he entered the cabin to retire; that Lewis remained alone out there in the woods two or three hours, garbed in old and tattered garments which presumably either he or Pernia had dug out of one of the trunks; that Pernia either did not know that his master was wounded and dying or had so little concern for him that he waited until after daylight to do anything about it; that the servants went off into the woods to hunt for him, and found him and brought him to the cabins; that Lewis, supposed to be deranged, in one moment begs her to look at his wounds and in the next tries to cut his throat; and that after all these hours of suffering he was decent enough to die. Thirty years is indeed a long time, but we will say with the school teacher that it is still wrapped up in a mystery.

Malinda, the slave, says she was there with Mrs. Grinder in the cabin the night Lewis was shot. No doubt she told her story many times. One version was taken from her lips by a Tennessee lawyer and written down.

So now we shall see what Lindy has to tell us.

# XIII

## Malinda's Story

J. H. Moore was an attorney in Hickman county who had read in a newspaper a story of how Lewis died, by another attorney named Webster, who believed that it was murder. Moore decided to reply to Webster and put the matter right, once and for all. His essay appeared in July, 1904.

His first five paragraphs summarize Lewis's career. Then: "Many accounts of Lewis' death have from time to time been published, nearly all based upon tradition, upon the alleged contemporaneous sentiment of the community in which the tragedy occurred, upon an absence of a motive for suicide, or the existence of a motive for murder, etc. Many of these accounts have been inaccurate and highly colored, and in some cases without any foundation whatever.

"On account of my long residence in a town not far distant from where Lewis died; my intimate professional connection with the descendants of Griner, who has been charged with the murder of Lewis; and my frequent discussion of the subject, not only with them, but with many of the oldest citizens of the locality, particularly the old negroes, Pete and Lindy (slaves in Griner's family and present at Lewis' death), I deem it proper to submit the information I have obtained."

In a footnote he says, "The correct spelling of the name is 'G-r-i-n-e-r, but it is usually pronounced 'Grinder'."

He then continues: "These facts will be conceded: That Lewis, while Governor of Louisiana, with his seat of office at St. Louis, smarting under an actual or imagined injustice done him at Washington (said to have been the refusal to honor his drafts for money to meet the necessities of the organization and government of the new territory), started down the Mississippi River by boat, carrying with him many vouchers and public documents and expecting to take a vessel from New Orleans to the East. At Chickasaw Bluffs (Memphis) he was led to believe that war with England was imminent. Fearing capture and, above all, the loss of the papers on which he relied for his vindiction, he procured horses at Chickasaw Bluffs and started over the Natchez Trace for Nashville, intending probably to go thence to Washington by way of Lexington or Louisville, Ky. He had two servants—one, a foreigner named 'Perney' or 'Pernea'; the other, a negro.

"Major Neely, Indian agent at Chickasaw Bluffs, accompanied the Governor until the loss of two pack horses. He stopped to search for them, agreeing to join Lewis at the next white man's house on the road, which was Griner's. Lewis reached the place during the afternoon of October 10, 1809, and that night received two or more gunshot wounds, which caused his death early the next day—whether inflicted by his own hand, as I believe, or by that of another, as many writers have claimed, is the question which has been discussed at intervals ever since.

"One of the earliest statements of the details of the death of Governor Lewis was given to the public by the great scientist, Dr. Alexander Wilson, who, passing through Nashville on his way to Natchez, Miss., stopped at the Griner Stand, where Lewis died, and obtained from Mrs. Griner an account of the tragedy, which was printed in the Portfolio (a magazine published in Philadelphia, Pa.) for January, 1812. His letter was dated 'Natchez, May 28, 1811'—about eighteen months after Lewis' death and about two years before the date of President Jefferson's 'Memoir of Lewis', prefixed to 'The History of the Lewis and Clark Expedition.' I have seen the letter in print only in the Portfolio, though it is quoted freely by Dr. Elliott Coues in his edition of the

history of the expedition (1893); and I, therefore, copy in full
that part which refers to Governor Lewis' death. Its chief value
lies in the fact that it came from an able and highly intelligent
man, a personal friend of Lewis, and, therefore, interested in all
that concerned him, who received his information directly from
an eyewitness of the tragedy, in the room where it occurred, and
not very long afterward."

As the reader has perceived, Moore has a number of minor
errors, and he now loses sight of the fact that the "eyewitness"
was also one of his clients in this defense! So far as we know,
Mrs. Grinder never said that she was an eyewitness to the shooting, or actually knew anything about what happened in the cabin
where Lewis was. So far as that goes, if he was so out of his mind
that, as Russell put it in his deposition, he thought he was about
to be destroyed by enemies "which had no existence but in his
wild imagination," then he could have been so out of his mind
that after having been shot two or three times by another person,
he could have believed that he had shot himself.

After giving the vital part of Alexander Wilson's report, he
continues: "Among my particular friends prior to his death was
Elijah Walker, of Savannah, Tenn., but a native of Hickman
County, a lawyer distinguished alike for his uprightness and his
ability. Chief Justice Nicholson pronounced him, in conversation
with me, one of the purest men and one of the best lawyers he
had ever known. He was judge of the Fourteenth Judicial Circuit
from 1870 until 1873. He knew not only the Griners, at whose
house Governor Lewis died, but practically all of the old people
living in the country at the time. He had given the death of Lewis
a thorough investigation, and was a firm believer in the innocence
of Griner."

One encounters in Tennessee again and again the statement,
either in published writings or from the lips of people, that the
death of Lewis was "thoroughly investigated." A retired judge
has recently made the statement that Thomas Jefferson made a
"thorough" investigation, but no one so far has brought forth any
evidence to support the claim.

Moore continues: "Nearly all of the accounts of the death
of Lewis agree in saying that there were present at the house,
besides the Governor and his servants, Mrs. Griner and her very
young daughter, and two negro children—Pete, aged about thir-

teen years, and Lindy, aged about twelve years. Probably the last two were too young to be of any aid to Griner in gathering the crop on the Swan Creek farm, some miles away, where he had gone, and were left to assist Mrs. Griner at the tavern. Pete, before the emancipation, was the servant of Judge Walker; and I have frequently heard him tell the story of the tragedy, which he remembered perfectly. It differed in no material way from the account given by Lindy, except that, negrolike, each claimed to have seen and heard more than the other; but the story of the one is the story of the other."

Moore seemed determined to lose his case at this point. On the scene he has a Grinder daughter, though two, possibly three, Grinder children were then born; and two slaves, one 12 and the other 13, though Neelly, on whom Jefferson seems to have based his conclusions, and on whom Moore leans, said clearly "the man of the house being from home, and no person there but a woman." And we must wonder what kind of witness we have here when he says that a male youngster thirteen years old was too young to help harvest a crop, or that, though Lindy and Pete each claimed to have seen and heard more than the the the other, the story of the one is the story of the other, and the stories of both are a trustworthy account of what happened. For we shall see in a moment that Lindy's story in some essential points flatly contradicts Wilson's, which Moore must have had before him, for he quotes in full that part dealing with Lewis's death and adds that it came from an able and highly intelligent man.

Moore says that "nearly all of the accounts of the death of Lewis agree" that there were present a Grinder daughter and Pete and Lindy, though Jefferson's account, which he had before him, or at least had read, did not mention any children or slaves, and could not have done so, since it rested on Neelly, who implied that none was present. The truth is that Moore seems to be the first one to bring Pete into it. Pete may have been there but it has not been possible to find any trace of him among the Grinders. He seems not to have been sold as a Grinder slave after Grinder died in 1848. It is, of course, possible that he had been sold earlier. Nor was the name of Pete found among slaves in the Hickman county area, in the records examined. But if Pete was present and was thirteen years old, it is nonsense to say that he was too young to assist Grinder on his farm on Swan Creek.

Moore continues: "When Pete died, Judge Walker suggested to me that Lindy was the last living witness of the death of Lewis; that my father had been a member of the legislature which authorized the erection of the monument to Lewis, was instrumental in securing the appropriation for it, and was chairman of the committee appointed to build it; and that, as the descendants and relatives of Griner had long been my neighbors, friends, and clients, it was almost my duty to see that the true story of the deplorable tragedy was preserved. I, therefore, visited Lindy and took full notes of the conversation with her, which I still have. Upon these notes I based a communication to the Maury County Sentinel, and it was also published later in the Hickman Pioneer in a condensed form. I have these two, but have been unable to secure a copy of the paper furnished to the Sentinel."

Here is Lindy's story, as Moore understood it:

"Lindy stated that late in the afternoon the Governor rode up to the house alone and asked Mrs. Griner if he could stay for the night. She replied: 'Yes, but there is no man here to care for your horse.' He replied: 'That makes no difference, as my servants will be on in a short time.' Soon thereafter the two servants, one white and one black, came up on horses, with one or two pack horses. She says that the white man's name was 'Perney' and that he was a Spaniard or some sort of 'furiner'. The servants, after removing the packs, took charge of the horses and repaired to the stables."

Even if Pete was not on the scene it is absurd to imagine that on a frontier Lewis's horse could not have been cared for by Lindy, if she was present; or even by the Grinder daughter, who was about ten. On the frontier where this writer was born, a child, male or female, even younger than the Grinder daughter would have thought nothing of taking a horse to the stable, to water and feed it. And why didn't Mrs. Grinder do it? What was she in business for?

"The Governor at once began to walk up and down the yard, talking to himself and muttering. His conduct was so peculiar and his appearance so strange and unusual that Mrs. Griner became alarmed, so much so that she went, carrying all the children—that is, her child and Pete and Lindy—to the kitchen, which was several yards from the 'big house', as she called it. Soon after, Mrs. Griner and Lindy went up to arrange the beds for the night. The Governor said they need not prepare any bed for him, as he preferred to sleep on his buffalo robe on the floor (which he had done on the entire trip), and they spread the robe down for him. The servants said they were afraid to stay in the house with him, as he had been acting strangely for the last two or three days, and went off to the barn to sleep."

If Malinda was on the scene we must assume that she was with the Grinders until she was sold in 1848, and that during all these years she heard Mrs. Grinder tell her story a number of times. If this was so, one would think that the slave would have copied her mistress, and that Mrs. Grinder's favorite version would at least have been Lindy's. The words, "which he had done on the entire trip," are revealing of Lewis and of his mental condition at least during the moments when he uttered them. They may indicate that he had earlier in the evening talked to them about his expedition to the ocean and that he told them he had slept on buaffo and bear robes the whole way out and back; or it may have been only an offhand remark which meant that he had slept on such robes on the way from Fort Pickering over.

In Malinda's version there is nothing about asking for a drink, nothing about supper; at once the governor began to pace and talk, and the alarmed Mrs. Grinder carried a ten-year-old, a twelve-year-old, and a thirteen-year-old to the kitchen. Soon thereafter she and Lindy went to the other cabin to make the beds. If we put with all this the new factor, that the servants were too afraid of Lewis to stay in the same house with him, we may have a story that down the years was steadily embellished and improved, to the advantage of the Grinders.

"The Governor did not lie down; he continued to walk—sometimes in the house and then in the yard—continually talking to himself and repeating, 'They have told lies on me and want to ruin me'. The children soon went to sleep, but Mrs. Griner could not and sat up all night. Just before day all were aroused by the report of firearms. Two shots were fired in rapid succession. Immediately Perney came running to the house, and the Governor crawled to the door and called for water. They all went together to the house, and found the Governor writhing in pain on the floor. Mrs. Griner asked: 'Why in the world did you do this?' He replied that if he had not done it, someone else would. 'They are telling lies and trying to ruin me.' He was bleeding profusely from a wound in the body near the heart. He drank great quantities of water, and would immediately throw it up. He lingered in great agony until twelve o'clock, when he died. He was buried just outside of the inclosure where the monument stands."

Moore would have been on safe ground if he had argued that two persons telling the same story, both speaking the truth as nearly as they knew it, might differ in minor details. But that is not the kind of case we have here. Moore had before him Wilson's account. He knew that Mrs. Grinder told Wilson that Lewis came begging for water and she kept the door barred against him; that he came a second time; that she was so frightened that she did not dare stir until daylight, and then sent two of the children to summon the servants. Yet without a word of comment on the discrepancies, he puts before his readers Malinda's version, in which immediately after the shots they all went to the cabin where Lewis was and gave him all the water he asked for. If Moore had not been so intent on clearing the Grinders of all suspicion, surely he would have pointed out the discrepancies and made some effort to explain them. For he told his readers in the beginning that Wilson was an able and intelligent reporter, and that Lindy's story was the "true" story of what happened.

That true story concludes with a fantastic improbability: "The next fall, Lindy said, two of the sisters of the Governor came to the Stand and stayed with the Griner family six weeks. They planted roses and other flowers on the grave. Upon leaving, they made Mrs. Griner several presents as keepsakes, including a drinking cup, which was kept in the Griner family until the Civil War, when it was taken off, with other property. I think she said from the house of Mr. Albert Griner's son, who was at the time in the Confederate Army. Old Lindy said the Lewis visitors were 'fine ladies', and seemed very thankful for the kindness and attention shown their relative in the last hours of his life."

Such pure invention discredits Malinda as a witness. What we should possibly suspect is that in competing with Pete in telling the story, as Moore naively admits that she did, the old Negress looked far and wide for embellishments that would put the best light on the Grinders. Mrs. Grinder may be the one who invented the visit of the sisters.

Having given this incredible story of how the two sisters made a long and difficult journey to offer heartfelt thanks and gifts, and a drinking cup (what a lovely irony!), for the kindness and attention shown their brother by a woman, who herself said that she would not open the door to him or give him so much as a drink of water, Moore then says: "Mrs. Griner, the widow of Capt. Robert Grinder, who was a son of the owner of the Griner Stand, was present at the interview with Lindy, and said the story was substantially the same as she had heard it often told by her mother-in-law." Since the story is different in fundamental details from the story Mrs. Grinder told Wilson, and the school teacher, it takes an act of faith to accept her, or the slave, as a witness.

Moore went on to tell his readers that the "idea that Governor Lewis was murdered by Griner was given wide circulation by an article which appeared in the Nashville American of September 6, 1891, over the signature 'John Quill' , . . . It was written by Mr. James D. Park . . . a gentleman of the best character . . . he permitted himself to be imposed upon by a garrulous and sensational old woman . . . who, when Park saw her, was seventy-seven years of age."

Park's evidence, for what it is worth, will be considered later —we take a brief look at him now, in passing, only because Moore did his best to discredit him. Wheeler says that Park "seems to have as thoroughly investigated the whole matter as was then possible" and that his father declared that "The further my son investigated the matter the more certain he believed that Lewis was murdered." But Moore says flatly that Park's story "was based entirely" on what was told him by a garrulous and sensational old woman. This is what happens to people, including lawyers, when they can see only one side of a thing. It was pretty foolish of Moore to dwell on the age of Mrs. Anthony, who was 77, when his own witness, Malinda, was born in 1797, and in 1879 when Moore interviewed her was 82 or 83.

Still trying to convince his readers that all the Grinders were worthy people, Moore now turns to the history of Hickman county by the Spences, and reveals even to his most loyal partisans the kind of tricks he had in his sleeve. He quotes the Spences on the death of Lewis, as we have earlier, and finds compelling significance in their statement, "This account of Lewis' death is substantiated by a statement made in 1879 by Linda, a negro woman who was born in 1797." Seventy years had passed, yet Moore says that Linda's was the true story, and the Spences accepted her as a dependable witness.

Moore continues: "As a matter of fact, the family has lived in Hickman County for nearly one hundred years. While few of the names have been prominent, they have been substantial and respectable people. Robert E. Griner, son of the owner of the Stand, was the senior captain in the Thirty-sixth Regiment of Tennessee Militia in 1834; another son, Albert S. Griner, was captain in the Ninety-seventh Regiment in 1837, lieutenant colonel in 1839, and colonel in 1840. Others of the name served in the Mexican War of 1845 and the Civil War of 1861-1865; others have intermarried with the Shipps, Easons, and other good families of the county."*

As an attorney, Moore must have known that a witness's motives fall under suspicion if he quotes from a source only that information favorable to his client, and conceals that which is not. He brought Albert up to 1840, when he was a colonel, and stopped. If he had turned only a page or two more in the Spence history and given the information there, he would have told his readers that by 1846 Albert was only a sergeant, and by 1850 had gone insane and killed himself. He would have told his readers that Noble, another son, went insane and killed himself—and he might well have speculated on whether there was more insanity in the Grinder family or in the Lewis family. He would have told them that the Grinder who operated the Stand often sold whisky to the Indians.

But all that was no part of his purpose. Nor was it his purpose, apparently, to give *all* of Linda's story. As Bakeless puts it, "About daylight, according to Aunt Lindy, the 'furriner,' Pernia, came to the kitchen and told Mrs. Grinder that Lewis was cutting the veins in his throat. If Mrs. Grinder would give him water, he would give up his razor." To have had Mrs. Grinder refuse

---

*We have seen (chapter 8) that if the Robert Grinder, Jr., reported in the 1820 Wayne county census was the son of the Stand's owner, he was at least 7 years old when Lewis rode up, for his age was listed as 18-26. If he was 7 in 1809 and was a senior captain in 1834, he was then about 32. It seems probable that he was older—that he was more than 7 years old when Mrs. Grinder is alleged to have told Lewis that she had no person with her who could take care of a horse.

water on such terms would have made a monster of her. As Bakeless says further, "Aunt Malinda asserted that after his arrival in Virginia, Pernia was accused by Mrs. Marks (whom she called Mrs. Lewis) of killing her son. Exclaiming 'I'll see Gov L before dark,' he 'cut his throat from ear to ear in Mrs. L's yard'."

This is only legend, of course, though on a later page we shall find Thomas Jefferson believing it. We don't know from whom Malinda got it. We don't know that Moore heard her utter these more sensational things but it is easy to believe that she babbled to him all that she had dreamed or heard of. He seems to have chosen only those details that would not reflect on the Grinders, quite as he chose only such details from the Spence history.

He comes at last to the report of the Tennessee legislative committee, and quotes the committee's own words: "The impression has long prevailed that, under the influence of a disease of the body and mind—of hopes based upon long and valuable services, not merely deferred, but wholly disappointed—Governor Lewis perished by his own hand. It seems more probable that he died by the hands of an assassin."

That appears to have been the unanimous opinion of the committee that examined Lewis's remains, or what the committee thought was his remains, less than forty years after his death. It is strange that the committee's statement has been wholly ignored or lightly brushed aside by nearly all writers on this subject. One of William Clark's sons had a little earlier written to a Tennessee clergyman to ask if he had heard that Lewis did not kill himself but was murdered. Moore says, "The legislative committee clearly indicates that the theory of suicide was general up to 1848; and while it does not say so, it no doubt got its impression of murder from the letter of Major Clark." He then dismisses the opinion of a Lewis relative, that a man who lived in the open as much as Lewis would have had no good reason to take his life, with the statement that such an opinion "carries no weight in view of the fact, as shown by statistics, that 'the rate of suicide for soldiers is enormously in excess of that for any other occupation'."

Moore seems to have been willing to invite suspicion of his intelligence, having already called its notice to his integrity, when he blandly said that a committee of men prominent in their area "no doubt" thought it "probable" that Lewis had been murdered, on no more than a letter from a Clark son saying he had heard it.

The Clark letter, which they had seen, and incorporated in their report, went on to say that he felt his honor to be involved, for the reason that he had been named for Meriwether Lewis. That seems hardly to be the kind of evidence that would prevail over the "theory of suicide [that was] general up to 1848," in the minds of middle-aged men who presumbably had been chosen for their task on the basis of experience and sound judgment. And not the least remarkable thing in all this is the fact that the chairman of that committee was Moore's father. As for the rate of suicide among soldiers, Lewis hadn't been a soldier for almost a decade.

It must be plain that Moore did the best he could for the Grinders.

# As Thomas Jefferson

# Told It

The third president of the United States was a great man, but as with so many great men (and men not so great), particuarly political leaders in emotionally immature countries where father-images seem as necessary as soap operas, he has been placed by a host of image-makers on a plane above suspicion and criticism. To discover how true this is one has only to read everything that has been published on the death of Lewis and observe how many of the writers have accepted Jefferson's view, not only without question but almost with a bow of reverence. Or one has only to read Professor Merrill D. Peterson's *The Jefferson Image in the American Mind,* which shows how this president has been raised to more than human eminence in an amazing number of fields.

The inventions of the myth-makers are so depressingly silly that we shall give only two. George G. Simpson of the American Museum of Natural History read a paper in 1942 to the American Philosophical Society in which he said (italics ours): "Thomas Jefferson has become a fabulous figure to paleontologists, few of whom know what he really did but most of whom consider him as the father or founder of vertebrate paleontology in America. . . . It should not be considered iconoclastic (*although I have already learned that it seems so to my colleagues*) to state that he was not a vertebrate paleontologist in any reasonable sense of the words, that he never collected a fossil or gave one a technical name, and that his scientific contributions were negligible or retrogressive."*

The second instance concerns the image of him as the Father of Perfect Domesticity. Jefferson's wife had told somewhere of a hundred-mile journey in January to the "horrible dreariness" of the little cottage at Monticello. The myth-makers could not let her two words stand, or the journey go unembellished. James Parton, America's "first professional biographer," in his life of Jefferson (1874) made of the wedding journey (says Peterson) "a delightful divertissment. The arrival on the bleak uninhabited mountain was not dreary at all but cheered by the warmth of young lovers, nestling in the cottage and reading the verses of Ossian. In one of his best-sellers, *Achievements of Celebrated Men,* Parton had the bride and groom leaving The Forest (the Wayless estate) after the wedding breakfast and arriving at Monticello sometime after nightfall—and he added a bottle of wine to the honeymoon picture! This fantastic tale—a one-hundred mile journey in phaeton and on horseback over the Virginia roads of 1772, through a blinding snowstorm part of the way, all on the day of the wedding, and the final merriment at Monticello—was repeated by nearly every writer for the next seventy-five years. By 1943, when Sidney Kingsley recreated the 'wedding night' in his Broadway play, *The Patriots,* the bride is playing the pianoforte and Jefferson the violin! 'Was there ever such a wedding night?' Jefferson's daughter Martha asks after the flashback. No, Martha, there never was. The meticulous scholarship of Jefferson's present-day biographer, Dumas Malone, shows how far the plain facts were from the picturesque story. Jefferson and his bride, it appears, stayed at The Forest for two weeks, dallied a while at Tuckahoe (his mother's old home) and finally arrived at Monticello late one snowy night near the end of the month." The time of the wedding was January 1: according to Paul Wilstach in his *Jefferson and Monticello* the snow was so deep "that they were forced to abandon their chaise . . . they pushed forward on horseback" and covered the hundred wintry miles during a day and

---

*See, for instance, D. J. Boorstin, *The Lost World of Thomas Jefferson.*

part of a night. It is obvious that Jefferson and his wife should have been pony express riders.

By 1900 the image of Jefferson as a "beautiful domestic character was well formed." As the perfect man in all ways, Professor Peterson, with his piles of evidence before him, might well have said. What did the image-makers do with Elizabeth Walker and Maria Cosway? Closed their eyes against them, no doubt. And so have practically all the biographers, except Nathan Schachner and Dumas Malone.* When Jefferson was twenty-five, one of his closest friends was John Walker, at whose marriage to Elizabeth Moore Jefferson was an attendant. Some four years later, when Walker's duties called him away from home, Jefferson "offered love" to his friend's wife. Professor Malone does his best for Jefferson when he says that Jefferson was "full of physical strength and vigor, and for four months his friend was away from home." When, years later, Mrs. Walker told her husband about it and the matter became a public scandal, Jefferson "candidly admitted to certain particular friends" that "I plead guilty . . . that when young and single I offered love to a handsome lady. I acknowledge its incorrectness." It is true, as Malone says, that when in his sixties Jefferson "did what he could in private to make amends to his alienated friend, and to relieve Walker's mind in a time of embarrassing publicity by exculpating the lady from all blame. Such action was in full accord with his strict code of manners and morals."

Jefferson's affair with Mrs. Cosway when she was about 27, and he was a widower of 45 with two small daughters and was living as the minister to France in Paris, deserves, in our opinion, a study by a qualified psychologist. We give the story in the words of Professor Malone. Practically within the hour of meeting Maria, Jefferson "conspired" to spend the remainder of the day with her, "even though this involved the shattering of engagements on all hands. In this mad moment he sent a 'lying messenger'** to the old Duchesse de la Rochefoucauld d'Anville, saying that, just as he started on his way to dine with her, important dispatches arrived requiring his immediate attention . . .

---

*Nathan Schachner, *Thomas Jefferson*, 2 vols., 1951; Dumas Malone, *Jefferson and His Time*, vol. 1 1948, vol. 2 1951.

**Jefferson's term for it later.

difficult as it is to get far beneath the surface of the record, there can be no doubt that he fell deeply in love that golden September, and there is no reason to suppose that the lady was displeased. . . . James Boswell . . . accused her of treating men like dogs. It is hard to see how she could have failed to be a flirt. . . ." The "delicious expeditions" with Maria (and without her husband) "ended abruptly and rather ingloriously when the middle-aged widower fell and dislocated his right wrist."* When some time after the accident "he did venture from his chamber . . . his purposes were wholly personal and the results were bad . . . his highly indiscreet day was followed by an excessively painful and long dialogue between his Head and Heart," for if, says Malone, "his fall did not shock him into a consciousness of folly her departure did." He had "no consciousness of sin, no concern over any disregard of the proprieties . . . he gave no sign of regretting his delicious adventure in irrationality which ended with a broken wrist . . . . his 'folly' had revealed to him anew the limitations of sheer intelligence . . . . this highly intellectual man recognized in human life the superior claims of sentiment over reason." In the long dialogue which he sent to Maria, the Heart, as Malone points out, had the last word: "Let the gloomy monk, sequestered from the world, seek unsocial pleasures in the bottom of his cell! Let the sublimated philosopher grasp visionary happiness while pursuing phantoms dressed in the garb of truth! Their supreme happiness is supreme folly; and they mistake for happiness the mere absence of pain. Had they ever felt the solid pleasure of one generous spasm of the heart, they would exchange for it all the frigid speculations of their lives." The first homage of his recovered right hand he told her he owed to her, but he had used exactly the same words in a letter to George Washington. During the many years that followed they exchanged letters. He "embarked on no romantic adventure with anybody else" but though she "had to share his friendship with other women, . . . her position in his life and memory was unique, and in the more restrained and mature sense he loved her all the rest of life." It is our guess that he loved not Maria but an image.**

---

*How he broke his wrist Malone did not pretend to know; Schachner says Jefferson "chose to essay leaping over a large kettle that proposed an obstacle to him in the courtyard of his establishment."
**Professor Malone tends to disparage Richard Cosway by saying he

was ridiculous but successful and looked like a monkey. One of his enemies called him a monkey but in his self-portrait and in the drawing of him by George Dance he looks no more like a monkey than we or Professor Malone, though he was a small man and, like Chopin and some others in times past and present, a foppish dandy with airs that most men thought preposterous. He was a distinguished miniaturist whose earnings were very large and whose friends and acquaintances included many of the titled and noted persons of Europe. Maria's self-portrait shows her as a lusciously pouting and remarkably lovely woman in a delicate and doll-like way and her husband's portrait of her supports her own.

James Northcote wrote (sneeringly, says one of her biographers) that she had "a form extremely delicate, and a pleasing manner of the utmost simplicity. But she was withal active, ambitious, proud, and restless. She had been the object of adoration of an indulgent father, who, unfortunately for her, had never checked the growth of her imperfections. She had some small knowledge of painting, the same of music, and about the same of five or six languages . . . from necessity married Cosway, the miniature painter [he really means the painter of miniatures], who at that time adored her, though she always despised him."

Williamson (George C. Williamson, *Richard Cosway, R. A. and His Wife and Pupils,* London, 1897) says Northcote was sneering but admits that "Thoughtless and frivolous Mrs. Cosway appears to have been in the days of her glory, but the further accusations made by many writers against her moral character lack point and circumstance, and are in no way warranted by any traditions or evidence that remain." Elsewhere he says: "Maria records in her own letters that at first she feared him, then she worshipped him; later on she admired him, gradually grew to like to be in his company and to obtain his advice, and finally loved him with her whole heart."

Maria seems to have been a devout Catholic (though of English parents she was born in Italy and Italian was her first language). When in 1793 Jefferson heard she had entered a convent he wrote to chide her, saying it would have been better to seek "the god of the Universe" on a *"mountain-top"*—even on his own at Monticello. She had not then entered but was thinking of it; by 1803 it appears that she had emerged and was back in Paris where, as a baroness, she presided over a salon to which the brilliant and titled came. In her later years she was devoted to children (her only child, a daughter, died young) and welfare work, and to her husband in his last depressing illness. He first became insane and imagined that great men, living and dead, were coming to him to pay homage to his genius. He seems then to have become paralyzed.

What kind of family man was Jefferson? Perfect, say his image-makers. Schachner says that Jefferson's reticence concerning the nature of his wife "verged on the morbid. . . . Jefferson, who meticulously saved every scrap of paper, no matter how unimportant, during his long life, permitted no sign of her to remain behind after his own death." Bernard Mayo in his biography says: "None of the letters which he and Martha exchanged were allowed to remain even for the children to read. . . . For three weeks he kept to his room, pacing the floor almost incessantly day and night." Randall* dwelt at greater length than most on Jefferson's response to his daughter Martha's wish to enter a convent. In Paris, where she was at the time, Jefferson rode up to the Abbaye, and "poor Martha met her father in a fever of doubts and fears." After a private interview with the Abbess, he told Martha to come with him, and her "school life was ended." In their correspondence thereafter neither "made the remotest allusion" to her wish at that time to immure herself or to his rejection of it. Her proposal must have been extremely repugnant to her father who was a rationalist and free-thinker.

In his old age Jefferson wrote for his children a memoir about some of his people. A few of the things he stated as facts about his father suggest that a scrupulous regard for accuracy, or in any case for the credible, was not, at least in his last years, one of his traits. Certain important facts he seems to have omitted. Says Randall: "We have sometimes conjectured that he might have *forgotten* those facts when he sat down at the age of seventy-seven to write the Memoir." That may be. And it may be that

---

It cannot be said that at 43 Thomas Jefferson lost his head to a mere flirt, a self-indulgent adventuress, or a woman who detested her husband. Undoubtedly she was flattered by the ardent attentions of the American minister, as day after day they walked, and talked about music (his passion) and painting and architecture (in both of which he had a minor and, as in poetry, rather superficial interest). What a pair they must have made!—the small, graceful, and rather doll-like woman, and the gangling tall man who stood more than six inches above John Adams.

*Not long after Jefferson's death Randall wrote his famous biography to defend Jefferson against his critics. Though it is frankly partisan Professor Malone seems to think highly of it. Peterson gives it a fine appraisal.

he no longer had a very clear image of Meriwether Lewis when at the age of seventy or past he wrote some things about him that have been accepted as gospel. Professor Malone speaks of "the imperfect memory of an old man" in connection with a "much-quoted" statement that Jefferson made; and Professor Boyd, his present editor, has said that "It is pertinent to observe that Jefferson, whose memory in old age caused him at times to err. . . ."

We come now to a curious matter. The reader will recall Lewis's letter to the War Department (ch. 2), in which some writers have seen signs of mental illness. When criticism (it seems to have been mild) was directed at Jefferson because he did not attend the spring session of the General Assembly in 1782, Jefferson developed what Randall calls "morbid" feelings. "The self infliction which a proud and sensitive man will often bring upon himself, under such circumstances, by magnifying the blame imputed to him—by trying to fancy himself only half acquitted—are here well illustrated. . . . This was obviously the waywardness of wounded feeling; his motives had never been attacked."

Nevertheless, Jefferson wrote to Monroe that "by a constant sacrifice of time, labor, parental and friendly duties, I had, so far from gaining the affection of my countrymen, which was the only reward I ever asked or could have felt, even lost the small estimation I had before possessed.

"That, however I might have comforted myself under the disapprobation of the well-meaning but uninformed people, yet that of their representatives was a shock on which I had not calculated. That this, indeed, had been followed by an exculpatory declaration. But, in the meantime, I had been suspected in the eyes of the world, without the least hint then or afterwards being made public, which might restrain them from supposing that I stood arraigned for treason of the heart, and not merely weaknesses of the mind; and I felt that these injuries, for such they have since been acknowledged, had inflicted a wound on my spirit which will only be cured by the all-healing grave." A person studying the two letters, but unfamiliar with the name of either man, might conclude that the same man wrote both, or two men very similar in their natures. Nearly five years later Jefferson returned to the matter: "To apologize for this by developing the circumstances of the time and place of their composition, would be to open wounds which have already bled enough." He could write such words even though the Assembly had passed a resolution which paid "the highest compliment to his impartiality, uprightness, rectitude, and integrity," without a single word of objection or a dissenting vote!

The two men *were* much alike in some ways. For one thing they both had what in contemporary psychological terminology is called identification with the opposite sex. Randall pointed out more than a century ago that in some ways Jefferson was soft and womanly. Alexander Hamilton called him "womanish," and William Graham Sumner and Henry Cabot Lodge "thought no single word better characterized him."[*] "He loathed cold. . . ."[**] Practically all his adult life he suffered from periodic and severe headaches. We would conjecture that his wife and at least his older daughter were not strangers to those "hypochondriac affections" which he told the world were found in Meriwether Lewis, and we suspect that it was schizophrenia with his sister Elizabeth, and not that, as Schachner put it, "if not wholly imbecilic, she was perilously close to that unfortunate state." For the person looking for abnormal traits, it is our opinion that the Thomas Jefferson family is a better hunting ground than the Meriwether Lewis family.

Having taken this great man off his pedestal and looked at a few of his frailties, and his failure of memory in his old age, we are in a better position to determine how dependable he was as a witness. Coues is typical of prevailing opinion when he says, as quoted by Wheeler, that Jefferson was a "wary and astute man of the world, accustomed to weigh his words well; one who must have been satisfied in his own mind that he had the facts of a case beyond his personal knowledge; and one who had every imaginable reason—personal, official, or other—to put the matter in the most favorable light." There were things about Jefferson that Coues had no knowledge of, and one of them is to be found in Robert Penn Warren's shrewd conjecture that for Jefferson Lewis was the son he had never had.[***] If that is so, it was almost inevitable, and above all in his old age, that he should have seen in Lewis certain personality disturbances that in his own family had been a cause of grief.

---

[*]Peterson, 232.    [**] Malone, II, 206.
[***]See Appendix A.

It has not been possible to learn on what he based his unqualified statement that he knew exactly how Lewis died. To be
sure, he received Neely's letter, for on the back of it he wrote
in his own hand, "recd. Nov 21." Presumably he received Brahan's
at about the same time, and early the next year the two from
Russell. We know that he saw Pernia, but we do not know if he
asked him any questions. We do not know whether the two Russell letters raised any doubts in his mind, or if they did not, why
they did not. There is no reason to believe that he knew Neely,
or had ever heard of him before.

In an earlier chapter appears a part of Jefferson's statement
on Lewis's death, which appeared in the 1814 Biddle and Allen
edition of the Lewis and Clark journals. He told the world that
from early life Lewis had been "subject to hypochondriac affections," and that this was a "constitutional disposition" in all the
nearer branches of his family. He said Lewis inherited it "more
immediately" from his father. Our search of the records has found
no facts to support Jefferson's implication that he was famiilar
with Lewis's early life. The Lewis family has always rejected the
idea that "affections" existed in such strength as to make them
seem abnormal. One is forced to wonder whether in his old age
Jefferson was projecting into Lewis those "affections" so obvious
in the faces of some members of his own family.

In that portion of the statement which we gave earlier, Jefferson says that when Lewis was in Washington he had "sensible depressions of mind"; that on his journey to the ocean he was so
physically active that these "distressing affections" were "suspended"; but that on taking up a sedentary residence in St. Louis "they
returned to him with redoubled vigor, and began seriously to
alarm his friends." If evidence to support these statements exists,
nobody has found it. Bearing in mind that in 1809 St. Louis was a
small river outpost of only a few hundred persons, it is necessary
for emphasis to say again that if Lewis was acting in a manner to
alarm his friends it is inconceivable that his tireless enemy Frederick Bates did not know it, or that, knowing it, he did not communicate it to his intimates.

Though Lewis arrived at Fort Pickering September 15, Jefferson says he arrived the 16th. It seems likely that he deduced
this error from Neely, who wrote him that he arrived at the fort
"on or about the 18th September" and that Lewis "had reached

there two days before me." If Jefferson could be so positive
about a matter when the evidence before him was not explicit,
are we to bow before his name and assume that in all his details
he was right? As a matter of fact the question is a more embarrassing one than that: presumably he had before him Russell's
letter in which it was said that Lewis "came here on the 15th September." Further, he had before him Neelly's letter in which the
name Neelly is unmistakably clear in its spelling, yet Jefferson
spelled it Neely. Though for a long time he had been familiar
with the name of George Rogers Clark and knew that William
was his brother, he always spelled William's name as Clarke. If
a person is not careful of small details, it is far-fetched to assume
that he is invariably careful of large details.

Take, for instance, his bland statement that on arriving at the
fort Neelly found Lewis "extremely indisposed, and betraying
at times some symptoms of a derangement of mind." Neelly did
*not* write him that, nor did Brahan, nor did Russell. Neelly told
him that he found Lewis "in very bad health." Russell told him
that in a few days Lewis "was perfectly restored in every respect,"
but Jefferson told his readers only that Lewis "appeared somewhat relieved." Possibly that part of it he based on Neelly's
statement that Lewis had "recovered his health in some digree."
He says health, not mental faculties, and this suggests that mental derangement did not occur to Neelly until after the party had
left the fort. Jefferson goes on to say that "Mr. Neely kindly determined to accompany and watch over him." Neelly did *not*
tell him that and Russell wrote him the exact opposite of that.
It may be that Pernia told him that (and if he did, it would seem
that he lied), or it may be that in his old age the thing that his
emotions told him should have been done became the thing that
was done.

Jefferson went on to tell his readers what happened at
Grinder's Stand, in the manner of one with no doubt at all that he
has the facts. "He stopped at the house of a Mr. Grinder, who
not being at home, his wife, alarmed at the symptoms of derangement she discovered, gave him up the house and retired to rest
herself in an out-house, the governor's and Neely's servants lodging in another. About three o'clock in the night he did the deed
which plunged his friends into affliction, and deprived his country
of one of her most valued citizens..." It was his concluding

words that settled the matter for practically all his readers: "I have only to add, that all the facts I have stated are either known to myself, or communicated by his family or others, for whose truth I have no hesitation to make myself responsible . . ." With his enormous personal prestige he guaranteed the matter. He even implied that some of the facts, if not indeed the whole substance of his essay, were corroborated and supported by members of Lewis's family, but we haven't found an iota of evidence to indicate that between the time he received Neelly's letter and the writing of his essay he was in touch with any member of the family.

The unqualified finality of Jefferson's statement was probably not intended to shut off all appeal, but for a long time that is exactly what it did.

Had Jefferson seen Wilson's account of the matter? We know that Paul Allen wrote Jefferson to call his attention to it, for Coues says he saw the letter. If Jefferson did not bother to read what a distinguished scientist had written about it, or if he read Wilson and saw no discrepancies between his version and Neelly's, we can only wonder about him. As Schachner says, "He could be vigorously logical, and simultaneously wildly inconsistent." Perhaps that is it. Wheeler wrote, "It is a matter for regret that Jefferson did not particularize more as to his sources of information . . . and the precise reasons for his conclusions, for there is no doubt that the weight of his name alone has given the suicide theory a force it otherwise would not possess."

Did Jefferson change his mind later? A legend says he did. Bakeless puts it this way: "There is some rather dubious ground for believing that Mr. Jefferson later gave up the idea of suicide and asserted that Lewis had been murdered. The letter in which he stated his revised opinion is said to have been in a volume of Jefferson MSS. compiled by Jefferson Randolph which came into the possession of Dr. William Randolph, by whom it was unfortunately 'loaned out'. Jefferson is said to have written that *'subsequent evidence* tended to prove Meriwether Lewis did not kill himself but was murdered'." Sarah Anderson, a member of the Lewis family, wrote Mrs. Eva Dye in 1902 that she was determined to find the letter but she never found it. Professor Boyd, editor of the Jefferson papers, seems strongly to feel not only that Jefferson never changed his mind but that he made "minute and

characteristically thorough investigations of known and accepted
details about Lewis's life and death." One needs to know by
whom the details about his *life* and *death* were accepted in 1814.
And one would think that if Jefferson made a minute and
thorough investigation there would be some trace of it somewhere.

So there is our witness: how trustworthy is he? And though
of the highest quality, how seriously should we take him? On
that we will let Ernest Newman, the Wagner scholar, make a
point.* Discussing *The Truth About Wagner* by Hurn and Root
(which reveals an "innocence so vast that one almost feels compunction in drawing public attention to it") he says: "They had
not even learned the first lesson in historical science—that no
statement, however simple, however plausible, by whomever
made, and made in whatever good faith, is to be accepted without investigation if anything depends upon it; for human nature,
even when honest, is fallible." A little later he speaks of the "im-
possibility of the careful historian accepting any statement, however plausible it may seem on the face of it, however high the
general reputation for veracity of the person who made it may
stand, without confirmation of it from some other source."

After citing fantasies given as facts by Lilli Lehmann, Clau-
dina Couqui, and Mathilde Wesendonck he says that "A few
experiences of this kind of thing will convince him [the biogra-
pher] that all evidence is suspect unless and until it is confirmed
from some other sources. Good faith on the part of the teller of
a story counts for nothing, for the most honest people are subject to the common human infirmities of memory, unconscious
prepossession or prejudice, liability to suggestion, the impulse
to believe what they want to believe, and proneness to allow
their recital of a fact to be colored by their desire to establish a
thesis."

Judged by such standards of evidence, both Neelly's statement and Jefferson's need confirmation from strong sources before they can be accepted as facts.

*Fact and Fiction about Wagner, passim.*

# XV

# *As the Newspapers*

# *Told It*

The Indexes list as extant no copy of the Frankfort *Argus* for October 28, 1809, but we know that it said that Lewis died by cutting his throat. William Clark was passing through Shelbyville when he picked up the newspaper and read the news. He wrote his brother Jonathan to tell him about it. His words, "I fear the weight of his mind has overcome him," indicate that he believed at that moment that Lewis had taken his own life. It has been said that Clark later became convinced that Lewis was murdered. If this is so, we don't know whether the change in him came from love and loyalty, or from evidence. One of his nieces has left the words, "Uncle had a great love for Lewis, & he never spoke of him without the tears coming into his eyes. he never believed he committed suicide . . . "

It is obvious that some of the newspaper stories were based on Neely directly, or by way of Brahan, or by way of Stoddard through Brahan. November 2 the *Missouri Gazette* said: "By last mail we received the melancholy account of the premature death of his Ex'y. Governor Lewis; he landed at the Chickasaw Bluffs much indisposed, and shortly after set out on his way to the Federal City via Nashville; about 40 miles east of the river Tennessee, the party stopped for the night and became much alarmed at the governors behavior, he appeared in a state of extreme mental debility, and before he could be prevented, discharged the contents of a brace of pistols in his head and breast, calling to his servant to give him a bason of water; he lived about two hours and died without much apparent pain. The governor has been of late very much affllicted with fever, which never failed of depriving him of his reason; to this we may ascribe the fatal catastrophe."

Our next report returns to the throat-cutting. It appeared in the *National Intelligencer,* at Washington, November 15, with this prefatory note: "Extract of a letter from a gentleman in Russellville, to his friend at present in Lexington dated Russellville, October 20, 1809." The names of the gentleman and his friend seem to be unknown. The Russellville gentleman wrote, only the second day after Neelly and Brahan wrote their letters to Jefferson, and only a little more than a week after Lewis died:

"A gentleman from Nashville informs me that he conversed with a person who had seen governor Merriwether Lewis buried on the 12th inst. about 40 miles beyond Nashville on the Natchez road.—The accounts are, that Governor Lewis arrived at a house very weak, from a recent illness at Natchez, and showed signs of mental derangement. After a stay of a few hours at the above house, he took his pistols and shot himself twice, and then cut his throat."

It is not easy to put faith in the words of a gentleman who wrote to a friend that a gentleman from Nashville informed him that he had talked with a person who had seen Lewis buried. If it is true that Lewis was buried on the 12th and that Neelly saw him buried, as he told Brahan, Neelly was at the Grinder place at least two nights. We now have two newspapers, published far apart, saying only shortly after Lewis's death that his throat was cut. Is it more probable that his throat was cut and that at least a few persons saw the wound, or that a rumor based on nothing sprang up and found its way as fact into newspapers? If Lewis was murdered, and a story of suicide was invented, with or without Neelly's knowledge, it seems to us that the more plausible story is the one that Neelly told Jefferson, that Lewis shot himself twice with his pistols. A less plausible story would be that he shot himself twice without killing himself and then seized a knife or razor to complete the job.

This newspaper account of the death goes on to tell us that "The above unfortunate intelligence is confirmed by a gentleman present in this place. It is added, that Governor Lewis, in addition to shooting himself twice in the body, and cutting his throat, shot himself in the head, and cut the arteries in his thighs and arms." All this is supposed to have come from a man who was on the scene and saw him buried. We don't know that he actually saw the corpse but this seems to be implied in his story as it reached the newspaper.

Our impression is that if this story is true, it sounds like a bungled murder in a dark cabin.

This story continues: "We have been unable to procure any satisfactory intelligence of the circumstances which led to this unhappy event." After saying he had heard that Lewis had some vouchers protested, the editor interrupts his account to insert, in brackets, the following: "[After the above was put in type [a] gentleman politely hand us a Nashville paper of the 20th inst. from which we have made the following extract:–]"

The extract from the Nashville paper is as follows:

"To record the untimely end of a brave and prudent officer, a learned scholar and scientific gentleman this column of the Clarion is ushered to the world in black. On the night of the 10th instant Meriwether Lewis, esq. Governor-general of Upper Louisiana, on his way to Washington City, came to the house of a Mr. Grinder near the Indian Line in this state—called for his supper and some spirits, of which he partook and gave to his servants. Mr. Grinder not being at home, Mrs. Grinder retired to the kitchen with the children, and the servants (after the Governor went to bed, which he did in good order) went to a stable about three hundred yards distant to sleep—no one in the house with the governor—and some time before midnight Mrs. Grinder was alarmed by the firing of two pistols in the house—she called to the servants without effect—and at the appearance of daylight the servants came to the house when the Governor said he had now done for himself—they asked what and he said he had shot himself and would die, and requested them to bring him water, he then laying on the floor where he expired about 7 o'clock in

the morning of the 11th—he had shot a ball that grazed the top of
his head and another through his intestines, and cut his neck and
arm and ham with a razor. When in his best sences he spoke
about a trunk of papers which he said would be of great value
to our government. He had been under the influence of a derang-
ing malady for about six weeks—the cause of which is unknown,
unless it was from a protest to a draft which he drew on the secretary of war, which he considered tantamount to a disgrace by
government."

This version of his death appeared in a Nashville paper *only
two days* after Neelly and Brahan wrote to Jefferson, and only
nine days after Lewis died, if he died on October 11. It does not
sound as if it came from Neelly, for in a number of important
particulars it differs from his story. Neelly, for instance, said
the shooting was at three in the morning and not before midnight, and that Mrs. Grinder awakened the servants and they
came.

It takes, in our opinion, a lot of willingness to find this *Clarion* version plausible. We are asked to believe that Lewis spent
six hours or more with guns and a razor trying to kill himself, and
when daylight came had not yet accomplished his purpose. We
are asked to believe that he was so incredibly clumsy with a pistol
that he only grazed the top of his skull, and with his second effort shot himself through the guts, of all places. And after all
those hours of shooting and slashing he seems to have been
rational! We suspect that those who are willing to accept this
kind of story know of guns only what they have seen in shop win-
dows and museums.

A week after the *Clarion* story appeared, *The Farmer's
Friend*, in Russellville, published the following:

"It is with extreme regret that we have to record the melancholy death of the excellency Merriwether Lewis, Governor of
Upper Louisiana, on his way to the city of Washington. The following particulars, are given to us by a gentleman who traveled
with him from the Chickasaw Bluffs.

"The governor had been in a bad state of health, but having
recovered in some degree, set out from the Chickasaw Bluffs and
in traveling from that to the Chickasaw nation, our informant
says, he discovered that the governor appeared at times consider-

ably deranged, and on their arrival in the nation, having lost two horses, the governor proceeded on and the gentleman detained with a view of hunting the horses. The governor proceeded on to a Mr. Grinder's on the road, found no person at home but a woman; she observing something wild in his appearance, became frightened and left the house to sleep in the stable. About three o'clock the woman says she heard the report of two pistols in the room where he lay, and immediately awakened the servants, who rushed into the house, but too late he had shot himself in the head and just below the breast, and was in the act of cutting himself with a razor. The only words he uttered, was 'It is done, my good servant give me some water,' and expired in a few moments after."

That version must have come from Neelly, though here she aroused the servants immediately and he died almost at once. It is well to recall that she told Wilson, only a few months later, that she was too terrified to venture out, and did not send for the servants until daylight, hours after she heard the shots. She told Wilson that Lewis lived until the sun was above the trees, and the *Clarion* says he lived until seven o'clock. Malinda told us that he lived until noon. It seems probable that Neelly did not tell Brahan that Lewis was cutting himself with a razor. Whatever the facts, the story that a knife or razor was used appeared too many times independently of one another to be put aside as mere legend.

In this version, as in the *Clarion's*, he was rational when the servants came. If he was, it seems unlikely to us that he would have been cutting at himself with a razor or knife, when presumably he had a rifle at hand, or in a few moments could have reloaded a pistol.

# XVI

## *As the Old Timers*

## *Told It*

All oral tradition related to Lewis's death Historian Phelps dismisses with the words "My Grandpa told me." It must be admitted that this is about all such tradition deserves, though hidden in the legends and lore, the inventions and embellishments, there may be facts, if only we could dig them out. Some of these witnesses were undoubtedly only rumor-mongers, but some were sober persons who made an honest effort to discover the truth. Mr. Harrison Smith, for instance, who is our first witness here, was in his time a well-known artist in his area and a highly respected citizen. He spent a lot of time investigating Lewis's death, and he came to certain conclusions. His devoted daughter, an elderly maiden lady, Miss Carrie E. Smith of Columbia, has her father's papers, some of which she so treasures that she keeps them in a bank vault. These are now pretty fragile, but she allowed Dr. Bakeless to examine them, and she allowed us to do so. The following are notes which we made on reading them.

These papers say that the Neelly servant was named Tom, and that the Grinder kitchen was twelve feet from the other cabin. "Lewis claimed to have lost his pocket-book & was looking for it under the bed after supper." There is a tradition of long standing that Lewis's purse disappeared soon after he arrived at Grinder's, but under the bed seems to be an unusual place to look for it, unless he hid it there before going to bed. "About 9 o'clock first shot heard—five minutes later second shot. Three shots fired. Piece of skull blown off forehead at first fire, stuck to bullet & lodged over mantel—2nd and 3rd shots just over his heart two inches apart."

Later Pernia came into the kitchen and told Mrs. Grinder Lewis said if she would give him water he would give up the razor. Mrs. G told P to give him only a spoonful. Pernia did, and L gave up the razor. "Lewis died about noon that day." Most of this seems to be more nonsense than sense. A man shot twice just above the heart isn't going to live from nine in the evening until noon the next day, and trading a razor for only a spoonful of water again introduces farce into the story. It is not known who told Mr. Smith these things; he is said to have interviewed as many of the older residents of the area as pretended to know anything about it. "Just before the shooting Mrs. G heard French & L talking in L's room. Mrs. G asker Fr next morning what they were talking about, Fr denied it, Mrs. G then told Fr he was dressing himself up in Govs clothes asked him why he did it; Fr said Gov. gave them to him." A part of that is, of course, what Mrs. Grinder told the school teacher; if it is facts and not legend, it points to Pernia as a probable murderer.

These papers go on to say that when Lewis was found he had on old clothes that were not his own. "Mrs. Grinder told Frenchman that he had killed the Govr, but he denied it but he looked guilty. Tom has left." Mrs. Grinder asked Lewis what made him shoot himself and he said if he had not done it, somebody else would have. Pernia left just after Lewis was buried. Malinda was on the scene and was about twelve years old.

The Smith papers give, as though it actually happened, the visit of Lewis's sisters to the Grinders, as well as Pernia's going to Lewis's mother, who charged him with killing her son, whereupon he cried, "I'll see Gov. Lewis before dark!" and cut his throat. The scraping of the bucket for water is also here.

"Mr. Sam Whiteside who held the inquest over Lewis told his grandson Grif Whiteside (who now lives near Cove Spring) that he was to remember that Lewis was murdered and that all the information gathered at inquest was written out in full on his docket. The docket has been destroyed or mislaid. Grif White-side says that he remembers his grandfather very well & remembers him telling him that Grinder proved an alibi beyond the question of a doubt but that there were moccason tracks found around the old crib about 100 yds from house also the print of a rifle in the dust and the patch found half way between crib and where the body was found. The tracks corresponded to those made by Runnions and the print of the rifle in the dust fitted to the rifle belonging to R. The rifle was very peculiar and there was not another one like it ... the print in the dust could not have been made with any other rifle than Runnions.

"Consequently the above proves that there was someone at the crib with a rifle .... Robt Smith, father of R.O. Smith is buried south of Lewis mounment, next grave to Lewis." It is not known if Harrison Smith saw the school teacher's report of his interview with Mrs. Grinder. If not, then certain elements in that story must have become a part of oral tradition, indicating that Mrs. Grinder told that version more than once. As for the Whitesides, only this can be said with any certainty, that they were one of the more prominent and respected families in the area.

Our next item is taken from the notebook of W. W. Southgate and is dated July, 1883.

"Mrs. Christina Anthony is 70 years old (and living in Lewis county, Tenn.) was acquainted with Polly Spencer a Servant at the House Grinders Tavern. Grinder who was part Indian was charged with the killing of Meriwether Lewis. Polly Spencer was there at the time of the killing at night washing dishes while his waiting boy was in the stable caring for the horses. She heard the first pistol shot went in and found him dead. He had just arrived and retired. Grinder was missing the next day and was arrested on Cane creek brot back tried and got clear.

"It is thought he suicided."

Mrs. Anthony is the one whom J. H. Moore called a garrulous old woman. Polly Spencer may have been at some time a Grinder servant but it is doubtful that she was on the scene when Lewis died.

Our next is a statement from F. Cooper Frierson in December, 1924, to John Trotwood Moore, at that time Tennessee State librarian.

"After talking to you I came home & talked to some of my friends & here is what I found out, with what I knew before. When I was in my teens I became very much interested in hearing Mr. Scott Mayes talk of Merriwether Lewis & his murder as he called it and talked of it as murder. he said that they tried to connect the Grinders with it but never could get evidence to convict or arrest. Some thought that his Servants were guilty. Messrs Bruce & Alfred Cooper, both old men Mr. B 86 years old. They told me that Mr. Robt O Smith, who was mail rider on the Natchez Trace found his remains lying near the road, as he was passing on his route early in the morning and told it. The Coopers also told me that when they were boys, that one of their playmates & friends who lived close told a Mr Whitesides that the jury were cowards & were afraid to bring a Verdict of Murder, which they all knew they should have done. I could not imagine what they were afraid of! But someone said that the murderers had Indian Blood in their Veins, & they were afraid they would meet a similar fate. I have heard Mr Thos. S Cooper an older brother of messrs A—B—say that when the Commission who put the Monument up wanted to locate Lewis's Grave, sent for his father Robt M Cooper who lived on west fork Bigby Creek about 15 miles from the Grave. He caught his horse to go back with them. Mr Thos C says he was a barefooted boy & asked to ride behind his father. Which he did, he told me his father told them that if they did not locate it, That there was one way that he Could tell that there would be Iron Nails or spikes in the Grave Mr Cooper was a Black Smith & said that they came to his shop & he made the nails and spikes & they were used. Mr R.M.C. said the reason they wanted Iron Nails was that they could not find any lumber to make a Coffin, & that they cut a tree near where he was found. They found one that would split easy cut it down & cut it in proper lenght hughed all four sides & made it smooth as they could then split it up about 2 inches thick & spiked it together Coffins in those days were made with wooden pegs. Mr Cooper said that when they dug down they found a few bones A Button or two an ornament of some kind & nails The men who were there went a short distance to a spring branch and dug up a flat Rock that was soft. they chiseled or cut a hole large enough to put Bones everything including the nails in put in

Grave got a smaller stone & some wet clay & stuck the two stones together."

The Cooper account of the burial and the opening of the grave and the second burial all has the ring of authenticity. One may wonder why an oak coffin would completely rot away in less than forty years: we can assume that this was due to the nature of the soil or that wild hogs dug up the corpse and that only the bones were returned to the earth. We have seen that Wilson wanted a fence put around the grave and paid Grinder to do it but we don't know that it was ever done.

Among papers at the Monument is one, author unknown, which says: "Later, when students of Lewis' life came to visit the final resting place of the explorer they found a number of traditional accounts which would indicate that Lewis was murdered, with the story made up to indicate suicide. Some accused Robert Grinder because he came to Tennessee with no known finances and yet in 1814 moved to Centerville and bought some of the best land nearby. It is claimed that he was tried for murder but acquitted for lack of evidence. A Maury County Coroner's Jury supposedly met and gave verdict of death by gunshot without specifying the method. The page recording this verdict has been reported as torn from the Maury County records. Smith, the post rider is supposed to have found the body some distance from the house with mortal wound in the back and with wadding at the stable. The servants were supposed to have vanished."

That statement and those that now follow were made by investigators who presumably belonged to the Historical Records Survey of the Works Progress Administration. They interviewed old-timers who were still alive and made these notes:

"Silas Stockard who said his father had held county offices, clerk, registrar, and circuit judge; had to pass G's Inn every morning when he went to work, often stopping for a cup of coffee. Silas knew nothing of significance concerning Lewis' death but his father believed that he was murdered by Grinder'."

We don't know when the Grinders left their Stand but by 1814 they seem to have been back on Duck River. If Silas was 85 (his age is unknown) in 1934 when he gave this statement, and if his father was only 25 when as a justice of the peace he stopped for coffee at the Stand, in, let us say, 1810, then the father was about 67 when Silas was conceived. It may be that the man interviewed was a grandson.

"Mrs. Nancy H Higgins, who was 86 in 1934. She said her father was one of those who opened the grave and her father noted particularly a bullet hole in the forehead of the skeleton. Mrs. Higgins said it was a belief of her father that Lewis was murdered.... She talks rather fast, but with intelligence and deliberation."

"Olan Duff Cooper who said he was a grandson of the Cooper who made the nails for the coffin. We were shown the site on which the blacksmith shop stood where the nails were made.... Mr. Cooper said that in his grandfather's opinion, Lewis had been murdered, but by whom Mr. Cooper did not recall hearing his grandfather say."

It is not easy to dismiss so many indications that those who opened the grave and examined the bones felt that Lewis had been murdered. A historian asks: "How could examination of a skeleton that has lain in the ground for a generation prove or disprove murder? Specifically, whether a man had been shot from in front or behind?" It is a valid question, but we have no way of knowing what the men found who opened the grave. We know that they said in their report that murder seemed more probable than suicide, and since they were men of standing in their community, who examined the remains, as we can not over a hundred years later, it would seem to be presumption to dismiss as worthless a conclusion on which they were unanimous.

"Mr Pinkerton a rather prominent lawyer of Centerville.... about sixty-five years of age.... twenty-five years ago he was superintendent of schools in Lewis county.... Mr. Pinkerton is a strong believer in the murder theory.... believes that Lewis was murdered by Major Neely.... stated that a few years ago he talked with an old man by the name of Whiteside who claimed to have been a grandson of the man who made the coffin that Lewis was buried in. According to Mr. Whiteside, his grandfather came to Grinder's Stand the day after the death of Lewis and that although Lewis had not been buried, Major Neely and the rest of the party had already departed."

"Tom Colley a lumber man of about seventy years of age . . . .
a peculiar character . . . . After discussing the Grinder family he
finally expressed himself concerning their morals. He said that
they were incorrigibles and drunkards in several generations . . . .
led us to believe that he was of the opinion that Grinder killed
Lewis, although he did not say so directly . . . . Mr. Colley referred to a Mrs. Wid Grinder, who had previously been insane, but
is supposedly well at this time. She was the wife of the grandson
of the owner of Grinder's Stand . . . . Most of these people whom
we interview delight in having one think that they know everything concerning the matter but few have significant facts of
value. Finally, Mr. Colley could stand the interruptions of his
wife and daughter no longer. He begged our pardon and with
drew to a back room . . . ."

"Hugh Webster, Lewis's body was found in the middle of the
Natchez Trace Road by Robt. O. Smith, who was a mail carrier
from Nashville to Natchez and was found about 100 yards northwest of the Inn. The barn where his horses were quartered was
about forty steps north east from where he was found lying in
the road . . . . It was told by Mr. Cooper to his children that it was
testified to before coroner's jury that a piece of patching used in
the rifle was found about halfway between the barn and where
Lewis's body was found. This piece of evidence indicates that
the person doing the shooting was stationed at or near the barn.
F. D. Smith at one time had the proceedings of the coroner's
jury."

If the barn was north of the Stand it was in the area where
Lewis was buried. It does not seem probable that he would
have been buried in the area of a stable.

"Grant Hale": they go to find him but encounter other men
and talk to them. "Gess says the old man never had a favorable
word for Grinder and related numerous stories of how oftentimes
guests at the Grinder Inn had awakened in the morning to find
their purses and valuables missing." The old man here was born
in 1832 "and knew many people who had known Grinder . . . .
The general impression gathered from Gess was that old man
Grinder was quite a bad character." When at last Grant Hale
came up he offered a new theory, "hitherto unheard of by either

Mr. Hagan or myself. That is that he was killed by a man named Runions who lived close to Grinder's Inn . . . . This story was given to him by a descendant . . . . of an old settler, who evidently had passed the story down to his children."

They then went to see a Mr. Milligan, in 1934 a man almost 80, whose father was born in 1817 and had lived in Maury county. Milligan "was a little more familiar with the Runions" and said that Runion had been a bad one. Both Hale and Milligan held the view that Lewis had been murdered and robbed.

So in this tantalizing realm of wraiths and specters, James Neelly becomes a suspect, as does a man named Runion or Runions.

# XVII

## *The Family Tradition*

Mr. Dawson A. Phelps, a National Park Service historian, says that "Except perhaps for the Lewis family, who in later years persisted in believing that their famous kinsman had been murdered, there appears to have been no disposition in either official or literary circles to question Jefferson's narrative prior to 1848." Mr. Phelps not only believes but seems to have no doubt that Lewis killed himself, and the use of such words as *perhaps, in later years* and *persisted* suggests the strength of his belief. To say that the family persisted seems to imply that they held a position in spite of evidence known to them which could overthrow it; to say that they did this in later years is to imply that they did not in former years. In regard to all that we simply do not know. He cites William Terrell Lewis, *Lewis Family in America,* "pp. 386, *passim*" and says that this Lewis "is inclined to agree with Jefferson."

When we told Mr. Phelps we could find no mention of suicide from page 386 to the end of the book he replied that "pp. 386 inadvertently slipped into the text. Terrell [he means W. T. Lewis] officially supports the suicide theory, but leaves the impression that he is not too sure." What this Lewis actually does is to give, on page 29, a brief sketch from a standard source of Rev. J. L. Blake, in which Blake, not Lewis, says that Lewis committed suicide. On page 52 he quotes George R. Gilmer, a former governor of Georgia: "... he stopped for the night at a little inn on the roadside in Tennessee. In the morning his throat was found cut and he was dead; whether by his own hand or others in search of his account of the place where gold was to be found, is not certainly known."

It has been said in the family that Lewis's mother never for a moment believed that her son killed himself, but to the day of her death was convinced that he was murdered by Pernia. The descendants of Jane Lewis Anderson, Lewis's sister, have maintained that on visiting Mrs. Marks Pernia was accused by her, and either then or within the year killed himself. This all sounds like family prejudice, pure and simple, but Thomas Jefferson heard that Pernia had killed himself and seems not to have had the slightest doubt of it.

The one person who more than any other made a determined effort to discover the nature of the master-servant relationship was Olin D. Wheeler, the indefatigable gentleman who spent so much time more than half a century ago trying to follow the Lewis and Clark trail and identify the campsites. He was a painstaking and level-headed investigator. He also went to Tennessee and adjacent areas to learn all he could about Lewis's death. He knew that Pernia had told Jefferson that Lewis owed him $240, a considerable sum of money in those years.

We have seen that both Neelly and Brahan gave Pernia a few dollars and sent him on his way from Nashville. We know that he appeared before Jefferson. It seems probable that he also went to see Mrs. Marks. No one has ever suggested that he had any motive in going to either person except money. Jefferson's endorsement on the back of the letter from Neelly reads, "recd. Nov. 21." Since Jefferson mentioned Pernia to Madison in a letter November 26, we may assume that Pernia appeared before him between that day and November 20. Whether Pernia took the cash Lewis had on him at the time of his death, or Neelly or Grinder or some other person took it, we may never know; but undoubtedly Pernia made the long tedious journey to Jefferson with the hope that he could collect his back wages. If that was

his motive, then it seems probable that he also went to Lewis's
mother, because from Jefferson he received only a few dollars.

If he appeared before Lucy Marks, it must have been quite a
scene. Her photographic likeness shows her to have been a rather
sharp-featured, shrewd, and, one suspects, quick-tempered woman. We don't know when she first heard of her son's death. If
it was from Pernia, she must have asked him more questions than
she would have asked if she had already heard about it. In either
case she must have wanted to know all the details. It is easy to
imagine how her sharp black eyes flashed as she drove him from
point to point with questions. It is easy to believe that she told
him flatly and with great emotion that she didn't believe his story,
and for any novelist, an attempt to portray this dramatic scene
must be an irresistible temptation.

Mrs. Marks was an aunt of Charles Meriwether, the father of
Mrs. Caroline D. M. Goodlett, who wrote Wheeler that her
father visited Lewis's mother when she was eighty years old,
"but remarkably vigorous in mind and body, rode around the
country on horseback like a girl, my father said, and was fond of
talking of her son. She said his letters written to her before
starting on his trip home were full of love and affection, and so
hopeful of a good time with his old friends, that *she never entertained the idea for a moment* that he had committed suicide. The
theory that the family have ever advanced is that he was murdered by his Spanish servant . . . We suppose that traveling together
for a long distance, it is probable that Meriwether Lewis, being of
a social and confiding nature, had spoken to the Spaniard of the
valuable papers and maps he was carrying to Virginia;—and knowing that the Governor of the State would not travel without plenty
of money, that the avaricious and treacherous nature of the servant
got possession of him and he determined to possess himself of
what valuables Captain Lewis had . . . . His family can attest to
the fact that there was no insanity in his branch of the family."

We assume that "his trip home" meant his journey to his
mother in Virginia. It seems likely that he did talk to Pernia
about his papers and maps, and if he did he must have said they
were valuable, for we know that he hoped to realize a small
fortune with their publication. We can imagine what ran through
Pernia's mind when he thought of the Lewis trunks and wondered
about their contents, and then dwelt unhappily on the fact that

Lewis owed him in back wages a sum that in purchasing power was well over a thousand dollars today.

The members of most families are invariably eager to attest but they are usually worthless as witnesses, particularly when the matter reflects, as insanity does, and suicide by many is thought to, on the character of the family. The relative quoted above says that Pernia disappeared soon afterward and was never seen again. This, as we shall see, contradicts another family tradition. But except for one improbable appearance in Mobile or New Orleans, he seems within a year or so to have vanished from the scene and from history.

We suspect that the family tradition of murder began with Lewis's mother. It was nearly forty years after Lewis's death that William Clark's son wrote the letter in which he said he had heard that Lewis was murdered. Mrs. Mark's opinion could have remained wholly within the family for a long time. Wheeler reported that one R. T. Quarles of Nashville, onetime secretary of the Tennessee Historical Society, and a Lewis or Meriwether descendant, thought that Lewis was murdered by his servant. It was his belief that Lewis had in his possession not only a sum of money but valuable jewels as well. The notion that Lewis had jewels with him is a part of the family tradition, but no evidence to support it has been brought forth.

Wheeler also corresponded with B. R. A. Scott and his wife, of Galveston, and Mrs. S. E. Shelton of Waco. The two women were Lewis's great-nieces. Mrs. Shelton wrote: "After a lapse of years, perhaps as many as thirty, he (Pernea) sent a trunk of papers to my grandmother, Mrs. William H. Moore, née Mary Garland Marks, a half sister of Meriwether Lewis. In this trunk was a will, in which Lewis made her his heiress to lands, of the extent of which I am ignorant, but which are now in the midst of the city of St. Louis . . . she compromised her claim for six thousand dollars."

That is probably of a nature with the legend of the jewels.

A Chief Justice Moore of Texas, a son of Mrs. Moore mentioned by Mrs. Skelton, told the Mr. Scott, above, that his father, William Moore, had somewhere on the Mississippi river recognized a gold watch that had belonged to Lewis, in Pernia's possession, and had taken it and returned it to the family. We have found Mrs. Grinder saying that Pernia appeared the next morning with Lewis's gold watch, but no such watch seems to be known today.

February 6, 1903, Sarah (Sally) Anderson, who had married a descendant, wrote Mrs. Dye: "The one point about Wm. Moore & Mary Marks that was unfamiliar I am afraid arose from my own obscure hand writing—namely that 'Mary Moore as well as her husband) met the lost French servant of Lewis on the streets of Mobile.' Family tradition asserts Wm. Moore met this servant *some where* presumably in New Orleans or Mobile & obtained from him papers & some articles which were Meriwether Lewis's and which had disappeared with this servant. . ."

There are those who scoff at all family traditions, but such beliefs sometimes have a core of fact that is obscured or lost in embellishment and transmission. One version of the lost property tradition says that Pernia was surprised on a Mobile or New Orleans street not only with the watch but with Lewis's rifle. As Bakeless says, that would be a strange place for Pernia to be carrying a rifle. Anyway, we know that the rifle was delivered up to a half-brother by Mrs. Neelly.

Mrs. H. M. Conklin of Corpus Christi, Texas, another great-niece, wrote Wheeler that "the gun Uncle Meriwether used in the expedition was given to my father, Col. J. M. Moore. It was sunk in a boat with many other relics when the Federal gunboats attacked this place in 1862." This may be the actual rifle Mrs. Neelly gave up, for its whereabouts today seem to be unknown. Still another letter, this time from Kate Harlan (she says Lewis was a first cousin to her grandmother's father), February 20, 1886, declares that "The servant who was travelling with him said he was thirsty during the night & that he gave him water several times."

There are still other expressions of opinion from members of the family. In the Nashville *Banner*, February 22, 1925, Miss Harriet Talbot wrote: "At first it was thought he committed suicide, but investigation furnished proof that he was assassinated by his French servant, who had stolen his horses and money and disappeared and was never heard of again. His mother always believed that he was murdered." If in family tradition after 116 years Pernia stole the horses, in another hundred he may be found making off with the journals.

In an address at the celebration of the creation of the national monument, Major Meriwether Lewis Anderson said, as reported by the Lewis county *Herald*, September 14, 1933: "The criminal was never found or convicted, for although, at the time, there was a report of suicide, his family never believed it and much subsequent evidence has strengthened their belief and that of historians that he was murdered." The only historian who in recent years has written about it takes another view, as we shall see.

No one in the family, descendant or in-law, has been so industrious as Sarah Anderson, whose writings about the Lewis and Meriwether families include a large book. She says: "And now regarding the matter of Captain Lewis' death—his family always maintained that he was murdered. . . . Mr. Jefferson's theory of suicide was expressed before this evidence came out." She does not tell us what "this evidence" is. "I wrote widely to the scattered branches of the family trying to get more definite evidence but always met tradition with invariably the same story"—that his servant killed him.

"I have been told the tradition of the vicinity where his death occured is murder, and that Grinder, the owner of the house where he died, was suspected but there was lack of evidence to support the charge. I have heard the Grinders assert Captain Lewis's sisters visited them. This can not be true. His only full sister, Mrs. Jane M. Anderson, so far as known, never left Virginia. . . . The half sister, Mrs. Mary (Marks) Moore lived in Georgia, and in her old age with her numerous family emigrated to Alabama and Texas. She died in Texas. She believed firmly her brother was murdered and transmitted this belief to her descendants. She would not have visited a family she suspected of complicity in his death."

If all the opinions expressed by members of the Lewis and Meriwether families, soon after his death and for more than a century later, were assembled they no doubt would prove only that family tradition in such matters is for the most part stubborn and worthless. The farther the tradition is removed in time from the actual event, the less trustwothy it becomes. If, as seems probable, the belief originated in Lewis's mother after she faced Pernia, it can hardly be dismissed as completely worthless. Even if it is assumed that both James Neely and Thomas Jefferson questioned the man, though there isn't a scrap of evidence to support such an assumption, it must be admitted, in our opinion, that if Lucy Marks questioned him she got closer to the facts. If we were a prisoner in the dock we'd far rather be questioned by a James Neelly, who seems himself to have been dishonest, or a Thomas Jefferson, who in his ready acceptance of Pernia's death showed an unusual capacity for belief based on rumor, than by an intelligent sharp-eyed sharp-tongued mother who had been awaiting the coming of her son, and on hearing of his death must have looked deep into the suspected man's soul, and have persisted in her questions until she was satisfied that she had elicited the circumstances and a full image of the scene.

# XVIII

## Was There

## a Coroner's Jury?

It is easy to believe that there was not. Grinder's Stand was on the very edge of the Chickasaw nation; it was nothing but Indian country west and south of it, and on the north and east there were only a few settlers. This is southern Tennessee hill-ridge country and it is only sparsely settled today.

But there is a strong tradition that a jury of some kind was called. No jury would have been called if it had been an unmistakable case of suicide. If there was a jury, was Neelly present? If there was a jury and he was present, surely he would have told Jefferson or Brahan or both that a jury was called, unless he had some reason to conceal the jury's verdict. If he was not present, but was there for the burial, was the corpse taken from its grave after he left the scene?

Some who believe it was suicide scoff at the idea of a jury. Typical of this position is a statement by Mr. William K. Kay, a National Park historian: "Lewis's death at Grinder's Stand seemed not to cause any great excitement in the area. If, as folklore has it, there was a coroner's inquest, no formal record of it survives. Indeed, the confused state of folk tales, the lack of competent testimony concerning an inquest, and the absence of record indicate that no coroner's jury met."

As late as 1959 Mr. Kay wrote: "Dr. Phelps traced the development of a theory that Lewis was murdered from its wistfully hopeful beginning to its acceptance in some circles as an article of faith. In supporting the suicide theory, Dr. Phelps gathered evidence overlooked by previous writers. Phelps' research and the lack of formal reply points toward Lewis's having committed suicide." That is a rather curious piece of reasoning in view of the fact that Phelps says, in the essay which Kay has in mind: "That a coroner's jury was summoned to inquire into the manner of death is highly probable."

Dr. Bakeless, who spent a lot of time in Tennessee searching the records and talking to people, says flatly: "A coroner's jury was called together, an inquest was held, and a verdict was rendered. The records of Maury County for this period have disappeared,* including the inquest record, but the various jurors often discussed the case, and the oral tradition of their views has come down in several of their families with surprising agreement as to the main facts. The jurors were Samuel Whiteside (foreman), R. M. Cooper, George Vincent, a certain Sharpe (or Shipp), a certain Carroll, and a certain Johnson.

"Since every coroner's jury is given an opportunity to view the body, this one presumably did so, as tradition among their descendants clearly indicates. Descendants of both Vincent and Sharpe say that Lewis was shot 'from behind slightly'—exactly what the post-rider said. There were apparently two wounds in the side and one in the head. There were no powder stains on the clothing or on the flesh, as there certainly would have been if Lewis himself had held the pistol. . . . Descendants' stories leave little doubt that the jurymen really believed it was murder—and after all the jury had a better chance to find the truth than anyone else.

"Why did the jury believe one thing and report another? Their statements to their families explain that, too. The plain truth is that they were afraid." In support of this statement Bakeless quotes the Frierson who appeared among the old-timers— "that the Jury were Cowards and were afraid to bring in a verdict

---

*Not all of them.

of murder, which they all knew was what they should have done. I could not imagine what they were afraid of! But some one said that the murderers had Indian Blood in their Veins, and they were afraid they would meet a similar fate." Bakeless says: "People who do not live defenseless in isolated farms on the Indian border will find it easy to scoff at their timidity."

Presumably Mr. Bakeless interviewed as many as possible of those who claimed to be descendants of jurors, as well as an investigator here and there, like Hugh Webster, who had talked to them, or whose father had. The assumption in this tradition is that Lewis went to the stable to see if the horses had been properly cared for, and was shot on his return, somewhere between the stable and the cabins.

Mr. Charles Morrow Wilson, widely regarded as a Lewis biographer,* says that Grinder was taken for trial to a town that did not then exist. We are in the realm of legend, in regard to jury, arrests, and trials, so it may be well to have a word of caution from W. J. Ghent, who in his time, according to Allan Nevins, knew more about the Lewis and Clark expedition than any other man alive. In a letter to Mrs. Dye, April 12, 1933, he said: "I am interested in this incident because it has to do with the credibility of old men's memories. My experience in dealing with such recollections has made me profoundly skeptical of their accuracy. I do not believe that at 11 years an average boy's interest in the pronunciation of an Indian woman's name would have resulted in a last impression, and I further do not believe that a man's statement at 78 of a pronunciation he heard 67 years before would be worth much in a court of history."

Very well. First a word about the post-rider, that is, the mail-carrier between Natchez and Nashville, who by one historian has been dismissed as a glory-seeker who was not born until the year of Lewis's death. An unclassified paper in the Webster file at the Monument says: "The story handed down by Robert O. Smith who was a post rider between Nashville and Natchez and who was the father of Robert A. Smith who signed the report of the legislative committee, that he, Robert O. Smith, in the early morning after Lewis was killed, found his body lying in the road with the mortal wound on the left side of his back and that a piece of

---

*See Appendix B.

patching used to wad old muzzle loading guns was found about
half way between Lewis's body and the barn. This would indicate
that Lewis had gone to see about his horses and while returning
was shot in the back from the barn or thereabouts."

If he was shot from the barn it could as well have been
Grinder as anyone else, especially if, as in one of Mrs.
Grinder's versions, not only Lewis but the two servants went to bed in the
guest cabin. Lewis might have left the servants there and gone to
take a look at the horses. There is a tradition that neighbors observed a sudden improvement in the financial condition of the
Grinders: in 1814 Grinder paid $250 for 100 acres on Duck
River, and this was, as Bakeless says, a "large sum on the frontier
in those days." Russell may not have known how much money
Lewis had on him when he left the fort; he thought it was about
$120, besides the check. Anyway, four and a half years passed
before Grinder bought the land. Possibly he saved the money
while keeping an inn and selling whisky to Indians. Possibly part
of it was money in Lewis's purse that was never found. Possibly
he robbed other wayfarers.

It is said that Lewis died just over the Hickman-Maury line
in Maury county. Hickman county in 1800 ran from its present
northern boundary to the southern boundary of Tennessee. Its
county seat was a hamlet called Vernon. The Spences say that in
1823 "the county records were removed from Vernon to Centerville," the new county seat. The courthouse at Vernon, built of
hewn poplar logs, was also removed to the new site, eight miles
distant. So far as is known, no records have disappeared from this
county.

Maury county was established December 21, 1807. Its first
court convened the following spring, and by November, 1809, a
circuit court was established. Among the first jurors was a
Thomas Whiteside. John Spencer was the first sheriff. Judge Turner's history of the county, from which we have taken these data,
gives an account of Lewis's death that is in some respects like Mrs.
Grinder's; but he says "it was found that a pistol ball had entered
under his chin and passed out through his skull. Suspecting foul
play, especially by Lewis's French servant, President Jefferson
caused a careful investigation to be made. He reached the conclusion that Mr. Lewis committed suicide. While there has been
a great deal of discussion of the circumstances ever since, Chan-

cellor W. S. Fleming, in his address of July 4, 1876, at Columbia agreed with that conclusion. Colonel Robert M. Cooper, uncle of Honorable W. F. Cooper and former Circuit Court Clerk of Lewis County, made the nails used in making the crude coffin."

Judge Turner, like so many who have written on this subject, gives legends and traditions as established facts. In his history of St. Louis in 1888, Billon wrote: "At about 3 o'clock in the morning of the 11th, Mrs. Griner was awakened by the report of a pistol from the room occupied by Gov. Lewis, followed in a little while by a second. On entering the room the Governor was found dead in his bed, with a bullet hole under his chin up to and through his skull." In earlier sources only Billon seems to have said that Lewis was shot under the chin, and it may be that Turner got his notion of it from Billon. If Lewis shot himself, it seems more likely that the muzzle was held under his chin than that it was held in such a way that the bullet merely creased his forehead.

One way to approach the matter of the jury is to learn, if one can, whether the names given as those of jurors actually lived in the area at that time. We know that two Shipps married the Grinder daughters, but all the Shipps seemed to have lived in Hickman county. The Coopers were in Maury, and were one of the oldest and most prominent families in the area: Matthew established a school before he became of legal age. One descendant was a United States Senator; another was a justice of the Tennessee Supreme Court and a legal author of note. Edmund Cooper, born in 1821, studied law at Harvard, became in turn a member of the legislature, assistant secretary of the U. S. Treasury, and secretary to President Johnson. A Henry Cooper ran against the same Johnson for the United States senate. A R. M. Cooper was circuit court clerk in Lewis county, 1844-56, and may have been the R. M. Cooper who is said to have been a juror in 1809. The Whiteside family also achieved some eminence. Buried in Hickman county is a Samuel L. Whiteside, born in 1820, who may have been a son of the Samuel who is said to have been a juror. If there were Johnsons, Carrols, and Vincents, they left no records that are easy to find.

William J. Webster, an attorney in Columbia, the seat of Maury county, gave a great deal of time to an investigation of the circumstances of Lewis's death, and has left the statement that the body was found across the line in Maury county, and that all the jurors were from this county. He caused a search to be made in the Maury county archives for a record of the inquest, and reported that it had disappeared. A number of persons, including a Tennessee state historian, Dr. Bakeless, and this writer, have searched the records and found no criminal docket for the fall of 1809.

In a letter dated January 29, 1932, Hugh L. Webster, a son of William, and himself an attorney, said: "I have been conducting a search for the report of the Coroner's jury who held the inquest, and which paper was seen by my father among the old papers of the Maury County Historical Society. My father remembered the names of the members of the jury and what was contained in the report. It is very apparent that the committee of the Legislature of Tennessee who were appointed to erect the present monument, had access to this paper, because in their report and resolutions in 1845 they state what it contained."

Lewis county was created by an act of the General Assembly, December 23, 1843. In 1848 its seat was moved from Gordon to its present site, on the ridge between Big and Little Swan creeks. The new seat was located on a fifty-acre tract that was donated by Hugh B. Venable and Robert O. Smith. It was called Newburg. Grinder's Stand was on Little Swan creek, near the Trace crossing.

The Assembly had a monument erected to Lewis. The report of the committee said, "Great care was taken to identify the grave. George Nixon, Esq., an old surveyor, had become very early acquainted with its locality. He pointed out the place, but to make assurance doubly sure the grave was re-opened, and the upper part of the skeleton was examined, and such evidence found as to leave no doubt of the place of interment. . . . Witnesses were called and their certificate, with that of the Surveyor, prove the fact beyond dispute. . . .

"The impression has long prevailed that under the influence of disease of body and mind . . . Gov. Lewis perished by his own hand. It seems to be more probable that he died by the hands of an assassin."

We have noted the letter written by one of William Clark's sons to Rev. James Cressey in Maury county, in which he said, "Have you heard of the report that Governor Lewis did not destroy his own life, but was murdered by his servant, a Frenchman, who stole his money and horses and returned to Natchez and was never afterwards heard of?" The committee reproduced this letter in its report, and by some who favor the theory of suicide it has been assumed that the committee's statement that murder seemed more probable was based on this letter and nothing else. If so, it was a remarkably unintelligent committee. Clark's son didn't say that Lewis had been murdered; he asked only, Have you heard of the report?—and went on to say that it was an important matter to him because he wanted no stigma "upon the fair name I have the honor to bear."

Among the Webster papers is the following: "According to the report of the Coroner's jury which at one time was in the possession of Mr. Frank H. Smith, Secty. of the Maury County Historical Society, the wound from which Capt. Lewis died was in his back behind his left shoulder and the report of the Coroner's jury was not that he committed suicide but that he came to his death at the hands of an unkonwn person, and that 'he might have committed suicide.'" Webster said that this jury was composed of R. M. Cooper, "some of whose grandsons still live in this same neighborhood, George Vincent, a Mr. Whiteside, Mr. Sharp, Mr. Johnson, and Mr. Carroll." In one copy someone has written in the name Shipp for Sharp.

If there was a jury and if one of the Shipps was on it, possibly it was a Shipp who took the record from the Maury county archives—for we have seen that both of the Grinder daughters married Shipps.

As for Webster, he could have erred in some of his details but there is no reason to think that he invented. When the son says his father remembered the names of the jurors, and their report, we do not have the faulty memory of an old man, but of a man in early middle age. On being asked whether his father had a good memory, the son said that his father went blind but continued to practice law for fifteen years, and had such a photographic memory that he would have the cases which he wished to cite in evidence read to him a time or two, and then, even before the U. S. Supreme Court, astonished people with the accuracy of statement with which he presented a case.

At the time the Lewis national monument was created, there was a renewal of interest in his death, and a good deal of writing about it in the Tennessee newspapers. A headline March 6, 1930, in the Lewis county *Herald* asked, WAS LEWIS MURDERED? and concluded that the committee thought that the theory of suicide never gained a foothold among the citizens of the area. W. W. O'Guin said in the Chattanooga *Times*, May 15, 1932, that "there are many persons who have talked with the pioneers of that section . . . who hold that Lewis was murdered." O. T. Hagan was reported by the Nashville *Banner*, October 15, 1933, as having said that "in his research in the neighborhood of the monument" he found that "everyone in the section accepts the belief that Lewis was murdered by Robert Grinder." It seems that the theory of murder won wide acceptance on little more than hearsay and rumor.

About all we can say is what Mr. Phelps said, that it seems "highly probable" that there was a coroner's jury. If there was, we cannot now be sure of what it said.

# XIX

# James D. Park:
# It Was Murder

After a committee of the Tennessee Assembly said it seemed probable that Lewis had been murdered, the belief that he was killed rather than that he killed himself seems to have been the dominant one for a long time. Even so, another forty years passed before anyone, except our anonymous school teacher, made an effort to investigate the matter. From about 1890 until the present moment there have been a number of investigations, though some of them, such as Moore's based on Malinda and Pete, have been less an effort to dig out the facts than to support the bias of the investigator. Now and then an investigation has been little more than an attempt to discredit the conclusions of a previous investigator. The emotions of some people have run hot in this matter. Bakeless reported that "the murder question is still so ticklish in twentieth-century Tennessee that a Hickman county antiquarian absolutely refused even to meet the writer to discuss it in Feb., 1946!" Thirteen years later no one whom we approached refused to talk about it, though in some Tennesseeans there is a wish to let the matter sleep.

Most of the investigators a half-century or more ago depended largely on oral tradition. Most of them never saw Neelly's,

Brahan's, or Wilson's letters, much less Russell's. A person may be able to dig some facts out of oral tradition if he is close enough to the time and the scene. The ones who should have dug the truth out of tradition and legend were the members of the committee who examined the corpse only a generation later, when both the elder Grinders were still alive. If there was a coroner's jury, then surely some member or members of it were then still living. Persons were living then who in a later time, after becoming senile and garrulous, were eager to tell all about it, and did.

We don't know why James D. Park became interested in the matter. He was an attorney who lived at Franklin. Wheeler says that Park "seems to have as thoroughly investigated the whole matter as was then possible. . ." In 1899, hoping to obtain from Park additional information, Wheeler wrote him at Franklin, "and received in reply a letter from his father, Dr. J. S. Park, announcing his son's death in 1897. I quote a sentence: 'The further my son investigated the matter the more certain he believed that Lewis was murdered.' "

Park began his investigation in the next to last decade of the last century. September 6, 1891, he wrote in the Nashville *American* an article on the death of Lewis, under the pseudonym of John Quill: "A mystery deep and dark has always hung over the death of Merriwether Lewis. . ." That was a common misspelling of his first name. Park then gave a brief account of the expedition, a short biographical sketch, an excerpt from Jefferson's life, and continued:

"The account of the death of Capt. Lewis was written by Mr. Jefferson in the light of the information which reached him at his home far away in Virginia. It would be interesting to know the exact sources of his information, if that were possible, and to judge for ourselves whether they were entirely free from suspicion. Probably the information which was carried to him did not embrace the idea of murder and robbery in the then wilds of the Indian border . . . whether the details of the death of Capt. Lewis ever reached there in official form cannot now be learned. The newspapers and chronicles of that day contain no mention of the death, so far as a patient search of some of their files has revealed it to the writer."

That is a temperate and scholarly approach but it shows that he was working largely in the dark. He knew about Neelly, for he had read Jefferson's account of the death, but apparently he did not sense that Neelly had made an official report. Having no knowledge of the other letters, Attorney Park shrewdly wonders what evidence Jefferson had on which to base an opinion "for whose truth I have no hesitation to make myself responsible." Park had to suppose that the evidence Jefferson had was compelling, or that Jefferson didn't know much about evidence, for the reason that his own investigation pointed to a wholly different conclusion. Possibly the most significant thing in Park's words is the indication of how potent and far-reaching the Jefferson statement had been. Park did not have the research facilities we have today; about all he was able to find in a library on the subject was Jefferson's words. He was working in the dark of oral tradition, as all investigators were to work the next fifteen years.

He goes on:

"The conduct of Mr. Neely, the Indian agent, as mentioned in Mr. Jefferson's account, seems to have been very strange. He had at the Chickasaw Bluffs volunteered to accompany Gov. Lewis from there . . . in order to look after and watch over his distinguished guest, whom he had found quite indisposed, and, as alleged, showing signs of a disordered mind. They had servants and horses in their train, yet the recapture of two horses that had strayed from the camp was deemed by Mr. Neely of more importance than the welfare and safety of his friend, whom he permitted to go forward with the servants while he remained a whole day behind to look up the horses."

Other investigators have thought it strange that, if Neelly thought Lewis deranged, he would let him go on a full day ahead of him. It is not so strange when we remember that this error, so often repeated, like the misspelling of the man's name, is Jefferson's. It seems probable that the first meeting of Lewis and Neelly was at the fort, and if we are to believe Russell, Neelly did not go with Lewis to look after and watch over him.

Park next gives a brief history of the Trace, telling his readers that every thirty or forty miles there was a "stand," a crude inn that offered lodging. At the time he was there "the site of 'Grinder's Stand' is still seen, marked by the ruins of the old stone chimney, a mound of earth, and the remains of a garden, or small clearing in the forest. . . . Even at this day the nearest habitation is one and a half or two miles distant. North of the site of the

old house and about 150 yards from it, at the side of the old road,
is the great explorer's grave. . . ."

As we noted earlier, Park's judgment of distance supports
that of some others, and raises a doubt: if he and Coues were
right, either the site now given is not the actual site of Grinder's
cabins, or it was not Lewis's grave that was found.

Park goes on to say that it had always been the firm belief
of the people of the area that Lewis was murdered and robbed.
That, in any case, became the general belief after the committee
made its report. We don't know what the general belief was in
the area before that; it seems likely that it was mixed, with the
more thoughtful persons accepting Jefferson and suicide. Park
says, "The oldest citizens now living remember the rumors current
at the time as to the murder, and it seems that no thought of
suicide ever obtained a footing here. The writer recently had an
interview with Mrs. Christina B. Anthony, who lives some two
miles from the Lewis grave, and has lived all her life of 77 years
in the neighborhood. . . . Polly Spencer, whom she knew well before her death about forty years ago, was a hired girl at Grinder's
when Gov. Lewis was killed. Polly had often told the circumstances of the murder as far as she personally knew them."

Attorney Moore, whom we found to be strongly biased in
favor of the Grinders, said of Mrs. Anthony that she was a garrulous old woman, that one of her relatives eloped with a Grinder
and she never forgave it, and that she did not by any means live
all her life in that area. If in 1891 Mrs. Anthony was 77, she was
born about 1814, or five years after Lewis died. Polly Spencer is
supposed to have been about 15 at the time. If she was 15 in
1809, and died 40 years before 1891, she died at about the age of
57. Unless Mrs. Anthony was an outrageous liar or a fool there
must have been a Polly Spencer, but we don't know that she was
at Grinder's when Lewis died, or that she was ever there.

If we assume for a moment that Polly was present, what did
she see and hear, according to Mrs. Anthony?

"She was washing dishes in the kitchen after supper with
some of the females of the family when they heard a shot in the
room where Capt. Lewis was sleeping. All rushed into the room
and found him dead in his bed." That's essentially Malinda's story
in respect to the time of the shooting. "Capt. Lewis, being fa-
tigued from his journey, had retired immediately after supper.

His only companion, she said, was a negro boy, who was attending to the horses in the barn at the time. Old Grinder, who was of Indian blood, was at once suspected of the murder, ran away, was captured on Cane Creek, brought back and tried, but the proof not being positive he was released. Only 25 cents was found on the person of Capt. Lewis after he was shot."

It is a rule of evidence that a witness may tell the truth in some matters, but not in other matters because of ignorance or malice. We are dealing here with a witness who was 77 years old, and probably garrulous, but our best judge of her as a witness would seem to be the attorney who faced her and talked to her. Park next gives a wild rumor as fact when he tells his readers that soon after Lewis's death Grinder moved to the western part of the state and bought a number of slaves and a farm "and seemed to have plenty of money. Before this he had always been quite poor." We know that Grinder did nothing of the kind.

A curious thing about Polly's story, as it comes through the mind of an old woman more than forty years later, is that Lewis was shot soon after he went to bed, and not about three o'clock in the morning, as Mrs. Grinder told Neelly and Wilson. She told Wilson that Lewis crawled forth, wounded, and twice begged for water, which she refused him. A conjecture is that some time after he went to bed Lewis came to the other cabin door and asked for water, and that Mrs. Grinder incorporated this fact into her tale, to embellish it or to show her fright, or because she was stupid and got things mixed up.

Mrs. Anthony told Park that "the people always believed old Grinder killed Mr. Lewis and got his money. She had never heard of the theory of suicide until the writer mentioned it to her. Mrs. Anthony was a young married woman, boarding with the father of Polly Spencer, when Polly told her these circumstances. Mrs. Anthony thus heard an ear witness, so to speak, relate the story of the murder, which is pretty direct evidence. She is a bright, active, and intelligent old lady, and has for many years kept the little hotel at the hamlet of Newburg, the county seat of Lewis county, which is just two miles east of the monument."

So we have one attorney who says that she was a garrulous old woman of low character, and another who says she was a bright intelligent old lady. If Mrs. Anthony lived with Polly's parents when she was a young married woman, and if it was at this time that Polly told her story, then Mrs. Anthony might have been about 25 years old, and Polly around 45. The time would have been about 1839, or before the committee made its report. Polly may have told the truth, but unless Mrs. Grinder was an invalid it doesn't seem probable that the Grinders could have afforded a girl to cook, or as a domestic servant, when they had a slave girl 12 years old, and apparently not enough cabin space to house more than two or three lodgers at a time.

Park says he talked to other persons living in Lewis and adjoining counties, "who remember the general belief at the time, that Grinder killed his guest for the purpose of robbery. He must have observed that Capt. Lewis was a person of distinction and wealth; that he was almost alone, and that he probably had money with him." The story of suicide "was doubtless invented to cover up the double crime of robbery and murder, and seems to have been the only version of his death that reached Mr. Jefferson and other friends in Virginia."

Coues thought that the Park essay was "literally a lawyer's brief." It is plain that he had a legal mind. His father was a doctor. His was, then, a family of some importance and responsibility. But he proved nothing either way, any more than Moore did with Pete and Malinda. The deeper he dug into the matter the more he became convinced that Lewis was murdered, but possibly none of his witnesses was any more trustworthy than Mrs. Anthony. As for Polly, if she was present at the Grinder's, then Mrs. Grinder's story collapses. If she was not present, she was as big a liar as a certain Negro seems to have been, whom we shall meet in the next chapter.

## XX

## *Vernon S. Pease:*

## *It Was Murder*

There is little information to be found out about Vernon S. Pease. His article, which appeared in *The South Magazine* in February, 1894, or only two and a half years after Park's, is not of much interest except for the replies it brought forth. Here and there, as in the opening—"Mystery deep and dark has hung for a century around the death. . . ."—his choice of words indicates that he had read Park. But in some respects their versions of the death are quite different.

He starts off with an allusion to the "uncharitable and impossible theory of suicide"; gives a paragraph to the Expedition; extols Lewis's work and life; describes the situation of the grave "in the heart of an interminable forest, miles from human habitation, by the side of an old abandoned road"; describes the Monument "worn with age and honeycombed by the action of the elements. Its rough, porous surface makes an excellent ground for the clinging moss which already overspreads the inscriptions and threatens the very summit of the shaft. The stranger, unfamiliar with the epitaph once chiseled there, could never learn from the inscriptions for whom the lonely grave was made. To him it would stand a memorial of perfect solitude and desolation."

It is true that for nearly eighty years the grave and its small monument were almost forgotten.

"Near the road and some few yards distant from the monument is an old pit, as though it had been a cellar, now nearly leveled, with two piles of crumbling stone; marking the location of a settler's house of an early day with the inevitable rock chimney at either end. Other clearings, that were once the habitation of pioneers, are indicated by old cellar pits and crumbling chimneys at intervals of half a mile along the old road, showing that in an early day quite a colony had located here."

He gives a paragraph to Lewis county, "an impoverished area" which seemed never to thrive—and it can hardly be said to thrive even to this day. He comes then to the "octogenarians, those faithful choniclers of past events . . . the only living and authentic witnesses"; and having warned us that for him there is no difference between the actual facts of history and the tales of old-timers, he says that the true story of Lewis's death would never have been told, "but for the happening of a most unforeseen accident.

"A party of money-loving Yankees, land prospectors, stopping at the nearest railway town, were told the story of the treasure buried in the old cellar near the monument. With characteristic greed and energy they organized a secret expedition to hunt for the buried gold, and on a bright Sunday morning set forth. . . "

The people in the county seat, he says, had even laid aside the jack-knife and whittling-stick, so deep was their sense of peace and repose. Then there came a person from the Monument area to report "the desecration about to be practiced on the historic and legendary relic of the county. A council of war was not necessary to bring out the available martial force which, half a dozen strong headed by the sheriff, was soon bearing down. . ." The gold-seeking Yankees fled for their lives.

The reader is tempted to suspect that Pease was pulling the legs of as many people as would pay attention to him. He says that the Yankee invasion and the armed force that put it to flight was thought to be a joke in the outside world, but so aroused the people of the area that for weeks they could talk of nothing else. The discussions "brought out many facts generally forgotten or covered with the rubbish of backwoods tradition. A committee of responsible citizens went to the monument and removed a portion of the moss that the inscriptions might be read and dates ascertained. Old citizens became reminiscent, authorities were marshaled, dates compared, hearsay and legend rejected, until it was established beyond doubt that just eighty years to a day before the . . . attempt was made to raise the buried treasure, Captain Merriwether Lewis was cruelly murdered and robbed in the house that covered the spot marked by the old cellar."

Whether Pease intended a hoax or actually believed all this is not known. His bland statement that all hearsay and legend were rejected (what old-timers they must have been!) is enough to remind one of the words of a Mussolini biographer, Roman Dombrowski, who tried in vain to clear up the mystery of the Duce's death, and then wrote: "There are so many mysteries, contradictions and ambiguities connected with Mussolini's death, that we are driven at last to query whether there is such a thing as objective, historical truth."

If there is, Pease didn't care much about it, for he now becomes an authority on the Grinders and the kind of cabins they occupied. There were a "hundred" dangerous Stands and "Among these was old Joshua Grinder, a half-breed Indian. . . . His family consisted of a daughter and two sons—base by nature and thoroughly depraved by the long course of crime through which their unnatural father had led them. Then, too, he kept about him a retinue of desperate creatures, ready to join in any act of violence and plunder. His inn, like most of those that were built along the old trace, was of rough, unhewn logs, comprising four or five rooms of the rudest sort. . . .

"Judged by the standard of that section the 'Grinder Stand' was attractive. Its front was adorned with a porch, built from home-made boards with pole posts, and the front room was bespread with a rag carpet; luxuries then unheard of in that backwoods country. A white servant girl, famous for her fine cooking, was kept on the place, and the fame of the stand for dinners soon reached from one end of the trace to the other." It looks as if Polly Spencer will again be called as a witness.

From the first, he says, Grinder was regarded with suspicion by the settlers around him, and was spied on by a committee of citizens. "Ugly stories were soon abroad, charging the Grinder stand with the responsibility of the sudden and mysterious disappearance of several rich planters who were known to have crossed the Tennessee river and whose course could be traced to that locality." Grinder, knowing that he would soon be exposed as a robber, resolved to make one more haul and flee. There then rode up to his door—

".... a gentleman, well mounted and attended by a colored boy. . . . His manner, dress and traveling outfit showed him to be a man of unusual distinction for that lonely country. All appearances indicated that he was a man of wealth. . . . Before going to his room, Captain Lewis left instructions for the entertainment of his traveling companion, John Neeley, in event of his arrival during the night. . . . At supper he entertained them with tales of his travels and adventures while crossing the continent."

Possibly Pease took all this out of his hat, or possibly he got it from old-timers. He conjectures that during this friendly and mellow evening Lewis told of the mineral wealth he had found and fired the imagination of the cruel halfbreed. Putting on the trappings of the writer of romantic fiction, he proceeds: "He had been in his room but a few minutes, the members of the family being still engaged in their various duties about the house, when the sharp report of a rifle rang out on the night air." The Grinder family and servants rushed to the guest chamber and found Lewis dying, with a bullet hole in his left temple. The Grinders hastily buried the body back of the house, set fire to the cabins and fled. Drawn by the fire a hundred persons rushed to the scene. An inquest was decided on. The corpse was taken up and a man was chosen to act as coroner; and "After hearing the testimony of Polly Spencer, the servant girl who was in the house when the tragedy was committed, and other witnesses, a verdict was rendered of 'murder at the hands of Joshua Grinder'. . . . To this day the theory of suicide has obtained no footing in this place. . . ."

If it was his purpose to stir people up, he did not write in vain. General Marcus D. Wright entered the fray by reminding his readers that in *Ware's Valley Monthly* for June, 1876, he had settled the matter, after he had "consulted with Maj. Bolling Gordon, Hon. A. M. Hughes, Robert M. Cooper, and Robert O. Smith, all old and reputable citizens of Maury county. . . ." He appends part of a letter from Hon. John V. Wright, for three terms a congressman from the district of which Lewis county was a part.

John V. Wright undertakes to correct a "tissue of errors and mistakes." He had had, he says, a "long and exhaustive conversation with old Col. Robert M. Cooper, who at that time was one of the oldest and most intelligent, as well as the most truthful and reliable, men in the country, and he told me that it was suspected at first that Capt. Lewis' valet, a Frenchman or Spaniard, murdered him but he said it was finally settled in the neighborhood, and universally believed that Lewis committed suicide. Grinder was not suspected, and neither was he a half-breed Indian. . . . I never heard from any source that Grinder committed the murder. . . . There was an old Negro man living when the monument was built who made the coffin in which Lewis was buried. The old Negro pointed out the spot where the grave was and described the material out of which the coffin was constructed, rude oak planks, and nails made in a black-smith's shop by the old negro. Cooper was an old man, perhaps over seventy. This was in 1854 or 1855, and Col. Cooper was a citizen of Lewis county and clerk of the circuit court. He must have been a grown man of twenty-one when Lewis was killed in 1809."

If there was a jury, and this was the R. M. Cooper who was on the jury, it is amazing that Congressman Wright did not mention the fact.

Another reply to Pease quotes Jefferson, as General Wright had in 1876, and concludes: "Could anything be more positive or convincing than this statement of Mr. Jefferson? . . . There is one additional fact, however, of an opposite character, which I feel it my duty to mention, although it does not alter my conviction that Governor Lewis killed himself in a fit of insanity. The fact I refer to was the published death at or near Charlottesville, Va., seven or eight years ago, of an old negro man who was a body servant of Governor Lewis in October, 1809 when the latter was killed. The papers reported the old negro as solemnly stating on his deathbed what he had for more than three quarters of a century often repeated, that his master, Governor Lewis, was murdered at the Grinder stand, in 1809. He was but a boy at that time, and in another room. . ."

This is the legend of the Negro servant, which has appeared in a number of places. If it is to be assumed, for a moment, that this dying Negro told the truth, then it must be assumed that he is the servant who went along to help with the Lewis trunks. If the Negro died seven or eight years before 1894, and was a youth of eighteen, say, the year Lewis died, he would have died at about the age of ninety-five. That is possible. And it is possible that he could have thought of himself as a Lewis servant, if it was understood that he was sent along to help Lewis with his packhorses.

To all of this Pease replied that he had hoped to be challenged; was happy to have so worthy an adversary as General Wright; had only summarized some of the local traditions, which he found more "reliable, and much more reasonable, than the historical accounts"; that his article was based on a dozen journeys through Lewis county, and discussions with "at least half a hundred old citizens of that and adjoining counties. Not half a dozen of the number had ever heard of the suicide theory, but said they always heard that Captain Lewis was murdered." He had had "a long talk on the subject with the late Captain Flannigan, who for more than a quarter of a century was clerk and master of the chancery court in Lewis county. He had heard of the suicide theory, but declared it to be an outside story not credited in the neighborhood." The story outside the neighborhood rested chiefly on Jefferson. Pease thinks that General Wright leaned too much on Alexander Wilson's account, in which he himself found a "vein of incredulity running through the whole."

He then makes this rather startling statement: "Captain John Nixon, the old surveyor of Lewis county who located the tomb and assisted to open it when the state of Tennessee built the monument, told his nephew, the late Chancellor Nixon . . . the same account of the murder that Mrs. Anthony gave me, and said that when the skeleton was unearthed the forehead was crushed, showing indubitable proof of a shot in that portion of the body. General Wright's account of a shot in the chin would be news to the Grinders and citizens of Lewis county. Captain Nixon must have been a young man at the time of the Lewis murder. His kinfolks describe him as a very intelligent man and a great stickler for the facts. The late Chancellor Nixon was famous for his probity."

So now we have Colonel Cooper against Captain Nixon, Chancellor Nixon against Congressman Wright, Polly Spencer against Malinda, and in a moment we will have Webster against Moore. Dombrowski concluded his somber reflection with these words, "and to wonder how many lies and distortions be concealed in the pages of history."

More, no doubt, than any man has ever dared imagine.

## XXI

# William J. Webster:

# It Was Murder

The liveliest of all the controversies over the manner of Lewis's death occurred in the fourth year of this century. It was precipitated by a letter from J. A. Cunningham in the Nashville *Banner*, May 12, 1904.

After saying that the facts about Lewis's death might be of interest to newspaper readers he proceeds: "My mother, Grace Cunningham, who would now be near 100 years old if living, was acquainted with the family at whose house Gov. Lewis died, and I have heard her repeat the story of his death many times as given to her by Mrs. Grinder, which was substantially as follows:

"Gov. Lewis, accompanied by his servants, came to her house in the afternoon and asked for entertainment. Her husband was not at home, but as they kept public house she agreed for him to stay. Soon after he stopped she discovered that he was acting strangely, and when night came she left her room and took lodging with a negress in a cabin only a little way from her house, where Gov. Lewis was. In the night she heard a pistol shot and soon afterwards heard him groaning. She opened the door of her cabin and saw him crawling on his hands and knees, coming towards her. When near her he said to her, 'Good madam, will you please give me some water and heal my wounds?' She gave him water and asked him why he shot himself. His reply was that if he had not done so someone else would. No doctor was near and he died before they could get one."

That is still another version of Mrs. Grinder's story. We don't know how old Mrs. Cunningham was when she heard the story: if she was 35, she heard it at about the time the school teacher heard it, but this version is not at all the one Mrs. Grinder told the school teacher. It is likely that Mrs. Cunningham heard it much later than that. We don't know how much it was transformed in passing through Mrs. Cunningham's mind, or how much he left out in his letter to the newspaper. In the Cunningham version we are asked to believe the preposterous story that Lewis would shoot himself and then beg Mrs. Grinder to heal his wounds.

At the time Cunningham sent his letter to the *Banner*, William J. Webster, an attorney living at Columbia, had been for many years investigating Lewis's death. Bakeless says, "The late William J. Webster . . . who devoted a great deal of study to the death of Lewis, who lived near the scene, and who interviewed many descendants of the coroner's jury, is supposed to have seen papers showing exactly what the verdict of the coroner's jury was." As has been noted in an earlier chapter, Webster seems to have been largely a self-educated man; he does not express himself with the fluency of a Park or a Moore. But the strange thing is that having spent so much time investigating the death, he had accepted so many errors which his research ought to have corrected.

He read Cunningham and published a reply in the Nashville *American* for May 23, to which the editor gave a number of subtitles, including this:

> Col Wm. J. Webster, of Columbia
> brings out some facts to prove that
> Mrs. Grinder, Gen. Lewis' hostess, did
> not tell the truth.

Webster begins by saying that he does not agree with Cunningham, yet admits that it will be "only theory against theory"; and then says:

"It is true that Thomas Jefferson thought he committed

suicide. This thought was based on the idea that the man was imbued with a principle and intended to carry it out. But, after ages, we can think that, if the man was imbued with only one principle, to get to Washington as quick as he could, this ought to have been a full explanation against any suicide theory."

That is curious reasoning in a lawyer, but so it was in Moore, too. Webster says it is true that Lewis was given to "abstracted thought and isolated himself from the world while thinking, and on that theory the suicide is based.

"Mr. Cunningham presents the theory that at 3 o'clock at night he shot himself and crawled back for water. Against this theory we present the following: He was found dead on the roadside about 100 yards from the house; there had been no outcry and nobody to find his body until, about 10 o'clock the next day, Robt. O. Smith, then a mail rider, found his body about 150 yards from the Grinder house and near where his monument now stands; and if Mrs. Grinder knew that Lewis had committed suicide at 3 o'clock the night before, why did she wait until Robt. O. Smith found him on the roadside at 10 o'clock the next day?"

If Lewis did die by the Trace, either north or south of the cabins, it seems reasonable to imagine that he was buried in the area where he died, since there were no cemeteries near. The curious thing in the Webster version is that Lewis was north of the cabins, whereas it is today assumed that the stable was south.

Webster says that it "is a part of history that the husband of Mrs. Grinder was arrested and accused of the murder of Lewis," and he finds it "strange that Mr. Cunningham relies only on the testimony of the wife of the man accused. . ." He says the distance between Grinder's and Washington was 1500 miles (an amazing exaggeration) and that Jefferson could have known less of what actually occurred than any citizen in the area where Lewis died. Jefferson knew "only the idiosyncracies of the man."

He returns then to the thought that Lewis was in haste to get to Washington; that he had decided to go by horseback instead of water because it was faster; that he had already "ridden down the man who was with him"; and that it must be assumed that the governor of "the whole Louisiana Purchase" had a considerable sum of money on him. "He had an Indian guide and a Spanish body servant, and was going as fast as he could to Washington. He was found on the roadside by the mail rider, Robert

O. Smith, with no money, no watch nor trinkets, only papers were found on his person. . ."

So it is his theory that Lewis, out for a stroll, was shot; his Indian guide and servant rushed to his relief and were also shot and hidden, "in order to create the impression that they had committed the murder, and ran away, but they were never found or arrested." That is almost as fantastic as some of Mrs. Grinder's versions. Webster says he is 56 years old, and had talked to persons who would be much over a hundred years old, if still living. He concludes with a plea for justice to the memory of a great "Anglo-Saxon."

A number of persons replied to Webster. W. W. Southgate, who in 1883 had told about Polly Spencer and Mrs. Anthony, summons Polly again as a witness, and has her tell substantially the story he had her tell twenty-one years earlier. J. W. Hensley wrote the newspaper to say, "I have often talked with old men on the manner of Gov. Lewis' death. My great-grandfather, Hickman Hensley, settled on Swan Creek over a hundred years ago, in five miles of the Lewis monument. I have frequently heard my father, Dr. E. H. Hensley, say that it was thought that Gov. Lewis was murdered. Another tradition is that he killed himself. Maj. J. H. Akin is of the opinion that Lewis killed himself. He bases his conclusion on a statement made by his grandfather, who was one of the oldest settlers of Wayne county." Hensley concludes by saying that the Lewis grave was identified by discovery in it of shop-made nails—but possibly some other coffins in the graves north of the Grinder cabins had been put together with such nails.

E. C. Lewis of Nashville also had his say. In 1890 business caused him "to spend a good deal of time in Lewis county" and while there he became interested in Lewis's death. In 1902 he determined to investigate it; he wrote to "the oldest citizens. . . . talked with a great many and got up a correspondence with a number through the efforts of Judge Weatherly and D. L. Voorhies, both of Lewis county. I never met a man among the old and constant residents of Lewis county who believed that Capt. Lewis killed himself."

He brings forth a Paris Cooper, over 80 years old, who had written him that "Capt. Lewis' wrists were both cut clear through to render him helpless. This was likely done while in bed. A Mrs. Chronister, who is quite an old lady, wrote that her father was about 14 when Capt. Lewis was killed and lived near. Mrs. Chronister says that often her father told her that when found Capt. Lewis was sitting by a tree shot in the mouth and dead, with both wrists cut—'and it did not look reasonable,' said her father, 'that Capt. Lewis could have killed himself with both wrists cut clear around.'" But that's as reasonable as the assumption that murderers would bother to cut his wrists to make him helpless.

Lewis says he had wanted to have the body exhumed a second time to see if it could be discovered by an examination of the bones whether it was suicide or murder. Paris Cooper wrote him that he was at the second burial, but "the skeleton had almost entirely gone to decay, only the teeth were intact, and some of them were filled with gold. So little was then left that no coffin was used, but a hole was made in a large rock, the remains deposited in this cavity and the monument erected over.

"Grinder . . . was tried for his murder and cleared, but if they clear people at this day who murder it cannot be expected that they did any better or worse a hundred years ago."

On June 2 Cunningham replied to Webster. He finds Webster's argument peculiar, again quotes Jefferson, and says: "Robert O. Smith told him that he was a mail rider at the time and found the body of Lewis on the side of the road. . . . But within ten days . . . he gets out a second edition, and says his first was not right. Between these publications someone who knew informed Mr. Webster that Robert O. Smith was an infant only a year old at the time of Mr. Lewis' death. . . . It will be remembered that Mr. Webster says that Smith told him this in 1875, which was about twenty-nine years ago, yet he never found out that it was not true until about ten days ago, and we may reasonably suppose that during these twenty-nine years Mr. Webster has been repeating this story of the death of Lewis as told to him by Mr. Smith—believing all the time that it was true. This is no reflection whatever on Mr. Webster, but is a striking illustration of the absolutely untrustworthiness of what may be designated 'chimney corner' history. . . ."

July 22 Cunningham wrote: "Capt. Joel P. Morrison, who is now 81 years old, was born and raised in Hickman county, and lives near the Lewis county line and was well acquainted with the people of Lewis county long before Mr. Webster was born.

"Capt. Morrison is now present as I write and authorizes me to say on his authority that Mr. Grinder was not arrested for the murder of Gov. Lewis. He has known the Grinder family all his life and feels morally certain that he would have heard of the arrest of Mr. Grinder years ago if it had ever occurred. He says all this talk of murder and the arrest of Grinder has originated within the last thirty-five or forty years."

He gives some facts about Morrison's past and continues: "Horatio Clagett, who is now 85 years old, is president of the First National Bank of Centreville. He has lived in Centreville sixty-seven years, and during this time was well acquainted with the people of Lewis county. . . . He says: 'He is sure Grinder was never arrested for the murder of Lewis . . . no breath of suspicion has ever been whispered against them. Clagett says he had repeated talks with Pete, a negro who was owned by Grinder and was present at the time of Lewis' death. His version was substantially as that given by Alexander Wilson. . .'"

This, of course, is the Pete who, according to Attorney Moore, competed with Malinda in telling the story.

Cunningham says that the "negro girl who was present lived to be very old. She told substantially the same story up to the time of her death about twenty years ago. A short time before the death of this negro she was visited by the Hon. W. P. Clark of Centreville, and Col. J. H. Moore . . . who took her statement. . .

"Maj. James H. Akin, of Williamson county, says his mother . . . was four years old at the time of Lewis' death. She lived to a ripe old age, retaining her mental faculties to a remarkable degree and always said she understood it was suicide. . ."

Though rejecting "chimney corner" history, Cunningham rested his case on it. Webster had no talent for sarcasm, or the case did not emotionally disturb him. Undertaking to "answer the various articles" with "facts obtained from conversation from numbers of people" he made one more statement and called it a day.

"Lewis must have fallen on the east side of the road because members of the jury of inquiry came from the Maury County side of the line between Maury and Hickman. I have had diligent search made for the papers in Maury County, but, so far, fail to find any report from the jury of inquiry." He names the members of the jury and goes on: "I have talked with Grif Whitesides, grandson of Mr. Whitesides, and he said his grandfather believed it to be a case of murder. I have talked with Mr. Johnson, grandson of Mr. Johnson, of the jury of inquiry, and he believed the same." The descendants of Vincent and Sharp "give some very minute details as to the wounds; both of them agree that he was shot from slightly behind, the ball passing out in front on the opposite side in a straight line, and that there were no powder stains on his clothes or flesh. One other thought he had two wounds, one through the side and the other through the mouth. . . . I am a busy lawyer and haven't time to hunt up all of them, but I don't believe the others will vary much, if any, even after this long lapse of time, in their statements at to what their ancestors informed them.

"It may be considered as settled that he was buried on the side of the Natchez Trace Road where he was found, as some reports say, leaning against an oak tree." He says Lewis was buried where he died, which was where his monument stood; and "it is a physical fact that this is 150 yards from that house, where it formerly stood, as shown by the remains of the 'old rock chimney', . . . Tradition in this county even goes further and names the man who they think killed him; Grinder was not at home, and it is not believed that he was a participant actively in the crime, but he is shadowed with suspicion that he was a particeps criminis. . . .

"They dispute that Robert Smith, Sr., the father of Robert O. Smith, was mail carrier on the Natchez trace road at that time. Recently, in a conversation with two of the grandsons of Robert Smith, one of them Robert Smith Aikin, in the presence of one of the parties who doubted it, stated to me in Columbia that his grandfather most certainly was mail carrier on this road, and added that 'he lies buried by the side of Meriwether Lewis, in Lewis County.' He is a grandson of Robert Smith and a nephew of Robert O. Smith; his brother was with him and confirmed this statement—so this is also settled.

"Now we come down to a case of special pleading. The suicide theorists, Mr. Cunningham, Alexander Wilson's report and Thomas Jefferson's letter, are all traceable to one and the same source; Mr. Cunningham gets his information from his mother, who talked with Mrs. Grinder; Alexander Wilson's report was made from conversations with the Grinders; Thomas Jefferson obtained his information from Mr. Neeley. . . . So that all sources of information of suicide evidently emanate from Grinder's stand. . . .

"Mr. Cunningham is disposed to make light of my communication and hurled at me the ipsi dixit of Thomas Jefferson. . . . I am not a man worshipper. . . . I don't care how high the authority; I want to know his means of knowledge and his opportunity of speaking the truth, and whether it is what he thought or what he knew. . . . There are people who would think it almost sacrilege in an humble citizen to do this, but he is regarded so highly that he is almost worshipped, but let an intelligent public look at the source of his information and judge it.

"Now, I am done with this discussion. I am satisfied in my own mind whether I have satisfied anybody else or not, and so drop the matter."

Not all those who argued one way or the other dropped it at that time, and there have been many expressions of opinion on the matter since; but not until recently has an investigator again attempted to arrive at the facts. We will not look at the conclusions of Mr. Dawson A. Phelps.

## XXII

# Dawson A. Phelps:

# It Was Suicide

The reader has seen with how little or how much cogency two attorneys argued for murder who were familiar with only a part of the evidence presented in this book up to this point. He will now see with what cogency a noted historian argues for suicide, who again did not have all the evidence that has been laid before the reader.

In the Oregon Historical Society are these words over the signatures of Douglass Adair, formerly editor of *The William and Mary Quarterly*, and Dawson A. Phelps, National Park Service historian: "Apparently most of Lewis's contemporaries who knew him well (Jefferson, William Clark) were either not surprised to learn that he had killed himself, or had extremely persuasive evidence that his death was suicide. Does the murder theory reflect the unwillingness of American scholars (the frontier specialists in particular) to admit that a man as great as Lewis had shown himself to be . . . could become so spiritually desolated or mentally ill that he could kill himself?"

Mr. Phelps felt that he settled the matter in an essay in the above quarterly. He starts off, as a number of others have done, by saying that the death "was put into authoritative form" by

Jefferson; dismisses as worthless the family tradition; and declares that almost nobody thought it was murder before William Clark's son wrote the letter to the Columbia clergyman.

He thinks that two events in the 1840's, the creation of Lewis county and the erection of the monument, "revived speculation concerning the manner of Lewis's death." If speculation was *revived*, opinion could hardly have been unanimous before that time. He finds it "not remarkable, considering nineteenth-century moral attitudes, that many persons living in the vicinity should have dismissed the possibility of suicide, substituting in its stead the more exciting, dramatic, and perhaps more acceptable stories of murder which, embellished and enlarged in the passage of time, became established folklore."

He thinks that such stories began to appear in the 1890's because in 1893 Coues published a new edition of the Biddle and Allen journals, and repeated the story that James D. Park had recently told. Though Park said he had many informants, Phelps says his "informant" was Mrs. Anthony, and that the best comment on her story is that by Coues, who found it "second hand, indirect, and circumstantial only; thus being fatally defective." If Polly Spencer was on the premises when Lewis was shot, Mrs. Anthony's story is no more second hand than Neelly's to Jefferson. The Coues edition, Mr. Phelps thinks, evoked a series of articles, letters, and "highly colored stories" of Lewis's death. "One story was that Lewis had crawled some 150 yards from the inn before death overtook him; that his body was suffered to lie there until late in the morning when a passing post rider found it. This tale was told in 1875 . . . by a man claiming to be the very post rider himself. Subsequently, it was learned that the glory seeker had not been born until the year 1809."

The story said *not* that Lewis crawled 150 yards but was shot down at the spot where he died. It was Mrs. Grinder, whom Mr. Phelps accepts as a witness without question, who in one of her versions said that Lewis crawled away. As we have seen, Webster first gave the name of Robert O. Smith, but when challenged by Cunningham said that Robert O. was the son of Robert Smith, the mail carrier. Mr. Phelps surely knew that Webster had corrected himself, that he had got Robert O. and Robert turned around. We wrote Mr. Phelps to ask on what he based his statement that Robert O. or Robert was born in 1809, and he replied:

"The birth date of Robert Smith is taken from a letter of J. A. Cunningham. . . ." Cunningham did *not* say that Robert was born in 1809, but that "Robert O. Smith was an infant only a year old at the time of Lewis's death." Whether born in 1808 or 1809 is a trivial matter. The important thing to know, if this were possible, is whether there was a mail carrier at the time named Robert Smith. We spent a lot of time, and members of various Federal departments spent a lot of time, trying to learn if there was a Robert Smith on the Trace in 1809.

Mr. Nyle M. Jackson, executive assistant to the Postmaster General, says, "these post riders were employed by private companies who contracted with the Post Office Department to transport the mail. . . . the Department would not necessarily have kept a record of the individual riders." After members of his staff had searched through various records, Dr. Robert H. Bahmer of National Archives advised us that "Colonel Benjamin Joslin of Nashville, Tennessee, was the contractor for conveying the mail on the Natchez Trace" in 1809, but "there is no reference to his post riders. The incoming letters from contractors and others to the Post Office Department, which might have contained some references to Lewis's death and the rider on the route at the time were disposed of many years ago before the National Archives was established and possibly were lost in the Post Office fire of the 1830's."

Mr. Phelps says next that "Another story concerned the inquest. Several men living in the 1890's claimed to be grandsons of members of the coroner's jury. While they unanimously admitted that their ancestors had found a verdict of suicide, they now maintained that, because of some unnamed fear, the jury had brought in a verdict which it did not believe to be true. That a coroner's jury was summoned to inquire into the manner of death is highly probable. Yet even this is conjecture, because all the judicial records of Maury County have disappeared. Statements by men who believed or claimed to believe that their ancestors were on the coroner's jury have little value as historical evidence."

It depends on the quality of the men. In a letter to us, Mr. Phelps says he "should have added a qualifying clause and said 'judicial records concerning the death of Lewis.' Actually, Maury County has carefully preserved its records. They are stored in the Court House and run to many hundreds of cubic feet in

volume." How well we know it, for we examined tons of them.
But the point here is that the record of the coroner's inquest is
supposed to have been among those at a historical society.

Mr. Phelps thinks it highly probable that there was an inquest, and that the grandsons said the jurors thought it suicide.
If it is assumed that there was a jury, and that the grandsons of
the jurors agreed on what their grandfathers said, it is going pretty
far to say that such evidence has "little value." As for the unnamed fear, we have found Dr. Bakeless saying that people who
do not live defenseless on isolated farms next to Indian country
"find it easy to scoff at their timidity." It may not have been
timidity. We have noted the tradition which said that the jurors
thought it murder but agreed that it could have been suicide. We
cannot look into the minds and emotions of those six men, if
there were six, but it is easy to imagine why in their circumstances
they would favor suicide as the more prudent and expedient
choice.

Mr. Phelps now comes to Grinder, who "as a respected citizen
raised a large family," some of his decendants becoming "locally
prominent." Mr. Phelps in such statements leans on attorney
Moore, whom we met with Pete and Malinda. Though in Tennessee histories many names of people are given who lived in
Hickman County, the name Grinder or Griner does not appear
except in the book by the Spences. Mr. Phelps finds Malinda's
story, as given by Moore, to be "substantially the same as Jefferson's." It should be the same, if the source of both is Mrs. Grinder.
He thinks the story of the death as a murder filtered from folklore
into "standard treatises"; and after citing a few of these he says
that prior to the appearance of the Coues edition, "those writers
who had occasion to treat the life of Lewis accepted Jefferson's
version without question." We don't know how many of them
accepted it without question. After all, they were in no position
to spend months or years investigating the matter, and so took
what possibly seemed to be the best statement on the subject
they could find. Persons who accept as fact a statement merely
because it was made by a famous man can hardly be said to have
any sense of scholarship or of history.

Mr. Phelps now approaches the heart of the thing. He says
that when Lewis went to Washington in 1806, soon after his return from the ocean, he was acclaimed, but that as governor a

year and a half later he "was abruptly plunged into a startling change in atmosphere. Lewis found himself beset with the boring and frequently sordid details of a colonial administrator. . . . To make matters worse, all was not well in his official family. He quarreled bitterly with his second-in-command, the territorial secretary, Frederick Bates." On first glance those seem to be fair statements, but the fact is that we don't know that Lewis found his task boring and sordid, or that he quarreled bitterly with Bates. Bates from the first seems to have been the aggressor, and Lewis time and again seems to have done what he could to conciliate him. Bates's letters suggest that one thing that kept him in a smouldering fury was Lewis's unwillingness to quarrel with him.

Mr. Phelps now says that having "arrived at the age of thirty-four without yet acquiring a competence, Lewis plunged into land speculation in an attempt to make his fortune. He soon exhausted his meager capital and, as security for his debts, pledged his income for many years." All that except the concluding statement has been covered. Lewis did *not* pledge his income for "many years." Mr. Phelps did not tell his readers that in the settlement of the Lewis estate the assets were more than enough to cover the debts; that it was not speculation but a stupid blunder in the War Department that brought the crisis on him; and that the Federal Government eventually confessed the error by paying to the estate, with interest, the sum it had denied.

He next takes up Lewis's "bitter and despairing reply" to the Secretary of War; the pledging of his assets; and his departure. Somewhere along the way "rumors became current that, being 'indisposed', Lewis stopped at New Madrid, Missouri. If such was the case, he apparently improved, and in the words of the *Missouri Gazette,* October 4, 1809, he 'set off in good health for New Orleans.' . . ." But when he arrived at Fort Pickering he was in a state of mental derangement, and there his friend Gilbert C. Russell "took the suffering man into his own quarters. . . . The fact that Lewis was mentally unbalanced at the time of his arrival at Fort Pickering cannot be doubted."

Two standard dictionaries on our desk define deranged as "disordered, insane." If Lewis arrived at the fort with malaria he may have been mentally unbalanced, though as we have seen he told Madison only that he arrived very much exhausted from the heat of the climate. He took some medicine and felt better the next morning. Unless by derangement is meant temporary impairment of faculties by debility and fever, it hardly seems likely that he would arrive deranged in the afternoon, and the next morning write a rational letter.

Mr. Phelps based his statement of derangement on the letter of Captain James House, which was considered in an earlier chapter. It seems to us strange that a historian can accept without question a statement by a man about whom he knew nothing, not even how to spell his name,* based on a statement by a second person, whose name in unknown to us, yet dismiss as of little value the statements of grandsons, some of whom were substantial citizens in their area. It seems even stranger to us that Lewis's word on the matter is rejected in favor of that of anonymous persons. In a letter to us, Mr. Phelps said that Attorney Moore "was a distinguished lawyer, lived at Centerville [a very small town], and knew the Grinder descendants well." He scornfully dismissed Attorney Webster, a more distinguished lawyer. As for Captain James House, we know nothing about him. His handwriting suggests that he had had little formal schooling and was a rather unimaginative man. We don't know if he wrote Bates because he belonged to the Bates faction, or for another reason.

In the opinion of Mr. Phelps, Russell's letter (the first) was "somewhat restrained," by which he may have intended to imply that Russell softened the facts. If Mr. Phelps had seen Russell's second letter to Jefferson it is strange that he ignored it, for it is more significant than the first. He says that Lewis had a "desire to have Captain Russell accompany him" and so delayed his departure several days, during which he decided to proceed by land instead of water. We have seen that by the time Lewis wrote Madison the morning after his arrival, he had decided to go by land. As for the other, we have no more reason to suppose that Lewis wanted Russell to go with him than to suppose that the proposal was made by Russell.

Mr. Phelps then comes to James Neelly and says that "Jefferson was by no means restricted to what Neelly could tell him. . . . He also received the letter from Captain Russell, and one from Captain John Brahan . . . who had heard the details from Neelly's own lips in Nashville." If hearing a story constitutes additional

---

*Mr. Phelps spelled the name James Howe.

or stronger evidence, we must assume that if Neelly had told his story to a score of persons the case for suicide would override the most stubborn doubts. We are told that Jefferson "was able to interview John Pernier (Pernia), Nov. 26, 1809" and that in "all probability this evidence was supplemented by Wilson's report." We are told that Pernia was an "eyewitness" to Lewis's death. We simply don't know.

He feels that though "very little is known" about Neelly, the fact of "his appointment to a responsible office, and in the absence of evidence to the contrary," it can be said "that he was a man of good character, and presumably a competent witness." We have brought forth the evidence to the contrary. He says Neelly is the "only witness from whom we have a written report who was with or near the man constantly during the last twenty-three days, save one, before the firing of the fatal shots." We don't know that Neelly was at the fort all the time between his arrival about September 18 and his departure September 29, or that if he was he saw Lewis every day.

Mr. Phelps now gives the Neelly statement that he "furnished" Lewis with a horse to pack his trunks on and a man to attend to them, with no comment on Russell's denial of this. He says that at the Indian agency near the present Houston, "Neelly noted that Lewis 'appeared at times deranged in mind';" that they left the agency probably Oct. 6 and after "traveling about 150 miles farther they must have reached the Tennessee River on the evening of Oct. 8. Crossing either on the afternoon of the 8th or the morning of the 9th, they traveled throughout the day and camped at a point not far from what is now the village of Collingwood, Tennessee." If they journeyed fifty miles a day over that rough hill-country trail it was pretty good riding for a deranged man. "During the night, two of the horses escaped. At Lewis's request, Neelly remained behind." Neelly did not tell Jefferson that Lewis asked him to remain behind. Brahan told Jefferson, though whether because Neelly told him or he assumed it we don't know. The proponents of suicide are strong in their belief that Neelly and Lewis were friends and that Neelly went along to watch over him. But they bring forth no evidence to support either assumption, and we have found none.

Mr. Phelps says that Neelly determined the manner of Lewis's death "from the stories told him by the two servants and Mrs.

Grinder." We don't know how he determined it, or indeed whether he actually determined it. Though Mr. Phelps had read Wilson, to whom Mrs. Grinder said that she was *not* alone, and Moore, who put both Pete and Malinda on the scene, and Neelly, who said Mrs. Grinder was alone, he passes over this without comment.

He says that Brahan failed to mention what he calls "the highly significant remark which Lewis, after having fired the fatal shots, made as his servant entered the room: 'I have done the business my good Servant give me Some water.' These words could refer only to the action which Lewis had from time to time been contemplating since arriving at Fort Pickering." To say flatly that for weeks Lewis had been thinking of killing himself, without making the slightest attempt to reconcile what Pernia is alleged to have heard with other versions of a story by a woman who was either stupid or a liar, is to go farther than any other writer has gone in reading the mind of a man who cannot speak. Mr. Phelps assumes that Lewis was deranged when he shot himself, and a few moments later spoke clearly and rationally; that the servant correctly understood what was said; and that the servant told the truth. He even goes so far as to say, without a scintilla of evidence, that Jefferson had "from Pernier, an eyewitness, [a] detailed oral account of Lewis's death."

Mrs. Grinder's story as she told it to Wilson he finds "identical in its main outlines with those of both Neelly and Brahan." Why Mr. Phelps keeps bringing Brahan forward as a witness, who presumably knew only what Neelly told him, it is impossible to say. He thinks that "Additional details related to Wilson by Mrs. Grinder bear directly on the mental state of Lewis during the last hours of his life. . . . Unconsciously she revealed one of the measures which Neelly had deemed necessary to protect his friend; when Lewis asked for gunpowder, 'the servant gave no distinct reply'—obviously evading the issue." It must be said again that there is no evidence to support the view that Lewis and Neelly were friends. If the servant gave no distinct reply, it may have been indistinct only to Mrs. Grinder. In one version of the tale, there was a whole canister of powder in the cabin where Lewis is said to have been shot. But the strangest thing in Mr. Phelp's argument here is that if it is to be assumed that Lewis journeyed a whole day through dangerous country with empty guns and that his powder had been taken from him, murder becomes far more plausible than suicide.

Mr. Phelps in his essay almost never uses the words possible or probable, never conjectures or surmises, but from first to last makes positive and unqualified statements, taking from each version of the tale known to him those items which support his thesis and rejecting those which do not. His complete acceptance of Mrs. Grinder is dismaying. Her story to Wilson, for instance, gave Phelps the "impression that she had been a badly frightened and hysterical woman. This impression is strengthened by her verbose account of Lewis's last moments and her lengthy recital of his last words." On the other hand she may have been trying to hide something, or perhaps she was a gabby woman by nature.

He then comes to the "hypochondriac affections" and goes so far as to cite a droll and whimsical passage in Lewis's journal (given on an early page in this book) as evidence of a mood of depression. Those who hunt for insanity in Lewis drag forth things that are true of all men and would make them all insane. With obvious approval he gives Jefferson, on redoubled vigor and alarm to friends, without thinking it necessary to bring forth supporting evidence; and then says: "With this background, the statements of Neelly and Russell that Lewis experienced a mental breakdown were easily credible." One hardly knows what to make of such argument. The Russell letter which he cites did *not* say or even imply that Lewis had a "mental breakdown."

"Does it suffice?" Mr. Phelps asks, meaning his argument. "Proponents of the murder theory say no, alleging that both the Neelly and Wilson stories emanate from Mrs. Grinder. This is not true. The two servants witnessed the event." The two servants are supposed to have been asleep in the stable. Mr. Phelps thinks it inconceivable that Neelly should have accepted Mrs. Grinder's story "without the confirmation supplied by the servants." It may be inconceivable to Mr. Phelps that he would have, or to us that we would have, but it certainly is not inconceivable in a man with so little sense of honor that he made off with Lewis's weapons.

He concludes with the Natchez Trace, on which he is said to be an authority, and makes these astonishing statements: ". . . it was not, in 1809, a dangerous road. The mail passed over it regularly. No robbery had been reported for years." In frontier

areas the mail passed regularly over many roads that were dangerous. The absence of report of robberies has never necessarily
meant the absence of robberies. What does he do with Alexander
Wilson's statement a few months after Lewis's death?—"I met a
soldier on foot . . . who had been robbed and plundered by the
Chactaws." Even the National Park Service survey of the Trace,
which Mr. Phelps now and then quotes with approval, makes
note of the infestation by bandits; for instance, under the photograph of the Red Tavern it says: "Here was located one of the
stands which accommodated travelers over the Trace. According
to local tradition, many of the bandits who preyed on travelers
made a rendezvous at or near this place." Indeed, Mr. Phelps
himself in one of his published essays quotes a man named
Hildreth, who in 1805 wrote that the journey over the Trace "was
made in companies of fifteen or twenty men. . . traveling together
through the wilderness, that they might assist each other if attacked by robbers or sickness." What Mr. Phelps is telling us is
that only four years after Hildreth wrote, the Trace was a perfectly safe place, though the notorious Hare was caught about
1812; and four years after that William Cooke, U. S. agent to the
Chickasaw wrote the Secretary of War (September 22, 1816):
"No person that has traveled the road in the year 1815 from Nashville to Natchez has been a stranger to the complaints which
travellers frequently made of having their horses stolen by Indians. . . ."

John Bakeless, a scholar not given to highly-colored statements, spent years in research for his book on Lewis and Clark.
Of the Trace he wrote, "Robbery was frequent all along the
Natchez Trace. . . . Dark tales were afloat of purses that disappeared along the way, and there is no doubt whatever that
Lewis's purse did vanish on the night of his death, never to be
recovered."

That is only one of the significant things on which the proponents of suicide are silent.

Mr. Phelps concludes: "In the absence of direct and pertinent
contemporary evidence to the contrary, of which not a scintilla
exists, the verdict of suicide must stand."

# XXIII

## *Suicide or Murder?*

For himself and for some who read his essay, Mr. Phelps settled the matter. The reader who has come with us to this point may now favor one view or the other. We feel much as Coues felt nearly seventy years ago when he said that probably the mystery would never be cleared up, and as Wheeler felt ten years later when he said the evidence was too circumstantial and contradictory. We have evidence today that neither man knew about. Though the reader must have the whole picture clearly in mind by this time, it may serve some purpose to bring all the more significant facts, possibilities, and questions together in a recapitulation as brief as we can make it.

Those who argue for suicide present a pretty simple case. They accept without supporting evidence all that Jefferson said about Lewis, from early childhood to the day of his death. They believe that Lewis became deranged and made attempts on his life before he reached the fort, and while there; that he again became deranged at the Chickasaw agency; and still again at Grinder's, where he took his life. They not only accept Jefferson without question; they also accept Neelly, Mrs. Grinder, and Pernia, about whom they have known almost nothing at all. If

their witnesses were all unimpeachable, they could close their
case.

But all their witnesses fall under suspicion. Of Mrs. Grinder
it is impossible to say whether she was a stupid, bungling woman
or deliberate liar. Presumably she told Neelly on October 11 that
she was alone when Lewis rode up, but she told Wilson the children were there. Mrs. Cunningham and the teacher were silent
on this, but Malinda said she and Pete and Mrs. Grinder's children were present. Mrs. Grinder told Wilson that Lewis called
for spirits and drank a little, and then began to pace and talk. She
told the teacher that he sat by the cabin and was sociable, then
challenged two or three men to a duel, ate supper and retired.
She told both Neelly and Wilson that the two servants went
to the stable, the teacher that they went to bed in the cabin with
Lewis. It may be that she never knew where they slept. She told
Neelly that at three o'clock she heard a pistol fire and in a few
moments a second one; the teacher, that it was two or three hours
before daybreak. Malinda said the shots were fired just before
morning. Mrs. Grinder told Neelly (as reported by him) that
on hearing the shots she awakened the servants, but they came
too late to save him and he died in a short time. She told Wilson
only a few months later she was too frightened to do anything until morning, and then sent two of her children to bring the servants. She told the teacher she heard three shots, and a little
later watched Lewis crawl away to the Trace and disappear.
Malinda said that immediately after the shots were fired Pernia
came running, and they all went to the cabin where Lewis was.

Mrs. Grinder told Wilson that Lewis came to the kitchen
door for water and begged her to heal his wounds, and that she
refused him water and kept her door barred until morning. She
told Mrs. Cunningham that she opened the door and gave him
water. She told the teacher that Lewis begged for water in vain
and then crawled away toward Little Swan creek. Malinda says
they gave him large quantities of water, all of which he vomited
forth. Mrs. Grinder told Wilson that after the first shot Lewis fell
heavily to the floor and cried, "O Lord!" though this first shot is
said merely to have grazed his forehead. By the proponents of
suicide it seems to be assumed that she clearly heard what Lewis
said through two log walls, in a cabin twelve or fifteen feet from
the one in which she stood. She told Mrs. Cunningham that she

heard him groaning, and on opening the door saw him on hands and knees crawling toward her. She told the teacher that after the third shot she heard someone fall and say, "O Lord, Congress, relieve me!" Malinda's story is that there were two quick shots and Pernia came, though it is not clear whether she meant that he came from the stable, or from one cabin to the other.

Mrs. Grinder told Wilson that she peered between logs and saw him "crawl for some distance," then sit by a tree, return to the larger cabin, and at last come again to the kitchen door. She told Mrs. Cunningham that she gave him water and asked him why he had shot himself. If she was calm enough to give him water and ask why he had shot himself (and how did she know that *he* had?) she surely lied when she told Wilson she was paralyzed by fear.

She told Wilson that after daylight she sent children for the servants and they came and found him on the bed; and he then showed them his wounds and begged them to blow his brains out. None of this appears in her story to the teacher, or in Malinda's. It may be an absurd invention, for if Lewis was lucid enough to talk, and able to move, he would have been able to shoot himself again.

She told Neelly that Lewis lived but a short time; Wilson, that he did not die until the sun was above the trees; Mrs. Cunningham, that he died before she could get a doctor; the teacher, that sometime after daylight the servants went into the woods and found him and brought him to the cabins. In this version he died sometime during the forenoon; in Malinda's, not until noon.

In her story to Neelly, or Pernia's, Lewis said to his servant that he had done the business and wanted some water. In her story to Wilson he said, "O madam! give me some water and heal my wounds." Mrs. Cunningham had him say, "Good madam, will you please give me some water and heal my wounds?" It is possible, of course, that if he was shot and did not die at once he said a number of things, and that in one version of her tale Mrs. Grinder recalled one thing, and in another version, another. There presumably was a long interval of time between her story to Wilson and to Mrs. Cunningham. That in both she has Lewis ask for water and relief of his wounds suggests that there may be truth in this part of her story. If there is, in our opinion it points more to murder than to suicide.

It certainly can be plausibly argued that Mrs. Grinder suffered some confusion, and with the passing of time some failure of memory; but it is going pretty far in trying to produce an honest witness to say that confusion or poor memory or both explain all these discrepancies: she immediately aroused the servants, *or* did not call them till hours later; had him pace the yard and talk like a lawyer, *or* sit by the house and chat and rush forth to challenge men to a duel; refused him water, *or* opened the door and gave him drink; saw him crawl around in the yard and back to the cabin, *or* over to the Trace and out of sight; shivered with terror all night behind a barred door, *or* went to the other cabin to give him water and question him.

It is possible that she was an honest but stupid or very confused woman. It is just as possible that she was trying to cover up. It is not necessary to assume that her husband was guilty; it is only necessary to suppose that she was horrified at finding a famous man, the governor of Upper Louisiana, dead on her premises. To assume that her governing wish was to tell the truth and nothing but the truth would be unrealistic. Her first thought, if she was like the majority of people, was to get out of the predicament in the easiest way she could. A tale of suicide there, or anywhere, for a person running an overnight inn, is far better than a tale of murder. There is the possibility that some settler in the area, like the mysterious Runion or Runions, shot Lewis in the cabin or while he was on his way to or from the stable. There is the possibility that Pernia told her that Lewis had shot himself, and either that she believed him or thought his story for her and her family as good as any other. In either of these or a similar case, some of the words which Mrs. Grinder attributed to Lewis could have been remembered from his talk the previous evening.

As for Neelly, it is in our view childish to assume that because he was a Federal official he was a man of character and honor. A number of writers have shown a remarkable sensitivity when dealing with him and Mrs. Grinder, and considerably less than the same credulity when dealing with any of the proponents of murder. It seems clear in his letter that Russell had a pretty low opinion of Neelly. Even if it is assumed that Neelly had a fair claim against Lewis for services, he made off with Lewis property the

value of which was enormously out of proportion to any just claim
he could have made. As for Neelly's presence on the scene, about
that we know nothing. We don't know with whom he talked. We
don't know if he examined the guns to see if they had been fired,
or the corpse to determine the nature of the wounds. We don't
know if he was present when Lewis was buried or had gone on
to Nashville. And if Mr. Phelps is right in his conjecture that the
party rode 150 miles in three days, we don't know why it spent
five or six days covering the hundred miles from the fort to the
agency.

We know practically nothing about Pernia. In a standard
volume on evidence, circumstantial evidence is analyzed under
ten headings. Motive, Opportunity, and Means are presumed to
establish a prima facie case of probable guilt. Pernia had all three.
William Seagle, a distinguished attorney, says that "strong circumstantial evidence has always been regarded as more reliable
than direct evidence." The circumstantial evidence against Pernia
cannot easily be put aside.

Some have called him a Frenchman, some, a Spaniard. Mrs.
Grace Miller calls him a "free mulatto." He may have been devoted to Lewis. On the other hand, he may have been brooding
over a sense of injustice and wrong. We don't know how much
Lewis owed him in back wages, but apparently Pernia told Jefferson it was $240. In terms of the 1961 dollar, that was from twelve
to fifteen hundred dollars in 1809. Surely Pernia knew that Lewis's
creditors had come on him and that his master was in a desperate
financial situation. And so we must ask how he was feeling and
thinking. We must wonder why he did not remain behind to help
Neelly find the horses.

In regard to opportunity it makes no difference whether we
assume that Pernia went to the stable to sleep or to the cabin with
Lewis. In either case he had the opportunity, and Neelly, so far
as we know, was a long way from Grinder's Stand. Pernia could
have given the Negro a pretext for going to the cabin, and could
have told him later that while he was there Lewis shot himself.
A Negro slave with the slightest sense of prudence would have
kept his mouth shut. Pernia certainly had the motive; many
murders are committed in this country every year for only a frac-
tion of the sum that Pernia said was due him. And with Lewis's
pistols and knife, or with his own weapons (for he certainly didn't

make the long journey from Nashville to Washington unarmed),
he had the means.

Let us for a moment imagine what possibly happened. Pernia,
brooding over his back wages and fearful that he would never
get them—feeling perhaps that the most he could ever get was
the currency that Lewis had on him, and that this was the only
chance he would have to be with Lewis with Neelly off the scene—
resolved to kill his master. Whether he went to the cabin with
Lewis, as Mrs. Grinder said in one version of her story, and after
Lewis was dozing on his buffalo robes seized a pistol and fired
at him, or came from the stable and slipped into the dark cabin
and fired, hardly matters. Either way is easily conceivable. The
first bullet only grazed Lewis's skull. With the other pistol Pernia
fired again, shooting Lewis through the left chest, below the
heart. Lewis then came up from the bed to defend himself and
was attacked with a knife. Pernia slashed at him in the dark,
wounding him in arms and legs and at last cutting his throat.

He found Lewis's purse and possibly some other items and
slipped back to the stable. What did Mrs. Grinder do? If we
accept her story to Wilson, she kept the door barred and waited
for daylight. When Pernia came at daybreak, he told her that
Lewis had killed himself. She had no good reason not to believe
it. If neither Lewis's windpipe nor jugular was severed, it is possible that he did crawl forth and beg for water and ask for help.
Or possibly he had asked for water earlier in the evening. If it is
said that Mrs. Grinder would not confuse his asking for water
earlier with asking for water after he was shot the obvious retort
is that the different versions of her tale show that no limits can
be placed on her capacity for confusion. It is possible she got so
mixed up that she simply didn't know what happened.

Pursuing a little further this imaginary reconstruction of the
scene, it is easy to see Pernia looking into the Lewis trunks. It is
easy to see him taking some of the Lewis garments as a payment
on his wages. And when Neelly rode up, who was the first person
to meet him? Pernia, no doubt. If we are to believe Russell, both
Pernia and Neelly were immoderate drinkers, and urged drink
on Lewis. Possibly some comradery had developed between them.
And if Lewis because of illness or heat and debility had mani-
fested after leaving the fort a form of behavior that Neelly thought
irrational, how easy it would have been for Pernia to say that

Lewis went out of his mind and killed himself. If Neelly then
questioned Mrs. Grinder, what reason had she to tell him more
than Pernia had told her? When morning came did she send all
the children away to safety? Did she arouse Pernia at daylight,
or say that she did because she felt that she should have done it?
It doesn't matter. Pernia—to go on with the conjecture—told
Neelly that he entered the cabin and found Lewis wounded and
dying, and that Lewis told him he had done the business and
wanted some water. Did Pernia think he was making a stronger
case for himself when he said that Lewis confessed that he had
done it?

Is this conjectural reconstruction any less plausible than what
the proponents of suicide ask us to believe? They ask us to believe that a man familiar with firearms from childhood, the use
of which for him must have been almost second nature, aimed at
his head with a pistol (not a rifle), evidently intending to shoot
through his brain, and only grazed his skull. He thereupon fell
down heavily crying, "O Lord!" Taking the other pistol he fired
again, presumably aiming at his heart, but actually shooting somewhere below it, and as far down as his intestines in one account.
Instead of taking his rifle now, or reloading a pistol, we are asked
to believe something more incredible still—to believe that this
man, the soul of fearlessness, who wished to die, then crawled
forth and begged for help. That is exactly what he might have
done if he had been shot by someone else. Unless the knife
wounds are dismissed as pure legend, we are next asked to believe
that he staggered or crawled back to the cabin and hacked at his
arms and legs and throat in a clumsy and feeble attempt to finish
the job. And through all this the proponents of suicide have him
rational every time he speaks!

To those convinced of suicide it is pertinent to put a few
questions to which they have never attempted to give answers.

1. Without reservations they have accepted Attorney Moore
as a character witness for the Grinders. He put not only the
Grinder children but Pete and Malinda on the scene. Neelly saw
the children and the slave or slaves or he did not see them. It
would be our guess that he never saw them. If they were hidden
from him, the question is why? And what do the proponents of
suicide do with Mrs. Grinder's absurd statement that there was
nobody present who could take Lewis's horse to the stable?

2. If, as Phelps and Bakeless believe, and as we believe, it is "highly probable" that there was a coroner's inquest, why was Neelly silent about it? If he remained, as he told Jefferson, to see Lewis buried, was the body exhumed for an inquest after his departure? We simply don't know how long Neelly was at Grinder's. It was a two-day ride (three at the outside) from Grinder's to Nashville: if Neelly left Grinder's the 12th he must have spent three or four days in Nashville before he wrote to Jefferson.

3. Russell apparently knew that Lewis had on him when he left the fort about $120 in currency. That was six or seven hundred 1961 dollars. He could not have spent much of it on the way to Grinder's. Not a single writer known to us who has argued for suicide has mentioned the fact that a substantial sum of money disappeared, never to be found. Who got it? And why was James Neelly silent about it?

4. Why have the proponents of suicide been silent on all the matters in Russell's letters that either reflect unfavorably on Neelly or flatly contradict him? Why was Neelly so specific about gunshot wounds and silent about knife wounds? If there were no knife wounds, why didn't he put the rumors to rest?

5. Less than a year after Lewis died the story was abroad that Pernia had killed himself. August 21, 1810, Jefferson wrote to Captain W. D. Meriwether: ". . . you probably know the fate of poor Pierney his servant who lately followed his master's example." Is this another instance where "all the facts I have stated are either known to myself, or communicated by his family or others, for whose truth I have no hesitation to make myself responsible?" So far as anybody has been able to learn, it was only a rumor. If Jefferson could be convinced and positive on nothing more than a rumor, without supporting evidence, are all his notions of Lewis to be accepted as gospel?

So we come to the question to which nobody has yet found a satisfactory answer: How did he die? It may be that he was so sunk in despair and illness and impairment of his faculties that he did fantastically bungle the job of killing himself. It may be as Billon and others reported long ago, that he was found dead on his bed with a bullet through his mouth or under his chin. It may be as Nancy Higgins said, that when her father helped open the grave in 1848 he saw a bullet hole in the forehead of the skull. It may be that the Lewis grave was never found—that Grinder took Wilson's money and forgot the promise and that wild hogs found the corpse and scattered the bones or that Grinder himself scattered them. Or it may be as some members of the jury are alleged to have said, that he was shot from behind.

Mr. Phelps and his followers think suicide has been established as a fact, but in our opinion it must be said in all fairness to the evidence that we still don't know how he died. After his long search of the records, Bakeless wrote a Mrs. Roush, March 12, 1948: "My private vote is for murder, but as the evidence is inadequate I cannot make a flat statement." Nor do we. But if a gun at our head forced us to choose, the choice would be murder. It is a little too much tax on our credulity to believe that Meriwether Lewis, even insane, could have spent hours with three guns and a razor in an effort to end his life. Writing of Sacco and Vanzetti, convicted of murder and executed nearly forty years ago, Judge Musmanno says: "It is beyond reason that two men who bore, without contradiction, the reputation of being considerate, generous, and gentle in their everyday dealings with their fellow men could suddenly become skilled, hardened robbers and conscienceless killers."

It may be beyond reason but not beyond possibility. And there until we have more evidence the matter rests.*

---

*Mrs. Grace Lewis Miller, who for many years has been busy on a biography of Lewis, and who is said by some of her friends to have no doubt that it was murder, may know of evidence that has not been presented here.

# APPENDIX A

## *Opinions Pro and Con*

In general the early historians declined to take a position in the matter, saying simply, as Paul Allen said soon after Lewis's death, that "Captain Lewis died in 1809, on his way to Philadelphia to superintend the publication of his journals." But when a Tennessee legislative committee considered a proposal to erect a monument to Lewis, the question whether he had killed himself or had been murdered was forced into the open, though the reasons for this are not wholly clear. Historian Phelps seems to feel that the chief, perhaps the only, reason was the letter which Clark's son sent to the clergyman in Maury county.

In its report to the legislature, or assembly, the committee, as we have seen, expressed the view that "The impression has long prevailed that, under the influence of a disease of the body and mind . . . the Governor perished by his own hand. It seems more probable that he died by the hands of an assassin." It needs to be pointed out again that those words were written and signed by a committee of responsible citizens only thirty-nine years after Lewis died.

From this time until about 1890 an occasional opinion was expressed but there seems to have been little interest in the matter; but from 1890 until the present, opinions, pro or con, have been expressed by scores, possibly by hundreds, of persons, and in nearly all instances without an iota of evidence to support them. Those who have favored suicide apparently had read someone who said it was suicide, and those who have favored murder had read someone who inclined to that view.

Now and then one hedged his remark, as Theodore Roosevelt did: "Lewis . . . died, as was supposed, by his own hand, in a squalid log cabin on the Chickasaw trace—though it was never certain that he had not been murdered." On the other hand many were as unqualified in their statements as J. B. Killebrew, who like so many misspelled Lewis's first name, and said flatly, "Merriwether Lewis committed suicide. . . ."

Coues and Wheeler were two able and responsible men. As we have seen, they gave a lot of time to an effort to discover how Lewis died, and found themselves unable to reach a conclusion. It was in 1893 that Coues wrote: "The affirmation of suicide, though made without qualification, has not passed unchallenged into history; and the mystery of the tragic event will probably never be cleared up. Undoubtedly Jefferson wrote in the light of all the evidence that reached him in 1813; but it appears that his view of the case was far from being that of persons who lived in the vicinity of the scene at the time. That Governor Lewis did not die by his own hand, but was murdered and robbed, was common report at the time, as vouched for by some persons still living. . . ."

Wheeler wrote a decade later, after exhaustive research, that it was then too late "definitely and absolutely to decide this question." As we have seen in an earlier page, he thought all the evidence "circumstantial, contradictory, and indeterminate" but concluded that the "preponderance of testimony is hardly in favor of suicide." It was Wheeler who first expressed the view that "the name of Jefferson" had given "a fictitious weight to the theory of suicide. . . ."

In a book published in 1901, William R. Lighton reasoned along lines that have been popular with many writers: "Although several writers have given their best efforts to erasing what they seem to consider a blot upon his reputation, the weight of opinion seems to sustain Mr. Jefferson's statement that he committed suicide." By "several writers" he possibly had in mind Coues and Wheeler. It is not known what he meant by the weight of opinion; he did not go to the primary sources.

In its annual report of 1903, The American Historical Association said, "A guest, at the time, of a wayside settler some sixty miles southwest of Nashville, it was reported that he had committed suicide, a theory which Jefferson, possibly his closest friend, accepted without

question; but it was, and still is, believed by many that he was murdered for the small sum of money upon his person at the time."

Two years later one who wrote under the name John Swain began
in a popular magazine that embellishment which with certain writers[*]
has been carried to preposterous lengths. He told his readers that a
heavy storm was raging when Lewis wrapped a buffalo robe around
him and lay on the floor. A shot was heard. Lewis was found dying, a
pistol beside him. "Grinder circulated the report that Lewis had shot
himself. . . . At Washington then, and by many historians since, Grinder's story has been believed; but by the settlers of that vicinity and
by the women who lived at Grinder's, only one opinion was ever entertained—that Grinder had murdered him for his money." Swain
visited the site in 1905 and met, he says, an old-timer who, on being
asked about the monument, said, "Some chap was murdered up there.
The place is ha'nted."

In following opinion pro and con through the decades since Coues,
one cannot miss the heavy weight of Jefferson's words. Ripley Hitchcock wrote, "On a journey to Washington in 1809 he stayed for the
night at a rough wayside inn near Memphis, Tennessee. In the morning he was found dead, probably by his own hand, for he was subject
to attacks of great depression." Nobody ever said he was, except
Jefferson, and those who have blindly followed Jefferson.

By 1908 Dr. Perley Spaulding was writing in a popular magazine,
"While on a trip to Washington he suffered a temporary attack of insanity, and committed suicide. . ." This was to become the widely
accepted version of the matter, though there would be a dissenter now
and then. Louis Houck, for instance, in his three-volume history of
Missouri, published in the same year, said that "although Jefferson
accepted the report that he committed suicide this was not the case
with the people who lived in the vicinity of the Grinder place at the
time. On the contrary, it was the common report, that he had been
murdered and robbed and many circumstances pointed to that conclusion. . . . So strongly was Grinder suspected, that he was indicted
in the county where the death of Lewis occurred."

And Rufus Blanchard in his history of the cession of Louisiana
was even more positive: "Meriwether Lewis was murdered and robbed . . . by Joshua Grinder, Oct. 11, 1809. . . . It was rumored at this
time that he committed suicide, but doubtless this originated in the

[*]See the next appendix.

east, where he was known to be of a hypochondriac disposition, but which affliction had entirely disappeared with his active, out-of-door life in the west. It was theory, groundless and cruel, that even the perpetrators of the crime did not stay to urge in their own defense."

Hitchcock leaned on Jefferson, Houck probably on Coues or Wheeler. Historian Constance Skinner seems to have been leaning on someone when in 1920 she wrote: "Here he was shot. For a long time the impression prevailed that he had taken his own life in a fit of depression. Later investigations, however, have led to the conclusion that he was robbed and murdered by the half-caste, Grinder, who kept the inn. But the belief of Lewis's family was that the Governor had been done away with by his Spanish servant, not only for the money on his person but for the sake of certain documents which Lewis was taking to Washington. Whether Lewis fell a victim to the rapacity of the ill-reputed Grinder, or whether his death was but one more knot in the intricate skein of Spanish intrigue, will now, probably, never be known. But, at least, the theory of suicide no longer beclouds his name."

It was to becloud his name more than ever, though in the year that Skinner found his name in clear sunshine, Luke Voorhees supported her in his *Recollections*: "In October, 1809, Lewis . . . was proceeding to Washington . . . when he was murdered." Six years later, George R. Gilmer, a former Georgia governor and a friend of the family, was not so sure: "In the morning his throat was found cut, and he dead; whether by his own hand, or others in search of his account of the place where gold was to be found, is not certainly known."

In 1929 *The Pageant of America,* produced under a number of distinguished editors, says in volume two that Lewis "was murdered probably for the money and for certain documents on his person." Two years later Clifford Smyth was equally positive: "Jefferson's view of the tragic climax to a brilliant career was generally accepted until later investigations indicated that Lewis was murdered. . . . In the minds of historians today there is little doubt that murder and not suicide brought the career of America's great explorer to its untimely end." Two years later E. W. Gilbert in *The Exploration of Western America* was to say: "It has been generally believed that Lewis was overcome by depression and took his own life, but there are some grounds for the assertion that he was murdered."

About this time there appeared the book by Charles Morrow Wilson, which a lot of persons have accepted as a biography of Lewis.

It will be briefly examined in the next appendix. As late as 1959 Wilson wrote that "The weight of testimony, both recorded and traditional, is overwhelmingly in support of the but slightly varying accounts forwarded by John Neely, Alexander Wilson, and Thomas Jefferson." One would think that after twenty-six years Mr. Wilson would have learned that the name is James Neelly, and that Jefferson was not on the scene to forward an account. In the same letter to a Nashville librarian Mr. Wilson says that "the lack of substantiation for the murder theory is almost absolute, as I remember." Like Jefferson's, his views have prevailed over a lot of minds.

A few years after the Wilson book, Flora W. Seymour was saying, but not proving: "A trial failed to bring out the truth. Many believed that Governor Lewis, ill, dejected, despairing of justice, had died by his own hand. . . . But those who had been with the brave young captain on the long journey West felt that this could not be the solution. The Meriwether Lewis they knew did not lose his courage nor his head in times of trial. His younger half-brother John Marks came out to the lonely spot in Tennessee . . . but his investigations threw very little light on the subject. In his trunk were his papers and documents, but no money whatever. The gold watch which had been given him in Richmond was gone. Years later his half-sister Mary, a grown woman and married, met on the streets of Mobile the French servant who had been with Lewis at the last. She recognized that the man was wearing her brother's watch and carrying his well-known gun. Her husband demanded them and Fernier gave them up."

Thus does legend thrive. In *The American Past* Roger Butterfield says that "he was mysteriously murdered in a backwoods tavern in Tennessee." But W. J. Ghent, who Allan Nevins thought in 1934 was "the most careful living student of the Lewis and Clark expedition," wrote an Oregon historian, "I quite agree with you that the probabilities are in favor of Lewis having committed suicide." And so decade after decade the opinions have ranged from positive pro to positive con.

Williams and Shoemaker in their *Missouri* say: "That night Lewis was found dead and was reported as having committed suicide. President Jefferson accepted this report, it appears, but not so the people who lived in the vicinity. . . . Many were outspoken that Lewis had been murdered and robbed." On the other hand, William K. Kay, a National Park Service historian, quotes Jefferson and concludes: "At

Grinder's Stand in the early hours of October 11 he shot himself twice and died several hours later."

The Filson Club's "Historical Quarterly" offers this: "Grinder explained that the man had shot himself. His story was then believed, but later was not only doubted but also disputed by many."

The histories of Tennessee say, in general, that Lewis killed himself. Typical is the huge work *The South in the Building of the Nation*: "Lewis was called to Washington [this is not true], but committed suicide on the way." The *New International* says only that "while on the way met his death mysteriously in the cabin of a Tennessee pioneer." The *Britannica* (11th edition): ". . . it is said that in the unwonted quiet of his new duties, his mind, always subject to melancholy, became unbalanced, and that while on his way to Washington he committed suicide. . . . It is not definitely known, however, whether he actually committed suicide or was murdered." The first sentence is, of course, pure Jefferson.

The *Americana* says that "he died at an inn in central Tennessee. The true facts about his death, whether murder or suicide have never been known." The Chambers edition which this writer examined had nine Lewises, and Lewiston, the town named for him, but seems to have thought the great explorer not worth mentioning.

According to the *Dictionary of American Biography*, "On the night of October 11, at a rude inn in central Tennessee, he died. Jefferson later assumed it was by his own hand. His family and the people of the locality where his death occurred believed he was murdered and the weight of evidence seems to be with this surmise."

Because the Jefferson-Lewis relationship is germane to the problem, it may be well to look at a curious interpretation of it, for what it is worth, by Robert Penn Warren in his *Brother to Dragons*. In his Introduction Warren says: "There is some evidence, which does not strike me as completely convincing, that Lewis did not commit suicide, but was murdered, but Jefferson, in any case, believed that death was a suicide committed in despair and resentment at the injustice of charges brought against his administration as Governor of the Louisiana Territory. My election of the theory of suicide is governed, however, by thematic and not by historical considerations. . . . I am trying to write a poem and not a history, and therefore have no compunction about tampering with facts."

He has Jefferson say, "Yes, Meriwether had been a sort of son. He took my words and heeded, and I saw in him an image of the straight-

backed and level-eyed man who would come and be worthy of the
gleaming miles of our distance. But he was dead. Courage had failed
him."

He then has Lewis say: "I am the man you did give the bullet to.
I am the man you killed. You knew my name. I was your near-son
once. . . . I'll say the truth, for if I lived a lie, and lived the lie you
taught me, I died a truth. I cracked my head and let the lie fly wide—
look! It's gone, there's nothing. Look in the hole. Just the bloody pulp
that is the truth. You see the gap. You made it—"

Jefferson then cries, "Meriwether!" and has Lewis retort, "Yes,
Meriwether, murdered by your lie. It was your lie that sent me forth,
in hope. To the wilderness—" Warren even gives to Lewis the huge
Negro servant, York, who belonged to Clark.

In due time he has Lewis say, "Toward evening I came to the
miserable inn. Grinder's, the name. A work-sick woman with brats.
The husband away. Two huts in the wilderness. . . . I asked for drink
and took it, but not much. I ate the food she gave me, but not much.
I could not understand my own agitation." That so little resembles the
Lewis idiom that like the hole and the pulpy truth it is fantastic.

After going to bed, Lewis knew suddenly that "there was no
justice. No, not for me, nor any man, for the human heart will hate
justice for its humanness." And again his bitterness toward Jefferson:
"I hated you"—and so he shot himself, that the truth might wing its
way and let him sleep. As for the "lie" Jefferson had lived, Lewis
honored "more the axe in the meat-house, as more honest at least"
than Jefferson's "special lie . . . concocted for your comfort to prove
yourself nobler in man's nobleness . . . you'd be the noble Jefferson.
And if that is not vanity—" Warren has Jefferson say that he had been
lost in the dark, "who had dreamed there was a light." He has Lewis
again cry out of bitterness, "I knew who murdered me."

Precisely what was Jefferson's sin, as Mr. Warren saw it? Apparently a belief in man's innocence—his own effort to "contrive a form
I thought fit to hold the purity of man's hope. But I did not understand
the nature of things." The nature of things seems, in the Warren fable,
to be symbolized by Frederick Bates, whose "hell-heart is a sink and a
bog of ordure."

Warren's poem reads more like a libel on all three men than a
revelation of their motives, though Jefferson's understanding of the
human heart and soul did leave something to be desired. There may be

just enough truth in the Warren theme to make the reader wish that he had not carried it so far into romantic over-emphasis.

A book could be made of the opinions pro and con but it would leave the riddle as dark as before. Perhaps the only lesson we can take from it all is an appalled sense of the way history usually gets itself written, even when there is no intrusion of poetic themes that pay no attention to historical facts. A further revelation of this can be found in the two appendixes that follow.

# APPENDIX B

# *The Lewis Myth*

By the Lewis myth is meant that image of him during the last weeks of his life that has been built by various writers, largely out of their own fancies. This image has passed into American literature and become accepted in high places. Three of the persons who devoted themselves to this myth, of whom two are possibly its chief architects, will be considered in this chapter. The first is Mrs. Eva Emery Dye.

She seems to have been taken far more seriously as a scholar than she should have been. James K. Hosmer, for instance, interrupted his writing of an introduction for a new edition of the Gass journal, to write Mrs. Dye a letter of high praise of her book *The Conquest: The True Story of Lewis and Clark*, published in 1902. The Attorney Moore who introduced Malinda to us quoted her inventions as evidence in support of his thesis. It is true that she was industrious; she seems to have written to every descendant of every member of the Lewis and Clark expedition she was able to discover, and her voluminous correspondence with these people and others, now at the Oregon Historical Society, contains a good deal of information that is not to be found elsewhere.

In the chapter of her novel called *A Mystery* she tells the story of Lewis's death. After receiving the rejected vouchers if Lewis "raged at heart he said little. Though the dagger pierced he made no sign . . .

his haggard face and evident illness alarmed his friends. 'You better take a trip to the east,' they urged. 'You have malarial fever.'"

This may be the origin of the story that Lewis had malaria. He took the advice of his friends, said "farewell" and headed down the river. At the fort he was ill, and James Neelly told himself, "I must accompany and watch over him." This may be one source of the oft-repeated but wholly unfounded statement that Neelly went along to take care of Lewis. Mrs. Dye probably took the idea from Jefferson.

When Lewis comes to the Grinder Stand, he asks, "May I stay for the night?" and the woman replies, "Come you alone?" He said his servants were behind, and asked her to bring him some wine. He then dismounted, took his saddle into a cabin, touched the wine to his lips and turned away. He pulled off his "loose white blue-striped travelling gown" and waited for his servants, and Mrs. Grinder meanwhile "scanned her guest" and perceived that he was of elegant manners and courtly bearing. He began to walk to and fro and talk to himself. "His sudden wheels and turns and strides startled her."

We have found Mrs. Grinder saying in one of her versions that Lewis "talked to himself." Some writers have made a great deal of this, for whom "talking to himself" seems to be a sign of insanity. It is to be assumed that such writers never talked to themselves and have no notion of what it means. Franz Schoenberner, a European intellectual, was for a long while paralyzed because of a brutal beating and during this time thought out and dictated a book. In it he says, "It is true that it seemed also a bit embarrassing to talk to yourself—that is generally considered a sure sign of at least the beginning of a mental derangement. If by chance, somebody observing the scene through the window of my ground-floor apartment, should overhear me without understanding what it was all about, he would probably not be surprised to see bars on my window."

It is unfortunate that Schoenberner used the words "talk to yourself," for it is rarely that anybody talks to *himself*—those who are said to talk to themselves invariably talk to someone else. The creative novelist often does it when he is developing a scene: the one who writes these words has been surprised a number of times "talking to himself" and the story has gone abroad that mentally he was not all that he should be. We suspect that Lewis did talk to himself—that is, to the War Department—that he rehearsed the scene hour after hour, perfecting and presenting his case. In one version Mrs. Grinder said he talked like a lawyer. We can imagine it:

"President Jefferson wrote me that this matter weighed on the nation's honor, and that as quickly as possible I should take measures to return the Mandan chief to his people. Do you charge me with being extravagant?" he cried, flinging long arms in a gesture toward Washington, while Mrs. Grinder took two steps back. "I remind you that one expedition had failed, with loss of life, almost with the massacre of the entire party. I thought it only prudent to let Chouteau have some money with which to bribe and buy his way through, rather than fight it through by force of arms. . ." Possibly in his eagerness he almost stumbled over Mrs. Grinder, who with a gasp and a shudder again backed away from him. Possibly it was then that, becoming aware of her and her perturbation, he said, "Madam, this is a very pleasant evening." It is possible that Lewis had been declaiming, off and on, all the way through the wilderness, and that James Neelly thought this a sign of derangement.

Hear him say it!—"Then I was authorized to engage Chouteau, an experienced riverman, to go with an armed escort of sufficient size to deliver the chief and his family to his home. After I put through a draft for the sum of $7,000, I realized that he would need funds to buy presents for hostile Indians, across whose lands he would have to pass. So I put through a small draft, and you rejected it, and you impeached my judgment and my honor in a letter which says—for I know it all by heart—The President has been consulted and the observations herein contained have his approval. Oh, but did you give him all the facts?" It is conceivable that now and then he gave a cry of outrage, and that Mrs. Grinder thought he was crazy. If he was murdered, it is conceivable that if the Grinders thought him insane, this became one of the motivations.

In Mrs. Dye's novel Lewis said, after Pernia came up, "Where is my powder?" After taking "a mouthful of supper" he suddenly starts up, "speaking in a violent manner, flushed and excited." But at once, lighting his pipe, he sat by the cabin door and said, "Madam, this is a very pleasant evening." He smoked a few minutes, "then again he flushed, arose excitedly, and stepped into the yard. There he began pacing angrily to and fro. But again he sat down to his pipe, and again seemed composed." Looking into the west he said, "What a sweet evening it is!" For the person who has spent countless hours in what the aesthetics love to call "creativity," there is nothing surprising in that, and certainly nothing deranged. It is surprising that those who accept the myth have him step into derangement and completely out of it, time and time again, as though somewhere in his mind a switch was turned on and off.

After Lewis spreads his robes and goes to bed, Mrs. Dye has Mrs. Grinder say, "I am afraid of that man. Something is wrong. I cannot sleep." Lewis meanwhile paces in the other cabin or out in the yard, and Mrs. Grinder, listening to his words, says, "He must be a lawyer." She then hears a shot and a second, and a little later a voice at her door says, "Oh, madam, give me some water and heal my wounds." Inasmuch as Mrs. Dye spent a part of her life writing about the American frontiers and frontiersmen, one wonders how she could have accepted this scene as plausible—for Mrs. Grinder now "peers into the moonlight between the open unplastered logs," sees him stagger and fall, and still makes no move. Mrs. Dye has him come a second time to the kitchen, and Mrs. Grinder, trembling and peering, hears him trying to find water in an empty pail—"Cowering, terrified, there in the kitchen with her children the woman waited for the light." The next morning "there on his bearskins on the cabin floor, they found the shattered frame of Meriwether Lewis, a bullet in his side, a shot under his chin, and a ghastly wound in his forehead." But still alive. He begs Pernia to kill him and promises not to hurt him. One would imagine that Pernia, who possibly had been in more scrapes than he could remember, needed no such assurance from a man who had a ghastly wound in his forehead, a bullet through his side, and another under his chin and presumably through his neck or skull.

Three years after Dye, Octavia Zollicoffer Bond published *Old Tales Retold*, with an enthusiastic introduction by a prominent Tennesseean who said the book's contents were "not fiction. . . . One is often surprised at her strict fidelity to the details of history." It was so highly regarded in certain quarters that Vanderbilt University Press reprinted it in 1941. A Tennessee librarian called it to our attention with the assurance that the essay about Lewis is absolutely reliable as history.

Bond makes Lewis 38 years old, whereas he was 35; has "Mr. Neely . . . tarry at a point ten miles back of Grinder's," and has him "seriously opposed [to] Lewis's determination to go on without him. But though Neely argued of the unsettled state of the country, with the highway infested as it was with robbers and cutthroats, and reminded him of the personal responsibility he felt for his safety, he could not turn the Governor from his purpose. . . . Lewis hurried ahead, accompanied only by his Spanish body servant and an Indian guide." Mrs. Grinder appeared "in answer to Lewis's lusty halloo. She looked searchingly at the three men. Turning from the foreign face of the servant to that of the bronze savage, she took alarm, and was not reassured by a glance at the gloomy features of the white stranger. Her conclusion was that she could not give them entertainment in the absence of her husband. But after long parleying Lewis persuaded her to admit them on condition that the travelers should confine themselves to one of the two detached cabins in the yard, and leave her and her small children undisturbed in the family room."

It is perhaps a waste of time to wonder where persons who profess to write not fiction but fact pick up their details—such (in this instance) as having Neelly try to persuade Lewis not to ride on ahead, replacing the Negro with a bronze savage, and confining the three men to one of the cabins. Refusing them supper, "the woman shut herself in her cabin and retired for the night." She heard shots at three in the morning, someone groaning outside, and a voice saying, "It is hard to die." She heard a gourd scraping in the empty water pail. "It was pitiful, yet the woman dared not go out until broad daylight, by which time the noises had all ceased. Everything was quiet when she opened the door to find that the strangers had all vanished. Their horses were also gone from the stable, and there was no trace of them to be found anywhere. It was not until nearly noon that a clue of any sort was discovered. In the meantime Grinder had returned, and the mail rider, Robert Smith, had stopped at the stand on his regular journey from Natchez to Nashville. Together the two men made a search which ended in their finding the dead body of Meriwether Lewis lying under a tree near the house. His fatal wound had come from a bullet which struck him under the chin and passed out through the top of the skull. No one knew then or has ever learned certainly since how the great man came to his death. The matter was discussed throughout the United States, and there were many differing opinions expressed on the subject. Mr. Jefferson, after taking pains to collect all the evidence that he could gather at such great distance from the scene as to the cause of his friend's tragic fate, concluded that it was an act of suicide, committed in a fit of mental depression. But the family of Governor Lewis thought differently. . . . All the circumstances led them to believe that the Spanish servant (with the Indian probably as an accomplice) had murdered and then robbed their master."

Another theory, this writer gravely tells us, is that Grinder's son-in-law killed Lewis, though Grinder's older daughter at the time could

have been no more than ten. Bond gives one amusing fillip to the story
when she has Lewis groaning in the yard and muttering that it is hard
to die, and later shooting himself through the brain—for surely not
even a woman could imagine that a man could shoot himself under the
chin and through his brain and then crawl or stagger around the yard
after water.

But the fancies of Dye and Bond read almost like solid history
when compared with Charles Morrow Wilson's *Meriwether Lewis of
Lewis and Clark,* published in 1934, and catalogued in libraries from
coast to coast as a biography. The surprising thing about this farrago
of errors is not that it has deceived and misled so many and been so
potent in establishing the Lewis myth, but that apparently it has been
taken seriously by some able scholars. Wilson says that "Statute Records of Tennessee show that on October 7, 1810, Grinder was brought
before a grand jury at Savannah to answer a charge of having murdered Meriwether Lewis. . . . The case was dismissed for lack of evidence."
Bakeless must have had that statement or one like it in mind when he
wondered why "the case should be tried at such a distance" and concluded that "It is doubtful if there is any truth in the story." He seems
to mean that it is doubtful that Grinder was taken so far from his
stand for trial, not that it was doubtful that there was a Savannah.

As a matter of fact there was not, in 1810. No white persons
settled in what was to be Hardin county until the spring of 1816, and
the county was not created by the Legislature until 1819. No courts
were organized in it until 1820. The first county seat was Hardinsville,
established in 1822. So many settlers were dissatisfied with it that in
1826 Savannah was chosen as the site, though the "seat of justice" was
not moved to Savannah until 1830. In support of his statement, above,
Wilson cites *Statutes,* Commonwealth of Tennessee, Vol. 123, pp.
1174-78. Tennessee librarians and historians say there has never been
such a record in so many volumes, or with so many pages. The reference librarian of the Tennessee State Library made a thorough search
of all the stacks and found nothing even remotely like it—and in fact
felt from the beginning that a search would be an utter waste of time.
At our request—again she thought it a waste of time—she wrote Mr.
Wilson to ask where he had found such a volume.*

Without citing any source or giving an iota of proof, Mr. Wilson
says that while the governor was still in St. Louis he "was forgetting

---

*For his reply see notes to this chapter.

his appearance. . . . He had been seen drinking at common taverns. He kept no vestige of a coach. His two saddle horses were scrubby. He entertained but rarely, and he paid no attention to any woman except Julia Clark [William Clark's wife], and but precious little to her . . . his . . . hair was carelessly kept and but seldom combed."

He was "taken sick, seized with an ailment that turned his skin yellow and fired him with an unnatural heat." Clark, we are told, doctored him but he "grew thin and lost all his craving to be outdoors. Pernea, the Creole, became his nurse. . . . Lewis found life bitter. His competency was being questioned; more than that, his honesty challenged."

Of "Pernea" he says that the servant was "a half-starved and wandering Creole named Pernea, whom Meriwether Lewis had found homeless and hungry along the river front. Pernea was a gaunt, sad ne'er-do-well who had followed the muddy Mississippi since birth. He gave his trade as 'voyageur or waterman,' and in years past he had floated raft-loads of fur down river for the Choteaus [sic]. He had been shot in a saloon brawl, and flogged half to death at Natchez, by a band of Spanish vigilantes who had accused him of stealing a colt. The torture had left him a bit deranged of mind, and so he had taken to wandering from port to port, from saloon to saloon, hoping for the best and never finding it. He had begged from Meriwether Lewis, never dreaming that so plainly dressed a gentleman could possibly be the great Governor. But the Virginian formed an instant interest in the wistful, beseeching fellow, this son of humanity that was down-trodden and outcast, and gave him a room in which to sleep and a steady allowance for food and drink."

Though Mr. Wilson seems to have lifted all this out of his hat, no doubt it sounds wholly convincing to the unwary reader. He now tells us that Lewis resolved to go to Washington "to answer this insolence and tongue-wagging in person. That much was his duty as an Albemarle Virginian, as a soldier, and as a gentleman. He was short of money and sick of body and heart, but he was going to Washington. . . he most certainly would not flee before the yowlings of a pack of coyote bureaucrats." Clark tried day after day to dissuade him—"You're sick, man; you're horse sick." But Lewis would go, taking Pernea as "nurse" and Jim, a Negro, as "handy man." Lewis "struggled hard to stand straight. His thigh ached where he had received the bullet wound two years before. His legs seemed strangely unsteady. His forehead burned and his lips felt like leather." There was, of course, no Jim; Lewis was shot not in a thigh but in a buttock, and the time was three, not two, years before. Unmoved by Clark's entreaties Lewis "turned, leaning heavily upon Pernea" who had followed him "like a faithful dog." We are assured that York, Clark's huge Negro servant on the expedition, appeared and danced a jig, and that Clark gave Lewis a watch. This may be the origin of the two-watches story.

Lewis takes a boat downriver but hears rumors of war with Britain, and because he was "in no good shape to fight" and wished with all haste to get to Washington where the "hirelings were calling him a thief," he decided to leave the boat at Memphis. "Sick, sick. All of them said he was sick. . . . Maj. John Neely, Indian Agent for the Cherokee nation, a hard and discerning Army man, looked the Governor over, and like the rest, judged him sick." His name was not John but James, he was never an Army man, and he was agent not to the Cherokee but to the Chickasaw nation.

Lewis bought two pack mules, we are told, and borrowed three cavalry horses from the Army post. He "hitched on a brace of good pistols and slipped a razor-sharp bowie knife into his coat pocket . . . He was a sick man. His skin was sallow and his cheeks suspiciously flushed. . . . Pernea, with dog-like fidelity, lifted his master to saddle. . . . No coterie of rotten-hearted underlings could brand him a thief. . . . Maybe his health was gone. Certainly his money was gone. . . . Death would answer all the striving uncertainties of living." During this journey he had "come to think well of death . . . felt a strange burning sensation in his forehead. Pains like daggers of ice shot through his shoulders and back . . . was changing his notions of death all at once. Now he rather wanted it, wanted it worse than he had ever wanted anything before—even more than he had wanted Theodosia Burr."

This allusion alone is enough to establish the Wilson "biography" for what it is. Emerson Hough, in a trashy novel, had Lewis madly infatuated with the married daughter of Aaron Burr, whom so far as we know he never even met. This stupid "romance" was a calumny on both persons, and had been exposed as a piece of nonsense before Wilson wrote his book.

Lewis rides on (he has left the fort with Neelly) and has "a mighty roaring in his ears." He hears imaginary voices. His "two" servants, "plainly uneasy," and Neelly, who had spent the better part of his "fifty-two years" in the open woods, watch over the Virginian with increasing caution. "The Indian agent was weary of escorting a

sick man through the wilderness. He was resolved to ask a military
escort for the Governor as soon as they reached Nashville. This journey
was no picnic, even with healthy followers. With a sick man along it
was next to impossible to cover more than a dozen miles a day." It is
obvious that Mr. Wilson never looked at the map.

"Meriwether Lewis responded strangely to his malady. At starting, he had been too weak to mount a horse. Yet as the days followed
he appeared to gain strength, and although he ate but sparingly and
complained occasionally of pains in the head and chest, his determination to keep with the journey only increased; and he rode well enough,
mounting and dismounting without Pernea's help.

"John Neely noticed that the Virginian had occasional recourse to
conversation, but that his sayings were lacking in continuity. Sometimes he told of old Army days, of forgotten maneuverings and march-
ings, inferring the company of various Army officers of whom Neely
had never heard. He made gestures in Indian sign talk. Now and then
he would give orders, as if he were directing a boat crew, and then he
would gaze away into the forest and smile. Sometimes he would stop
to gather in grass-heads or late-blooming flowers."

Without citing any sources or any proof, he says of Neelly, "Certainly it is only justice to say that the tradition of our early Indian
service was high; that John Neely's official record was outstanding for
integrity and attention to duty, a record backed by long service in the
United States Army."

A page and a half later—it is now October 10: "The Governor was
a sick man. This gadding about in a storm would be flirting with death,
and if the Governor lost his life the papers would be of no help. John
Neely himself would round up the strays, with the help of Pernea and
Jim. In return for this he had just one request to make—that the
Governor ride on until he came to a house where he could dry himself
and take a lodging for the night."

So Lewis rides on ahead, and the "bared treetops nodded in stoic
acceptance. . . . Mud was as red as blood, and the raindrops stung like
hail." He approaches a log cabin where two Negro children and a
white child are playing. He "walked lurchingly to the door. He was
sick, and his forehead burned as if it were banked with fire." There
came to the door a "tall, angular mountain woman" who "stared at him
as if in fear." Mr. Wilson seems to be the only person to discover the
shape of Mrs. Grinder. Knowing so much about her, it is strange that
he calls her husband John, whose name was Robert—even stranger that

he wrote an entire "biography" of Lewis, and called his mother Ann, whose name was Lucy.

He concludes: "The weight of testimony, both recorded and traditional, is overwhelmingly in support of the but slightly varying accounts forwarded by John Neelly, Alexander Wilson, and Thomas Jefferson." One wonders how Jefferson could have forwarded an account, since he was not on the scene, and to whom he sent it.

Well, that is the Lewis myth. It is obvious not only that Mr. Wilson is its chief architect, but that he also is the chief source of the Neelly myth.

Professor Allan Nevins reviewed this "biography" in *The Saturday Review of Literature,* and Wilson wrote a long sharp reply, which appeared in that journal August 25, 1934. Mr. Wilson said that "from better than a hundred reviewers and historians" the reviews by Nevins and Constance Skinner "stand alone in fever of denunciation." In the same issue Professor Nevins replied to Wilson, saying:

"Mr. Wilson tries to bring a whole school of red herring into the picture. The central issue is of the reliability or unreliability of his book, and every chapter of it is utterly unreliable. I disclaim any heat in my review, though I confess that it is difficult to handle such a volume without sarcasm. I repeat that it is undocumented, for it makes the most extraordinary misstatements without the slightest attempt to cite authority—from the misstatement of the name of Meriwether Lewis's mother at the beginning to the invention of the dog Brewster (there was no such animal) near the end. If Mr. Wilson used the works of Wheeler and Coues, then not only his bibliography but his text fails to show the fact." Nevins says that W. J. Ghent, "the most careful living student of the Lewis and Clark expedition," agrees with him, and then quotes from a letter Ghent had published in the Washington *Post:*

"Most of its details happen to be absurdly wrong. Parts of it seem to be based on Emerson Hough's preposterous novel, 'The Magnificent Adventure,' and other parts are mere guesswork. The author has not taken the trouble to acquaint himself with the basic facts of that immortal journey. His geography is a kind of 'Alice in Wonderland' region; he has no knowledge, except in spots, of the region travelled; and he confuses the members of the expedition in a manner made familiar to us by Mr. H. I. Phillips's 'Garble Sisters.'" Nevins says that Ghent found the "inaccuracy of the book 'shocking.'" Ghent wrote to Stella Drum, at that time Missouri Historical Society librarian: "You have undoubtedly now read Wilson's book on Meriwether Lewis. If so, you have made acquaintance with the most slovenly mess of misstatements that has ever appeared in a professedly serious book." In one instance Mr. Wilson has defended his book in these words: "My Lewis book was published quite sloppily by a financially distressed book house. There are many printing errors in addition to author's."

But, like so many books, it will go on and on and it will be taken seriously by historians yet to come. There comes to mind Ernest Newman's protest against worthless books about Wagner. After telling us that Houston S. Chamberlain proved that Ferdinand Praeger's *Wagner as I Knew Him* was a "masterpiece of mendacity" he goes on to say: "The misfortune is that the evil can never be wholly undone. A book of this kind may be discredited in the eyes of the experts, but it is bound to come, for many years after its publication, into the hands of people who are completely unaware of its having been discredited; while even long after the book itself has been forgotten, some of the inventions it started will still be in currency among people who have no idea of the source of them. Much of the nonsense that is still floating about with regard to Wagner in this country is ultimately traceable to Praeger's work." Chamberlain wrote in the 1908 edition of his book that "the latest edition of Riemann's *Musik lexicon* actually cites, as historic facts, statements by Praeger that I showed fifteen years ago, by documentary edvidence, to be lies."

"Have you seen Wilson's biography?" was the question put to us by librarians from coast to coast. Yes, alas, we had.

# APPENDIX C

## *A Neglected American*

In the dedication of this book Meriwether Lewis is called a great American, and the most neglected American of his breed. Magnificent memorials have been erected to Thomas Jefferson, one of whose dreams was to bring into the United States what is now its northwestern part, before the Spanish or English could get their hands on it. The man he called on to explore and lay claim to it, a task that demanded the utmost in fortitude, intelligence, and valor, has had no magnificent memorials erected to him. Even Sergeant Charles Floyd, who did not reach the Mandan villages, but died August 20, 1804, on the first leg of the journey up the Missouri, has a shaft in his honor that towers far above anything that honors Lewis.

As James D. Park said in 1891, "The only monument erected to the great explorer in all this broad land he has served so well, is that built by the State of Tennessee." This monument, according to Coues, is twenty and a half feet high, a base of rough, unhewn stone eight feet high and nine feet square. On this rests a plinth of cut stone, on which are the inscriptions. On the plinth stands a broken column eleven feet high, two and a half feet in diameter at the base, and a little less at the top. The base is a form of sandstone; the plinth and shaft are of fine limestone, sometimes called Tennessee marble.

Park suggested that the Congress should authorize the erection of a suitable monument at the national capital. The Congress has never done this, though its fantastic appropriation of public funds for innumerable projects is one of the wonders of the modern world. A few years after Park published his essay, Mrs. Dye wrote in her novel that "In the lonely heart of Lewis county, Tennessee, stands to-day a crumbling gray stone monument with a broken shaft of limestone. . . . In solitude and desolation, moss overlies his tomb."

A National Park Service folder tells the visitor that February 6, 1925, the Meriwether Lewis National Monument was established, on 300 acres of Federal land. "Places of historic interest within the monument include a section of the long-abandoned Natchez Trace; the grave of Meriwether Lewis, and the site of Grinder's Stand." It is confessed that "except for a 'post fence' built in 1810, the plot was unmarked until 1848, when the State of Tennessee erected over the remains a broken column. . . ."* We don't even know that the column stands over his grave. In any case, for well over half a century the spot was then forgotten by all but the few who remembered the name of one to whom they owed so much. As Sherwood Anderson wrote in a letter to his son, it is chiefly the fakers whom this nation honors.

The National Monument is far more impressive in its title than in its fact. In Hohenwald, the town closest to it, inquiries revealed that the Monument has few visitors. Formerly there was an annual gathering in the Monument by the people of the area, but this is no longer so. In the Monument there is nothing to see, nothing to bring a person to this out-of-the-way spot, except the rather pathetic little monument, and what is pointed out as the site of Grinder's Stand. Nobody except a person with a sentimental interest in Lewis could imagine that his visit to the spot was worth it.

The Lewis and Clark expedition to the ocean "opened up seventeen States for trade, for settlement and for marvelous development— a fact which is scarcely noticed in the histories of the United States." We shall see in a moment how true that is. It opened, says Professor Albert Bushnell Hart, "half a continent." And as Charles Van Ravenswaay, director of the Missouri Historical Society, puts it, "The work of these great men has been too often neglected in general books on the history of exploration. There is no doubt that they deserve a place beside the great explorers of the world." That is an understatement: the question is how many of the so-called great explorers deserve a

---

*It is said a broken column was chosen to indicate a broken life.

place beside them. In the very Society which Mr. Van Ravenswaay supervises there are many books about St. Louis or Missouri, or both, in the indexes of which the name of Meriwether Lewis does not appear. His name *does* appear in *A New History of Missouri* by F. A. Culmer, page 62, but only in F. L. Paxon's unsupported statement that Lewis's presence in St. Louis "was in connection with a scheme of Jefferson's for the investigation of Louisiana." Frederick Bates, on the other hand, is given generous space and a full-page photograph.

As late as 1914 the custodian of the Monument reported "a population of 65 swine," as well as a considerable number of kine, sheep, and two mules "at large about the office and residence." The neglect of Lewis and the indifference to him is so well-established and accepted that the Park historians themselves don't bother to separate facts from fictions, in a folder on Lewis which is given away to visitors. For it is said that Clark was "second in command" whereas he had the same rank as Lewis's, in fact if not in the records of the War Department. It is said that on May 14, 1804, Lewis "led his band of 32 men up the Missouri River." That was not the number of men in the party at that time. It is said that the Corps "spent the winter in a Mandan Sioux village." It seems likely that the Park historian took such errors from one or more of a number of professors, whom we shall look at in a moment.

Said Park, "The existence of such a grave and monument is scarcely known outside of the State and to but few anywhere of the present generation." The Louisiana Purchase was an event of such magnitude that, as Henry Adams said, its results are beyond measurement. Not only "did it provide a potential that was certain to make us a great power, not only did it make equally certain that we would expand beyond the Rockies to the Pacific," as De Voto says, but it insured this nation's existence against hostile powers eager to absorb it. It took Jefferson's vision, but the vision would have been worth nothing without Lewis or a man like him. For as Coues says, "The story of this adventure stands easily first and alone. It is our national epic of exploration." It stands, says Chittenden, "as incomparably the most perfect achievement of its kind in the history of the world."

Very well. What do books on American history have to say about these two great men, Lewis and Clark, and their valiant companions? For the most part, nothing. If the reader wishes to determine for himself whether that incredible statement is true, he can get, as we did, stack permits to the American history section in such fine libraries as the Huntington, the Bancroft, the Library of Congress, and go through a few hundred indexes. Many of the older histories, such as the huge tomes by Hinton or Stephens, do not list Lewis or Clark, or their expedition, in their index. Neither is in the index of a history of the United States in *eight* big volumes, nor in one of three, though the first includes a "Judge Lewis." Woodrow Wilson's five volumes, *A History of the American People*, does not list them, but has a William B. Lewis. Hamilton's five volumes lists a Morgan Lewis but not Meriwether. In neither his four-volume history of the U. S. nor in his 600-page history for students does Professor Channing list either man or their expedition. Nicholas Murray Butler's fat tome on the building of this nation (what built it?) lists neither man. Beard's *The American Spirit* (what *was* the American spirit?) does not list them and his *A Century of Progress* gives them one sentence. Professor N. W. Stephenson's two volumes, *A History of the American People*, gives to Lewis and the expedition one short sentence. Professor Ralph V. Harlow in *The Growth of the United States* (850 pages) gives the expedition one short sentence.

Butterfield in *The American Past* reproduces the drawing of Lewis in Indian regalia but devotes his text entirely to Jefferson. James Truslow Adams in *The Epic of America* (and what *is* the epic?) allows Lewis and Clark and their great expedition to share one sentence with Zebulon Pike—though the truth is that Lewis or Clark or Pike, or any one of a hundred others of the same breed, was infinitely more important in the history of this country than most of the politicians to whom American historians devote their pages. One is compelled to the conclusion that this nation has a positive genius for paying homage to mediocrities.

In their large illustrated *The American Way of Life*, Faulkner, Kepner, and Bartlett give Lewis and Clark one sentence in more than 700 pages. Professor S. E. Morison's two-volume *The Oxford History of the United States* heaps upon Jefferson the usual plaudits but of Lewis and Clark's remarkable triumph says only that in 1806 they returned with "news of the untouched store of fur-bearing animals in the core of the continent." His book with Professor Commager, *The Growth of the American Republic*, repeats the above, exactly, and elsewhere says only that Lewis and Clark "fulfilled the quest of the gallant Chevalier." They give the book's frontispiece to Jefferson.

R. L. Ashley's *American History*, "for use in secondary schools," gives Lewis and Clark and their expedition eight words. Macdonald's

600-page *High School History of the United States,* which from time to time has been revised by various professors, gives Lewis and Clark and their expedition part of a sentence, but uses a photograph of such national "heroes" as Nathaniel Green, Anthony Wayne, and John Paul Jones. A. E. Martin in his two-volume *iHstory of the United States* has not a single word in his index for Lewis or Clark or their expedition, but in his index gives nineteen lines to W. J. Bryan, five and a half to Robert M. La Follette, six to H. L. Stimson, eight to Charles E. Hughes, and even a line and a half to Adlai Stevenson. Such books as C. B. Coleman's *The Undying Past* make this kind of statement, that "the expeditions of George Rogers Clark in 1778 and 1779 are of far greater importance in the history of the United States as a whole; far more spectacular, far more dramatic, than the Lewis and Clark expedition, interesting as that is." One would think that that said everything but we still have Beyer and Keydal and their enormous two-volume set, *Deeds of Valor,* which doesn't mention Lewis and Clark among more than 800 names.

And when Lewis and Clark are mentioned, the errors by professional historians, including nearly all those who write textbooks for our schools, are startling, to put it in the gentlest possible way. Indeed, it can be said that of histories written for use in our schools, which contain a few sentences or a paragraph or two, it is hard to find one that does not contain errors. Here are a few instances:

Professor Albert Bushnell Hart in his *School History of the United States:* "The party of forty-five men, for which Congress appropriated only $2500 . . . guided by the 'Bird Woman' . . ." There we have three errors in seventeen words. Professors Bourne and Benton tell students that "only one Indian had been killed," an error found also in Hall, Smither and Ousley *The Student's History of Our Country,* though Lewis wrote as plain as daylight in his journal that two Indians were killed. Professor Fite says that "forty-five members were included in the party" which reached the Three Forks the "next spring." Both statements are false. Casner and Gabriel say that the party wintered "in the lodges of the Mandan Indians" and were "guided by a French trapper and his young wife." Both statements are false. Professor David S. Muzzey in *An American History* says that Lewis and Clark left St. Louis "with a company of forty-five men"; Professors James and Sanford in their *American History* say it was a "party of thirty-five men"; and Professors Riegel and Hough in their *United States of America,* another text for schools, say that a "party of some thirty men" left St. Louis. Professor W. M. West's 900-page tome, *History of the American Nation,* gives the number leaving St. Louis as thirty-five, and says, as so many do, that the party was "guided by the 'Bird Woman.' "

Lewis chose Clark as his companion in leadership, but a common error is that Jefferson chose Clark; and it even appears in such books as *The American Hertiage,* with Bruce Catton listed as Editor and Allan Nevins as author of "Chapter Prologues"; in Professor T. J. Wertenbaker's *The American People;* and Beard and Bagley.

Sometimes the errors are simply staggering. Here are samples: Boyle, Shires, Price, and Carman in *Quest of a Hemisphere* say that "many times" the Indian girl Sacajawea "saved the white men when their lives were threatened by hostile Indians." In not a single known instance did she save their lives. Twaites, Kendall, and Paxson in their *History of the United States* (for the schools) say that "After many thrilling experiences with fierce currents, inclement weather, grizzly bears, they spent a long, bitterly cold, and almost starving winter not far from the present Bismarck, North Dakota." Thwaites at least should have known that the fierce currents, grizzlies, and all that came *after* the party left its winter headquarters near the present Bismarck. Professor Frederic L. Paxson (the same Paxson) in his students' edition of his *History of the American Frontier* says that when Lewis wanted to converse with the Indians "he was forced to rely upon his mulatto body servant, who by chance spoke French. This servant translated the message to Charbonneau." Lewis had no mulatto body servant and no servant of any kind. Paxson goes on to commit another whopper when he says that on "May 14, 1804, he led his band of thirty-two across the Mississippi and up the Missouri." But it remained for S. P. Lee, with Louise Manly, in their *School History of the United States,* to misspell both names (Merriwether and Clarke) and to say: "Up the Missouri and its great branches and through the wild mountain ranges of the northwest they pushed their way to the Pacific slope. Here they found the two rivers which today bear their names. Down these they went, until the two rolled together into the Columbia." If students who use the Paxson book look at the map of the Northwest they must conclude that it was Lewis and Clark who rolled together into the Columbia River.

If the samples given here are an average of accuracy in our textbooks of American history, one wonders what the image of this nation's past is in the heads of college graduates. We saw that Historian

Dombrowski was led to exclaim, "how many lies and distortions be concealed in the pages of history!" The explanation, of course, with many of our textbooks is that distinguished professors fall into the lazy and profitable habit of letting their students gather the data for their books.

# Acknowledgements and Notes

It would be a gesture if I were to name all the persons who assisted me and my wife during our research. To the able and willing staffs in such libraries as the Huntington, Bancroft, New York Public, and Congress any student must be grateful. Those who deserve special mention include Dr. Robert H. Bahmer, Archivist, Oliver W. Holmes, Chief Archivist, Social and Economic Records Division and Herman R. Friis, Chief Archivist, Cartographic Records Division, National Archives; Mrs. Dorothy Thomas Cullen, Librarian and Curator, and Miss Mabel C. Weaks, Archivist, the Filson Club of Louisville; Mrs. Brenda R. Gieseker, Librarian, Miss Dorothy A. Brockhoff, Reference Librarian, and Mrs. Ellen G. Harris, Assistant Archivist, the Missouri Historical Society, St. Louis; Mrs. Gertrude Parsley, Reference Librarian, Mrs. Hermione D. Embrey, Genealogical Reference Librarian, and Robert T. Quarles, Jr., Director of Archives, Tennessee State Library, Nashville; Josephine L. Harper, Manuscripts Librarian, Wisconsin Historical Society, Madison; Priscilla Knuth, Research Associate, Oregon Historical Society, Portland; Francis L. Berkeley, Jr., Curator of Manuscripts, Alderman Library, University of Virginia; Dr. Julian P. Boyd, Princeton University; Dr. Dawson A. Phelps and Mr. William K. Kay, National Park historians, Tupelo; John H. Saxon, Superintendent, Meriwether Lewis National Monument; Franklin J. McLean, Charlottesville, Va.; Miss Carrie E. Smith and Mr. Hugh Webster of

Columbia, Tenn. and Mrs. W. K. Edwards of Centerville, Tenn. I am specially indebted to three men who were more than generous with their time: to Dr. John Bakeless of Seymour, Conn. who again and again interrupted his work to reply to my many letters; to Jonathan Daniels, editor of *The News and Observer*, who while engaged with his own book on the Trace took time to read this book in manuscript and give its author the benefit of his wide knowledge; and above all to Mr. Donald D. Jackson of the University of Illinois Press, who not only read the book in manuscript but corrected a number of errors and offered a number of suggestions that were faithfully incorporated into a rewriting of the book.

These abbreviations are used in the Notes that follow:

| | |
|---|---|
| DDJ | Donald D. Jackson (see paragraph above) |
| B | John Bakeless The citations are from his excellent book on the Lewis and Clark expedition and on the lives of the two men, Chapter 26. |
| DAP | Dawson A. Phelps, National Park Service historian |
| FC | Filson Club, Louisville |
| HCL | A thick folder of newspaper clippings about Lewis, Houston and Crockett, at Tennessee State Library |
| LC | The Library of Congress |
| LPAND | Lewis Papers, 1821 and no date, MoHS |
| MoHS | Missouri Historical Society |
| MLNM | The Meriwether Lewis National Monument |
| NA | National Archives |
| NABa | Dr. Bahmer's office at NA; in it are typescripts of many letters and documents |
| OHS | Oregon Historical Society |
| Spence | A *History of Hickman County* by the Spences, Jerome and David |
| WHS | Wisconsin Historical Society |

Chapter 1: The materials for this sketch of Meriwether Lewis have been drawn from many sources, including DeVoto's edition of the Journals; Wheeler and Coues and Thwaites; Jefferson; J. E. Graustein, "Lisa and Nuttall," MoHS Bulletin, April, 1956; various genealogical accounts, often untrustworthy. "An American historian" is DDJ. McAllister and Tandy in their *Genealogies of the Lewis and Kindred Families* say: "His father died when he was a small boy, and his mother afterwards married Colonel William Marks, also a Revolu-

tionary patriot, and in a sort of exodus, so to speak, of the Meriwethers, Mrs. Marks, together with her second husband, and her Lewis children, removed to Georgia. . . . Mr. Jefferson, no doubt drawing upon his imagination, tells us of the early childhood of Meriwether Lewis, of his hunting the 'raccoon and opossum,' in the darkness of the night among the spurs of the Blue Ridge, and in this way accounts for his habits of hardihood in later life. Mr. Jefferson was doubtless ignorant of the removal of Mrs. Marks and her Lewis children to Georgia, and wholly ignorant of the early life of Meriwether Lewis, who had spent all of his coon-hunting days in Georgia, where Indians were the only game that the white man could afford to hunt, or at school, where coons were not to be found. . . . After the death of Colonel Marks, 'Aunt Marks' returned to Locust Hill, Albemarle county, Virginia, and shortly after her return Meriwether Lewis entered the United States army. He volunteered in 1794, with the troops called out to suppress the whiskey rebellion, and in 1795 entered the regular army." Commenting on this DDJ says, "Having misquoted Jefferson about the spurs of the Blue Ridge, McAllister and Tandy make the silly statement that Lewis wouldn't have hunted raccoon and opossum in Georgia, 'where Indians were the only game that the white man could afford to hunt. . . .'" He also points out that the name of her second husband was John, not William. "One of the ablest. . . .": this is Olin D. Wheeler.

Chapter 2: Billon, 374,377; Spaulding, *Popular Science Monthly,* Dec., 1908; the Phelps essay, "The Tragic Death of Meriwether Lewis," *The William and Mary Quarterly,* July, 1956, will be examined in a later chapter; DeVoto, xliv; Hecht, "The Burr Conspiracy," MHS *Bulletin,* Jan., 1956; Wheeler, I, 93-4-5; Jefferson letters, NABa; Billon, 53; Jefferson to Lewis, quoted by Gen. Marcus D. Wright, "Ware's Valley Monthly," III, 1876, 136. DDJ has pointed out that the additional sum made available to Chouteau was actually $940: Lewis to Sec. of War, 13 May 1809, in NA, Record Group 107, unregistered series.

Chapter 3: Marshall, Thomas Maitland, *Life and Times of Frederick Bates,* in two volumes; Tracy, G., *Frederick Bates and his Administration of Louisiana Territory,* a Univ. of Washington thesis, 1925. All the Bates letters used here are from the Marshall volumes; there are other Bates letters at MoHS. See also Carter, *Territorial Papers of the United States,* XIV, 339-340, note; 121; DeVoto, xliii; Billon, 284. The Treat letter is at MoHS.

Chapter 4:  Letter to mother, MoHS; Miller, "Expedition Finances," MoHS *Bulletin*, July, 1954; *His Excellency Meriwether Lewis and the First Publications West of the Mississippi River*, Univ. of Texas thesis, 1948 (Mrs. Miller says the information for her thesis she dug out of the Recorder of Deeds office in St. Louis and from records in St. Charles County, Mo. It is said by some who know her that for fifteen years, or more, she has been doing research for a biography of Lewis). Lucas, *Encyc. of the History of Missouri*, IV, 130. On land speculation see also Roy T. King, "The Territorial Press in Missouri," MoHS *Bulletin*, Oct., 1954; also April, 1951. The Lewis account book and nearly all his letters used here are at MoHS, though the July 8 one was taken from a photostat in the office of Oliver W. Holmes, NA. Papers on Colter are at MoHS; on Anderson and incomplete letter, Dye Coll., OHS.

Chapter 5:  On Bates, Marshall, *op.cit.*; Lewis account books are at MoHS; the four promissory notes are at WHS; on witnesses to will, Billon, 378-9; Dickson, NABa; DeVoto, xliv; Warner, LPAND; issue of *Globe-Democrat*, LPAND; all Bakeless citations in this book are from pp. 408-428.

"Unless evidence turns up . . .": Dr. Julian P. Boyd's editing of the Jefferson Papers may turn up evidence on this and on other matters, though at this writing Dr. Boyd doubts that there is anything in the Papers, now unknown, that will throw any light on Lewis's death.

Chapter 6:  Bullen, see DAP; Sept. 11 will, Will Book, No. 5, Albemarle County Clerk's office; Jackson, letter to writer; letter to Madison is in Carter, *Territorial Papers*, XIV, 269; Wheeler, I, 77-8; the two Russell letters to Jefferson in Jan., 1810, were copies in NA; there were so many missing words that it was necessary to go to the originals, but in a few instances it was not possible to determine what was written, and in a few other instances it was possible to correct the NA scribe. Jonathan Williams: this amazing document in which Russell did a complete about-face was called to the writer's attention by Mr. Jackson; a copy is at the Univ. of Indiana—it has not been possible to find the original. House letter is at MoHS; the writer is indebted to Mrs. Brenda R. Gieseker, MoHS librarian, for reading the signature.

Chapter 7:    Boyd, *The American Archivist*, XXII, No. 2, 174; Gilmer:
              see also William Terrell Lewis, *Genealogy*, 52; Leftwich,
George J., *Publications of the Mississippi Historical Society*, 1916; Olin
D. Wheeler, *The Trail of Lewis and Clark*, two volumes, and Elliott
Coues, *History of the Expedition*, four volumes, will hereafter be re-
ferred to as Wheeler or Coues; Natchez Park Historian is Dawson A.
Phelps: his widely discussed article in the *William and Mary Quarter-
ly* is considered in detail in ch. XXII; Phelps, an authority on the Trace,
has established the names and sites of most of the stands: *The Journal
of Mississippi History*, XI 4; see also Elizabeth B. Stanton, *Ye Old
Natchez Trace*, privately printed; Jonathan Daniels, editor of the
*News and Observer*, is preparing a book on the Trace; on the early
Trace see *Everybody's Magazine*, Sept., 1905; on banditry on the Trace
some of the following are highly colored but give an overall picture:
Robert M. Coates, *The Outlaw Years: A History of the Land Pirates of
the Natchez Trace*, New York, 1930; Edward J. Coale, *Trials of the
Mail Robbers*, Baltimore, 1818; James D. Davis, *History of the City of
Memphis*, Memphis, 1873; Josephus Conn Guild, *Old Times in Ten-
nessee*, Nashville, 1878; Thomas Speed, *The Wilderness Road*, Louis-
ville, 1886; Augustus Q. Walton, *John A. Murrel*, Athens, Tenn., 1885;
Otto A. Rothert, *The Outlaws of Cave-in Rock*, Cleveland, 1924; Joseph
L. French, *A Gallery of Old Rogues*; Anthony Gish, *American Bandits*;
George D. Hendricks, *The Bad Men of the West*; Emerson Hough,
*The Story of the Outlaw*; Edwin L. Sabin, *Wild Men of the Wild West*;
Frank Triplett, *History, Romance and Philosophy of Great American
Crimes and Criminals*; for Neelly's letter, Carter, *op.cit.*, XIV, 332-3;
Bechtle: for reading his difficult signature and for information about
him the writer is indebted to Josephine L. Harper, WHS librarian; on
the stranger whom Lewis met, Draper mss. I 81, WHS; Russell deposition: it is the opinion of Oliver W. Holmes of NA that this document
must have been drawn for some legal purpose in settlement of the
Lewis estate or of other matters: in regard to this Mrs. Ellen G. Harris
of MoHS called the writer's attention to an item in the files there—
Gilbert C. Russell to Charles Lucas, March 21, 1816: "Some years ago
a suit was instituted in my name . . . in one of your courts against the
administrator of the estate of Governor Lewis. . . .": it may be that
the document was drawn for this suit.

Chapter 8:    Phelps, *op.cit.*; all papers on the Stand prepared by mem-
              bers of National Park Service are at MLNM; Gordon's
Ferry, "Tennessee Historical Quarterly," March, 1943; Park, Nashville

*American,* Sept. 6, 1891; Kay, a monograph at MLNM; Coues, I, liii; Grinder purchase of land on Duck River, Hickman County deed book; on North Carolina and other Grinders, names, ages, insanity, sale of slaves, etc. see microfilm records and Tenn. minute books and census reports at TSL; Phelps, in a letter to the writer; Spences, Jerome and David, *A History of Hickman County Tennessee,* Nashville, 1900; Sallie Walker, an old-timer long dead, said there was a tradition of insanity: TSL, in a M. Lewis Miscellany.

Chapter 9:  Pernia saw Jefferson about a month after Lewis died. If Jefferson questioned him he apparently left no memo of it. Mr. Boyd in a letter to the writer says that "we did some time ago make a fairly systematic search of the Jefferson papers in the fall of 1809 and the early months of 1810 and we found nothing in addition to what I had already made available." In another letter Mr. Boyd says he is convinced there is nothing more in the Jefferson papers on the subject of Lewis's death than is known. In a letter to the writer Mr. Jackson says, "I think I have seen everything extant that Jefferson wrote on the subject. There is not a scrap dealing with any talks he had with Pernia."

The Neelly letter is copied from Carter, XIV, 332-3. On Neelly Mr. Phelps says in his essay: "By virtue of his appointment to a responsible office, and in the absence of evidence to the contrary, it can be said that he was a man of good character, and presumably a competent witness." When the writer asked Bakeless if he knew what became of Lewis's pistols he replied: "I don't know what became of the pistols, but you mustn't think too badly of Neelly on that account. Army officers often get shifted about and minor bits of property as a result don't get returned. The officer to whom I lent my expensive gold aguillettes when I left the Embassy in Turkey has never returned them. Not that he's a rogue but probably only because they got packed and never got unpacked." The two cases are in no sense parallel. After reading this book in manuscript Mr. Jackson wrote: "You have convinced me that Neelly was dishonest, and Mrs. Grinder was a real nut."

Chapter 10:  Brahan to Eustis: NA B/589 (4); the other two letters are from NABa; Salcedo: War Dept. Register of Letters No. 5, p. 30. In a letter from Isaac Coles to Jefferson, 5 January 1810, it is revealed that he and Clark opened the trunks—"every thing of a public nature was given to the Dept. to which it properly belonged, everything relating to the Expedition to Genl. Clarke, and all that remained is contained in the five little bundles now directed to you." Jefferson Papers at the Mass. Hist. Soc. Strange that he said nothing about the guns, tomahawk, dirk. The Russell document is copied from a copy at the Univ. of Indiana library, made by Jonathan Williams. Why he made a copy of it we don't know.

Chapter 11:  Coues, I, xliii, dates Wilson's letter May 18, 1811, and says it was published in *Portfolio* (Philadelphia), VII, No. 1, pp. 34-47, January, 1812. Phelps cites Vol. IX (1811) and gives May 28, 1811, as the date of the letter. Wilson's biographer, George Ord, *American Ornithology*, I, says the date was May 18, 1810. On Audubon see the *Life* edited by his wife, New York, 1869, 30-33. The Wilson letter has appeared in a number of places; our copy is that used in Wheeler, I, 64-6.

Chapter 12:  *Dispatch:* Draper mss., 296633, WHS. In a letter . . . historian says: DDJ.

Chapter 13:  Moore's article appeared in the *American Historical Magazine*, IX, July, 1904; Spences, 50-51; Bakeless, 422. On Lewis family tradition in this matter including the visit of the sisters see such sources as Sarah Travers Lewis (Scott) Anderson, *Lewises, Meriwethers, and their Kin*, Richmond, 1938.

Chapter 14:  On C. L. Lewis see Otto A. Rothert, "The Tragedy of the Lewis Brothers," The Filson Club *Quarterly*, X, 231 ff. This Lewis was not a Meriwether Lewis relative. Coues, I, xliv; Wheeler, 1, 66; Anderson, Dye Papers, OHS; Boyd, in a letter to the author.

Chapter 15:  *Gazette*, LC; *Intelligencer*, NABa; *The Farmer's Friend*, FC.

Chapter 16:  Southgate is at TSL in a folder of newspaper clippings, as well as Frierson; the interviews are at MLNM. The historian is DDJ.

Chapter 17:  Wheeler, I, 68; Goodlett, Wheeler, I, 66-7; Anderson, Dye Papers, OHS.

Chapter 18:  Bakeless, ch. 26; Kay, a typewritten monograph at Park headquarters, Tupelo, Miss.; Ghent, Dye Papers, OHS; Billon, *Annals*, 378; Turner, *History of Maury County, Tennessee*,

Nashville, 1955, 40 (when asked what evidence he had to support his statement about Jefferson Turner cited only the Fleming address); report of Monument committee, State of Tennessee House Journal, 1849, 238-240. Members of the committee who signed the report were Edmund Dillahunty, Barclay Martin, Robert A. Smith, Samuel B. Moore; if there was a post-rider named Smith in 1809 he may have been the Robert A. who was on the committee, and if this were so the committee probably based its statement largely on what he had to say. The letter to Cressey is in the committee's report.

Chapter 21: This writer talked with Webster's son, Hugh Lee, in October, 1959, and later sent him a question: "In a newspaper article your father said he talked to grandsons of about all the members of the coroner's jury. They all seem to have told much the same story. Were they all known to one another or not? As an attorney you no doubt will agree with me that if not all of them were known to one another, yet told the same story, it is more convincing evidence than it would be if they were all known to one another." Mr. Webster replied: "You have asked a very pertinent question and one which I cannot answer yes or no."

Chapter 22: For the Phelps essay see *The William and Mary Quarterly,* Third Series, XIII, 1956; it has been reprinted as a booklet and the writer bought a copy for 25c from Mr. Phelps whose address is National Park Headquarters, Tupelo, Miss. Natchez Trace Parkway Survey, Senate Document 148, 76th Congress, 3rd session; on Hildreth see Phelps, "Travel on the Natchez Trace," JMH, XV, 160; Cocke, *American State Papers, Indian Affairs,* II, 106; Kane, *Natchez on the Mississippi,* New York, 1947, 63; Bakeless, 415; Coates, *The Outlaw Years,* Part IV; Theodora Britton Marshall and Gladys Crail, *They Found It in Natchez,* New Orleans, 1939, 58 and 111. In regard to the Grinders, whom Phelps, like Moore, would clear of all suspicion, Bakeless points out that "The niece of Grinder's daughter-in-law long afterward accepted the theory that Lewis was murdered—a theory still much resented by Grinder's modern descendants. She averred that Grinder's son kept buried in a chimney corner 'the old man's pants', the legs of which were filled with gold." This is absurd nonsense but no more absurd than some of the things that have been printed in defense of the Grinders. Mr. Phelps accepted Moore on Grinder but on the other hand in this writer's presence was scornful of Webster, though one lawyer seems to have been as "distinguished" as the other.

Jackson, in a letter to the writer; Seagle, *Acquitted of Murder,* Chicago 1958, 40; in Lewis papers, MLNM. Whether Mrs. Miller will come forth with new evidence nobody knows; some historians are skeptical. This writer asked her seven questions and she replied: "As for the seven questions you have listed, no doubt I could answer some of them to your entire satisfaction. I don't think, however, that it would be to my interest to do so. The study of Lewis's life and his time is more than a hobby with me. I was indeed an amateur when I commenced my searches, but meanwhile I have professionalized myself as a historian and today regard my record files as my most valuable asset."

Appendix A: Paul Allen, *History of the Expedition,* New York, 1842, I, li; Roosevelt, *The Winning of the West,* VI, 261; Killebrew quoted by Coues, I, i; Lighton, *Lewis and Clark,,* 152-3-4; *Am. Hist. Assoc.,* 1903, I, 110; Swain, *Everybody's Magazine,* Sept., 1905; Spaulding, *Popular Science Monthly,* Dec., 1908; Blanchard, *Documentary History,* Chicago, 1903, 67; Hitchcock, *Lewis and Clark Expedition,* Boston, 1905, 116, note; Skinner, *Adventures in Oregon,* New Haven, 1920, 70; Voorhees, *Personal Recollections,* Cheyenne, 1920; Gilmer, *Sketches,* Americus, Georgia, 83-4; Smyth, *Lewis and Clark,* New York, 1931, 167-8; Wilson, *Meriwether Lewis of Lewis and Clark,* New York, 1934, 283 and a letter to and now at TSL; Seymour, *Meriwether Lewis,* New York, 1937, 237-8; Kay, unpublished monograph at National Park Headquarters, Tupelo, Miss.; Nevins and Ghent, attached to copy of Charles M. Wilson book at MoHS; Williams and Shoemaker, *Missouri,* I; Filson, X, 243; *The South,* 12 volumes, Richmond, 1909, XII, 96.

Appendix B: Hosmer to Dye, OHS; on Savannah and Hardin county see *History of Tennessee,* Nashville, 1887, many unnumbered volumes: Bakeless, 421. Besides calling Robert Grinder, John, Lucy Marks, Ann, the Neelly servant, Jim, Neelly, John, he gives the name of Mrs. Christina Anthony as Christina Ambrey. Research in St. Louis turned up nothing on the man Lewis called Pernia, Jefferson, John Pernier, and Wilson, Pernea. The Nevins and Ghent materials are in a copy of the Wilson book, MoHS, except the second Ghent statement which is at OHS. In his reply to the Tennessee librarian Mr. Wilson said, "My original notes have long been lost . . . do recall considerable delving in Tennessee statutes in and via the law library of my grandfather. . . ." It is in the same letter that he spoke of the sloppy publishing. In the Foreword to my novel *Tale of Valor* I said that DeVoto called the Lewis dog (on the Expedition) Brewster. John Bakeless says he did not and thinks I confused DeVoto and Wilson. That probably is true and I use this awkward place to make the correction.

Appendix C: For views of the importance of the expedition see the review of Coues, *The Nation*, Oct. 26, 1893 and Nov. 2, 1893; and the *National Republic*, October, 1931. Ravenswaay, MoHS *Bulletin*, April, 1946; Kay, *op.cit.*, 22 and 25.

# Index